SECOND BOOK
OF
MODERN LACE KNITTING

SECOND BOOK

OF

MODERN LACE KNITTING

BY

MARIANNE KINZEL

DOVER PUBLICATIONS, INC.
NEW YORK

Published in Canada by General Publishing
Company, Ltd., 30 Lesmill Road, Don Mills,
Toronto, Ontario.
Published in the United Kingdom by Constable
and Company, Ltd., 10 Orange Street, London WC 2

This Dover edition, first published in 1972, is a
corrected republication of the work originally
published by Mills & Boon Limited, London,
England, in 1961. It also contains a new Preface
by the author.

International Standard Book Number: 0-486-22905-X
Library of Congress Catalog Card Number: 72-86064

Manufactured in the United States of America
Dover Publications, Inc.
180 Varick Street
New York, N. Y. 10014

Contents

PREFACE TO THE DOVER EDITION

Since the first edition of my **Second Book of Modern Lace Knitting,** published by Messrs. Mills & Boon Ltd., has been out of print for some years, I am most grateful to Dover Publications, Inc., for this republication. I am sure that this new edition will acquire still larger numbers of enthusiasts for the art of lace knitting, especially in the United States of America.

The text in the Dover edition is unabridged. A number of corrections have been made, and the chart for the 'Rose of England' design, which was originally printed as a fold-out, appears on two facing pages. The Acknowledgements and Appendix in the original edition have been omitted because they are no longer applicable.

M.K.

July, 1972

Author's Introduction

In my FIRST BOOK I presented as introduction a short passage on the history of MODERN LACE KNITTING. At the same time I tried to inspire the needlewoman of today to understand the suitability of this craft to our present crowded and bustling life, to discover the delicate beauty of knitted lace, and the truly fascinating charm of working designs in this old art.

The FIRST BOOK I also made a book of teaching by explaining with the help of diagrams the basic knowledge needed to work articles of knitted lace and to bring them to perfection; and I presented a few very simple designs before going on to the more complicated samples. Thus the chapters were arranged in such a way as to give a real course on the subject.

This *Second Book of Modern Lace Knitting* now before you continues this course by introducing a number of new patterns of different shapes and designs which I was not able to incorporate in my first volume.

The General Instructions are in part similar to those in the FIRST BOOK. However, I have had to repeat them, although in a shortened version, for the benefit of knitters who are not acquainted with my previous publications. The greater part of the Basic Instructions is entirely new and devoted to the technique of working oval and oblong designs and to the application of lace knitting in wool, a subject not touched upon previously.

Diagrams are provided, as usual, to help to overcome difficulties, should any arise, in the working of the various articles.

From the pages on Abbreviations used in the working instructions the knitter will see what knowledge of knitting stitches is expected for the making of these new designs in this book, and although there are many more stitches than in the first volume, the average knitter should not have any difficulty in following the instructions of the patterns.

There are once again fully written instructions and charts for the knitting of each design. From letters received from my needlewomen friends, I know that many of them now prefer the use of charts and, therefore, they cannot be omitted. May I point out here that should a knitter encounter some difficulties in the working of a design, it will be of help to her to compare the chart with the written instructions or vice versa, according to the form of directions she has chosen to work from.

For the chart knitter I would also like to explain here why the presentation of the charts is in some cases slightly altered. Elaborate designs, and some of the patterns in this book are more intricate, often require very large charts. To print these, large folders are needed which would make the production of such a book more difficult and costly. To avoid such folders the reader may find that a chart line is continued sometimes over two pages, or that perhaps more than one knit stitch is drawn into one square, which reduces the length of the line considerably. It in no way complicates the reading of the chart.

Now for the choice of the designs and articles presented in this book. Only the 'Rose of England' and the 'Balmoral' are reprints of patterns I designed years ago. All other designs are entirely new and printed for the first time in this volume.

I had often been approached by my needlewomen friends to put into knitting stitches the 'Daffodil' and the 'Shamrock' in addition to the 'Rose' and the 'Thistle', and I thought it a fitting opportunity to do so in this book. Since the 'Rose of England' and the 'Balmoral' are out of print as leaflets I thought it most desirable to incorporate all the four emblems of the British Isles in this *Second Book of Modern Lace Knitting*, and it made me very happy that Messrs. Mills & Boon, Ltd, consented to such an arrangement.

At the same time I was able to give with the 'Trifolium' design the working of an oblong pattern in many variations which was also very often asked for by my customer friends.

All the other designs included in this book are likewise urgent requests I received in hundreds of letters during the past years. The Altar Lace, the Lace by the Yard, the Stole for Evening Wear, the Christening Shawl should be very welcome judging by all the demands I received.

It was also quite astonishing for me to learn how many Bridge enthusiasts belonged to my knitting circle. For these I designed for the first time Club, Diamond, Heart and Spade in separate squares which can be put together to the taste of the knitter, a technique of working lace pieces I have often been asked to present.

The oval design 'Lilac Time' was long overdue, too. It is not so easy to achieve in a design the same effect all round when part of the pattern has to be worked on the principle of round knitting and another part on the principle of straight knitting as is required in the building up of an oval design. Although 'Lilac Time' looks very simple, I would warn the knitter to be very observant when working this pattern since in the round section of the cloth are a few inconspicuous increases which could easily be overlooked.

Many suggestions received from my customers I could not accept, as it would need a very thick volume to deal with them. I also cannot comply with requests to produce individual designs. I think most of my readers will understand when I tell them that it is a very long way from an idea or a rough drawing to a finished pattern in lace knitting. With all the experience and skill, a design has to be thought out, charted and tried out, and if of elaborate nature, often knitted more than once before it is perfect. Some shapes which are requested just cannot be put into knitting stitches. Even when a design is finished, the chart and the instructions have to be made presentable to the knitter and this, too, often raises unforeseen difficulties and takes time. Designs of special nature like the 'Rose of England', the 'Scottish Thistle', the 'Daffodil' and the 'Shamrock' involve months of work, although they appear so easy to knit when finally printed.

It was a great pleasure to me to work out these designs presented to my readers in this book. I sincerely hope that all my needlewomen friends who so patiently waited for this volume will find something which suits their needs and appeals to their tastes.

To those needlewomen who take up lace knitting just for the pleasure of knitting I wish increased joy arising from this book.

To those knitters who work my designs to exhibit articles in shows and enter them in competitions, I wish further great successes.

And finally, to those friends of my designs, and I know from letters received there are many, who took up this craft of lace knitting to keep their fingers moving, or to occupy their minds, to take away the thoughts of sorrow and loneliness, may I send to them my sincerest sympathy and wish that they may be granted what they so much hope for.

M.K.

CHAPTER I

BASIC INSTRUCTIONS

ABBREVIATIONS USED IN WORKING INSTRUCTIONS

The abbreviations adopted in the working instructions of the designs are such as are most generally used in knitting patterns and will be familiar to any knitter.

K. = Knit.

K.1 = Knit 1 stitch.

P. = Purl.

P.1 = Purl 1 stitch.

K.1B. = Knit 1 stitch through the back.

Sl.1 = Slip 1 stitch from the left needle to the right-hand needle without knitting it.

Psso. = Pass the slip stitch over.

Yo. = Yarn over, i.e. bring the yarn forward between the needles and take it back over the right-hand needle ready for the next stitch. (In wool patterns this action is usually described as 'wool forward'.)

Yo.2 = Yarn over twice.

KM.1B. same as (K.1–M.1B.) = Knit twice into one stitch, this is into front and then into back, before slipping it off the needle.

(K.1 o.1) = Knit 1 stitch over the second, i.e. take the needle behind the first stitch and insert knitwise into the second stitch. Knit this second stitch and leave it on the left needle, and then knit the first stitch. Now slip both stitches off the needle. The final effect is that the first stitch crosses over the second.

K.2 tog. = Knit 2 stitches together.

Sl.1, K.1, psso. = Slip 1 stitch, knit 1 stitch and pass the slipped stitch over.

Sl.1, K.2 tog., psso. = Slip 1 stitch, knit 2 stitches together pass slipped stitch over.

K.3 tog. = Knit 3 stitches together.

P.3 tog. = Purl 3 stitches together.

Sl.2, K.1, p2sso. = Slip 2 stitches, knit 1 stitch, pass 2 slipped stitches over.

Sl.1, K.2, psso.2 = Slip 1 stitch, knit 2 stitches, pass the slipped stitch over both stitches.

Sl.2, K.2 tog., p2sso. = Slip 2 stitches, knit 2 stitches together, pass 2 slipped stitches over.

Sl.2, K.3 tog., p2sso. = Slip 2 stitches, knit 3 stitches together and pass the 2 slipped stitches over.

C.3R. = Cable 3 stitches, to the right, i.e. take 2 stitches on to a spare needle and keep them at the back of the work. Knit third stitch, and then knit the two stitches from the spare needle.

C.3L. = Cable 3 stitches, to the left, i.e. take 1 stitch on to a spare needle. Keeping this stitch in front, knit 2 stitches and then knit the stitch from the spare needle, so that it lies in front of the two stitches.

M.2 = Make 2 stitches into next stitch, i.e. knit 1 stitch and purl 1 stitch into the same stitch before slipping it off the needle.

M.3 = Make 3 stitches into next stitch, i.e. knit 1, purl 1, knit 1 into the front of the same stitch before slipping it off the needle.

M.4 = Make 4 stitches into next stitch, i.e. (knit 1, purl 1), twice, into same stitch before slipping it off the needle.

M.5 = Make 5 stitches into yarn over of previous round, i.e. knit 1 (purl 1, knit 1), twice into yarn over of previous round before slipping it off the needle.

M.6 = Make 6 stitches into double yarn over of previous round, i.e. (knit 1, purl 1), 3 times into yarn over 2 of previous round before slipping it off the needle.

M.8 = Make 8 stitches into double yarn over of previous round, i.e. (knit 1, purl 1), 4 times into yarn over 2 of previous round before slipping it off the needle.

M.9 = Make 9 stitches into next stitch, i.e. knit 1 (yarn over, knit 1), 4 times into front of the same stitch before slipping it off the needle.

st. = Stitch.	d.c. = Double crochet.
sts. = Stitches.	rep. = Repeat.
ch. = Chain.	incl. = Inclusive.

X = This sign in front of a round means: knit first stitch of round from first needle on to the third needle. Slip first stitch from second needle on to first needle, and then slip first stitch from third needle on to the second needle. Now proceed to knit the marked pattern round.

When using a circular pin knit the first stitch of round plain, adding it to the previous round, and then start to knit the marked pattern round.

XX = Do as explained above with two stitches.

L = This sign in front of a chart line means: do not knit last stitch of previous round but slip it on to first needle, using the stitch as first stitch for this round. Also slip last stitch from first needle on to second needle, and last stitch from second needle on to third needle. If using a circular knitting needle use last stitch of plain round as first stitch for marked pattern round.

LL = Do as explained above with two stitches.

* = Asterisk: Repeat the instructions between the asterisks as many times as stated.

( ) = Brackets: Knit the instructions inside the brackets as many times as specified after closing bracket.

MATERIALS

LINEN THREAD—CROCHET COTTON—WOOL

It is important to choose yarns of first-class quality for lace knitting, since most of the designs are worked in very open lace stitches, and are more liable to wear and tear than a closely knitted fabric.

The designs photographed throughout the book were worked either in white or light ecru crochet cotton or in white or naturally coloured linen thread. For the few articles knitted in wool a 1-ply or fine 2-ply wool of best quality was used. It is not in the lace-making tradition to use silks, rayon, or any other yarn of highly polished surface or very conspicuous colour.

For a beginner in lace knitting, it may be advisable to take a slightly thicker thread than stated in the working instructions of the chosen design.

KNITTING NEEDLES—CIRCULAR PINS—CROCHET HOOKS

Knitting pins and knitting needles required for lace knitting are the usual kind, available in every needlework shop. The size of knitting pins or needles is always given in the working instructions of the design concerned, and are usually either No. 12, No. 13 or No. 14 for articles worked in cotton or linen thread and No. 9 or No. 10 for lace pieces worked in wool.

For patterns worked on two needles, which require a large number of cast-on stitches, use the ordinary knitting pins with knob-ends, to prevent the stitches from slipping off the ends.

For knitting round, square, oval or oblong designs which are worked in the round, four double pointed knitting needles (sock needles) are needed for the start, and small designs are also completed on four needles. When knitting a lace piece of medium or large size it is absolutely essential to continue and finish the work with a circular knitting pin.

The most usual kind on the market is the nylon circular pin, an ideal tool for round knitting. Circular knitting needles are available in various lengths and in all sizes needed for our purpose. The length of the circular pin selected depends on the size of the design to be worked, and it is stated in the working instructions of each individual pattern which pin will serve to finish the particular article.

It is of great importance that the thickness of the circular pin is the same as that of the double pointed needles used for the commencement of the same article, for a different size of circular pin would alter the gauge of the stitches.

Crochet hooks needed for the crocheting-off are the kind of steel hooks obtainable in all needlework stores. No. 4, 4½, or 5 will serve for the finishing of any pattern worked in linen thread or cotton, and No. 2 or 3 are required when working with wool.

FOR AMERICAN KNITTERS

Needle gauge British size No. 12 is equivalent to the American size 11 in double pointed steel needles, and size 2 in American circular knitting needles.

British size No. 13 is equivalent to U.S.A. size 12 in double pointed needles, and size 1 in circular needles.

KNITTING ON TWO PINS

CASTING-ON

Designs worked on two pins require a certain amount of stitches for the start. These stitches can be obtained either by CASTING-ON or by KNITTING-ON and it is of no importance which method is used since it will not influence the appearance of the designs. If for some reason it is preferable to adopt one of the methods then it is specially emphasised in the working instructions of the design concerned.

When a great number of stitches is required for knitting an article, as for instance the Altar Lace, and the two knitting pins prove to be too short, it is possible to use instead one long circular pin of 36 or 42 in. length. Cast on all stitches on to this one circular pin and then knit to and fro, turning the work after each row, using the two points of the circular pin like two knitting pins.

GENERAL RULES

When an article is being worked on two pins, the front and the back of the fabric alternately faces the knitter. The front of the lace fabric is composed of pattern rows which are given in the written working instructions (as well as on the charts) and are marked with numbers. All rows of which the numbers are missing are back rows and knitted purl, thus making up the wrong side of the fabric.

Pay **special attention** if, in a pattern row, a 'yarn over' occurs twice in succession since in the following purl row the first corresponding stitch must be purled and the second stitch knitted. Knitters with slack tension should work only one 'yarn over' where this 'double yarn over' is given in the pattern, but great care must be taken that in the following purl row, two stitches are worked into its place, as explained above.

KNITTING ON FOUR NEEDLES OR
ON A CIRCULAR KNITTING PIN

The following directions apply to the working of round, square, oval and oblong designs.

COMMENCEMENT OF ROUND AND SQUARE DESIGNS

CASTING-ON

Commence from the centre of the cloth by casting-on the number of stitches stated in the working instructions of the chosen design. Divide the stitches on to three needles as suggested and arrange them to form a circle as when working a sock. Then always knit one round into the back of the stitches (to tighten the cast-on stitches) before following further instructions of the design concerned.

EASY-TO-START METHOD

The easy-to-start method, using a crochet hook, presents an alternative means of starting a round or square design and is an ideal way for beginners in the technique of round knitting, to overcome the difficulty of holding so few stitches on the needles.

The photo-diagrams Fig. 1 to Fig. 7 show the commencement of a design which requires 12 stitches for the start, but the same method can be applied to any round or square design using the number of stitches required for the particular pattern.

Fig. 1.   Commence from the centre by making 12 chain.

Fig. 2.   Join to a ring with a slip stitch through the first chain. This is the first stitch.

Fig. 3.   Draw 3 more slip stitches through the following 3 chain, which gives altogether 4 stitches.

Fig. 4.   Slip those 4 stitches from the crochet hook on to the first knitting needle.

Fig. 5.   Make 4 more slip stitches with the crochet hook through the following 4 chain.

Fig. 6.   Transfer them on to the second knitting needle.

Fig. 7.   Do the same with the remaining 4 stitches, and slip them on to the third needle.

Whether a design is started by casting-on or by help of the easy-to-start method, it is advisable to push little pieces of cork on to the points of the needles to prevent them from slipping out of the work. The knitter will find through experience that these pieces of cork, although so useful for the very beginning, can be dispensed with after a few rounds of knitting.

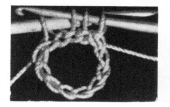

Fig. 1

Fig. 2

Fig. 3

Fig. 4

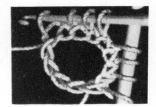

Fig. 5

Fig. 6

Fig. 7

The little hole left in the centre should be drawn together afterwards when the cloth is finished. Thread the long cast-on or chain-end into a sewing needle and make one overcasting stitch into each cast-on stitch or chain, all round the little hole, thus drawing it together, and securing the thread at the same time.

17

COMMENCEMENT OF OVAL AND OBLONG DESIGNS

Commence from the centre of the cloth by KNITTING-ON the number of stitches given in the working instructions of the particular design. Divide the stitches on to three needles as suggested in the pattern concerned, and arrange the needles to form a circle exactly as when working a sock.

Then knit one round of plain before following the instructions of the pattern. This first round of plain must be worked through the front of the stitches (not the back, as this would tighten the stitches) since a loose, loopy selvedge is desired (see Fig. 8). Also casting-on by thumb method is not suitable when working oval and oblong designs, since this would also give an inflexible tight selvedge edge.

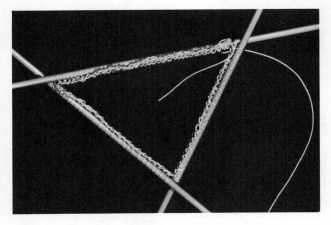

Fig. 8

When commencing a large Cloth or Runner with more than about 150 stitches to begin with, it is recommended to knit-on the stitches on to a circular knitting pin of 16 in. length (see Fig. 9).

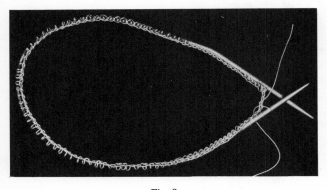

Fig. 9

Even when working a smaller mat and commencing with double pointed needles as described in the first paragraph, it is possible to transfer all stitches on to a 16 in. circular knitting pin after about 10 rounds of knitting (see Fig. 10).

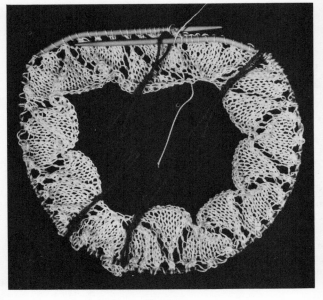

Fig. 10

When the article is completed and taken off the needles the large hole in the centre will appear as a slit and can be stitched together with overcasting stitches. Care should be taken to join the opposite side sections of the pattern, sewing together the corresponding stitches from each side. Thus a pleasing look can be achieved and the join will not disturb the general appearance of the design (see Fig. 11).

GENERAL RULES

When an article is being worked on four needles or on a circular pin the front of the fabric always faces the knitter. Never turn your work when knitting round.

Only pattern rounds are given in the written instructions (as well as on the charts), and they are marked with numbers. Every round of which the number is missing is knitted plain. In general you will observe that every alternate round is usually a plain round, and if not, special attention is drawn to this fact in the working instructions of the pattern. Nevertheless, the knitter should carefully watch the numbers of the rounds and not adopt the habit, so easily acquired by good knitters, of knitting on, automatically, one pattern and one plain round.

Special attention should be paid if, in a pattern round, a 'yarn over' occurs twice in succession, since in the following plain round, the first corresponding stitch must be knitted, and the second stitch purled or vice versa. Knitters with a slack tension may work only one 'yarn over' in place of the 'double yarn over' stated in the pattern, but great care must be taken that in the following plain round, two stitches are worked into its place as explained above.

18

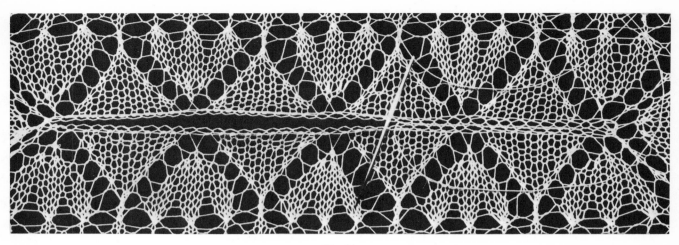

Fig. 11

TRANSFER OF STITCHES

When working a square or round design it is unavoidable to start with double pointed knitting needles. Only after a certain amount of rounds can the stitches be transferred on to a circular needle. The scale below may be a useful guide.

From about round 30 — 16 in. length circular pin.
From about round 45 — 24 in. length circular pin.
From about round 75 — 30 in. or 36 in. circular pin.
From about round 95 — 42 in. length circular pin.

When working oblong or oval designs one may be able to begin with a circular needle right from the start as explained in the COMMENCEMENT. If, however, the oval or oblong cloth had to be started on double pointed needles the stitches can be transferred on to a circular needle at an earlier stage as when knitting a square or round design, since there are a much larger number of stitches to start (see the scale below).

From about round 10 — 16 in. circular pin.
From about round 30 — 24 in. circular pin.
From about round 60 — 30 in. or 36 in. circular pin.
From about round 75 — 42 in. circular pin.

It is better to transfer the stitches on to a circular needle when knitting a plain round, and, of course, it is stated in the working instructions of each individual design which pin will serve to finish the particular article.

MARKING OF THE ROUND

In circular knitting, it is most essential that the beginning of the round is marked very clearly. When knitting with four double pointed knitting needles, draw in a coloured thread between the first and the last needle when the round is completed. When working with a circular pin mark your round again with a coloured loop, slipping it over the right-hand point of the needle before knitting the first stitch (see Fig. 10). This coloured thread will quite automatically move, with the stitches, all round the circular needle, since it keeps its position all the time between the last and first stitch. As the knitter finishes the round, the loop only needs to be lifted from the left-hand needle-point to the right-hand point before the first stitch of the next round is knitted.

It may be also very useful to mark the finish of each pattern unit with a coloured thread when working a round cloth, and it is especially recommended to mark the corner stitches when knitting a square or oblong design. (Also shown in Fig. 10.)

TENSION

A knitter used to wool knitting will find that a slight adjustment of tension is needed when taking up lace knitting. Fine threads usually require a tightening of tension but not to such an extent that the stitches will not move upon the needle. Neither should the needles be able to slip out of the work on their own.

In general, tension is something personal which cannot be forced, but watched and adjusted through experience. Therefore, beginners in lace knitting are advised to knit first one or two articles in a thicker cotton to get the feel of the thread,

before knitting with the finer yarn recommended in the pattern. Articles worked in slightly thicker cotton will be less delicate, but otherwise the general shape of the design will not be disturbed.

Very slack or very tight knitters can also control their tension by taking either finer or thicker needles than those recommended in the instructions. However, it must be borne in mind that needles which are too fine will not make the fabric appear lacier but closer and more compact, unless, of course, a much finer thread is used at the same time. On the other hand, needles which are too thick may widen the gauge of the stitches to such an extent that the design loses its shape.

A change over from needles No. 12 to needles No. 13, or vice versa, should be adequate to adjust the tension if it cannot be done by deliberate control.

Special care must be taken when working with a circular pin that the thread is not tensioned too tightly, otherwise the knitter will have difficulty in pushing the stitches over the join of the pin. Furthermore, it will cause unnecessary strain at the point where the flexible part of the circular needle is connected with the stiff pin-end.

FINISHING OF LACE

CASTING-OFF

Some of the articles like the Scarf, Stole, etc., require, when knitted, only a simple cast-off row as finish.

Any method familiar to the knitter can be used, provided it is worked to the same tension as the knitting and that great care is taken that the selvedge formed by the casting-off stitches stretches to its proper measurement.

To strengthen selvedge edges all round, a row of double crochet can be recommended, but is not essential and can be left to the discretion of the knitter and whether she is conversant with the use of a crochet hook.

CROCHETING-OFF

In Modern Lace Knitting, crocheting-off was adopted as a new method to give the lace pieces a more dainty finish. It achieves the most effective results when used for designs worked in round knitting.

This very simple way of securing the stitches does not require an expert knowledge of crochet; only the working of chain and double crochet is needed to follow the instructions.

After knitting the last purl row of a design worked on two pins, or last plain round of lace worked on four needles or a circular pin, we do not cast-off at all but start to finish the edge immediately, with a chain of crochet. Three, four, or even five stitches are crocheted together in a group with one double crochet and a certain number of chain are made to link those groups of stitches, working all along the row or round of the lace.

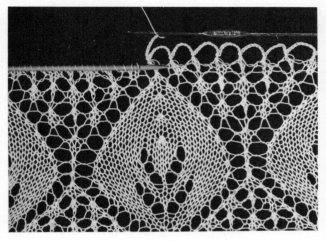

Fig. 12

The number of stitches taken together and the number of chain made to form the little loops, between the groups of stitches, vary and depend on the individual designs, as seen in the working instructions. The chain edge ought not to contract the outer edge of the lace but must allow for the stretching into a scallop, etc. A needlewoman used to very tight crochet work may therefore be advised to work, perhaps, one or two more chain than stated in the instructions concerned.

Fig. 12 shows the crocheting-off on a section of the design 'Lilac Time', worked as diagram in thick cotton. Most explicitly detailed instructions and diagrams of this chapter are given in the *First Book of Modern Lace Knitting*.

WASHING AND STRETCHING

Since the knitter has spent so many hours working a piece of lace, it should not be regarded as too troublesome to take another hour or so to complete the article in an expert way. So much depends on the proper finish. The gossamer-like appearance of a fine wool shawl, or the crisp lacy look of knitted lace worked in cotton or linen thread, results partly from the treatment which can be achieved with hardly any cost.

WASHING AND STARCHING OF ARTICLES IN COTTON OR LINEN THREAD

Wash the finished article in a warm lather of mild soap powder or soap flakes.

Do not rub hard but squeeze the lace gently and rinse well in lukewarm water before it is steeped into the prepared starch.

We are, of course, all aware that ordinarily starch is not used when treating lace, nor would I advise it, should the article concerned be a precious bobbin or a needlepoint lace. Since the designs presented in this book are not meant to be heirlooms, shut away in a glass case, but household access·ories to be used every day, starch will not harm the thread, and knitted lace needs this extra strengthening to retain a perfect shape for a longer time. The designs photographed are slightly stiffened with the warm water starch commonly used for table linen, etc. For small doilies, for instance, luncheon mats, a thicker solution of starch is recommended to keep them clean and crisp longer. A satisfactory method is to take one tablespoonful of starch to one pint of water. For larger cloths which should drape well, two or three spoonfuls of starch are sufficient to six pints of water. When the lace is washed, rinsed and starched, do not dry but leave it wet for stretching.

WASHING OF ARTICLES IN WOOL

Prepare a lukewarm lather of soap flakes, and gently squeeze the lace piece in the lather without rubbing. Rinse well in lukewarm water, and roll the article between two bath towels, to remove moisture without wringing the lace. The still damp piece is now ready for stretching.

STRETCHING

The working instructions of all the designs give accurate measurements to prepare the paper patterns which should be used for the pinning-out of the lace. Take white or brown paper which does not leave any colour when wet. Place the paper pattern on to a thick cardboard, card table, piece of felt or perhaps the wrong side of your hearth rug, in short, anything that will allow for an easy insertion of pins. For a very large cloth, the carpet may have to be used. Make sure to have rustless pins for the process of pinning out.

The photo diagrams Fig. 13 to 16 demonstrate, with the help of the 'Mat Trifolium', the method of stretching an oblong piece of lace. Since the method of pinning out is in principle the same, whether it is a large or a small cloth, a square or a round one, an oval or an oblong, the photo diagrams together with the working instructions of the individual designs should give a clear picture of the process.

Fig. 13. Draw an oblong according to measurements given in the working instructions of the selected design. Draw into the oblong the two centre lines as shown and then set all along the four sides the marks needed for the inner points of the scallops, their distance being always stated in each pattern.

Fig. 14. Take the washed, rinsed and starched cloth, pin down the middle join on to the centre line, at the same distance of each side from the middle. Then fasten with one pin only the two loops of chain on both sides of the corners on to the corner point of the drawn diagram.
Proceed with pinning down with one pin only the two loops of chain at the middle of each side.

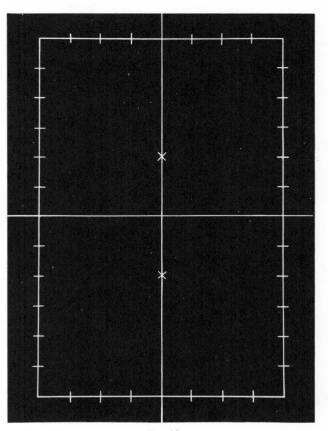

Fig. 13

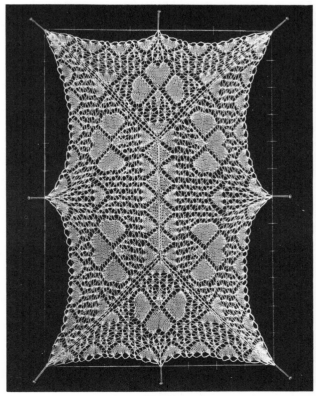

Fig. 14

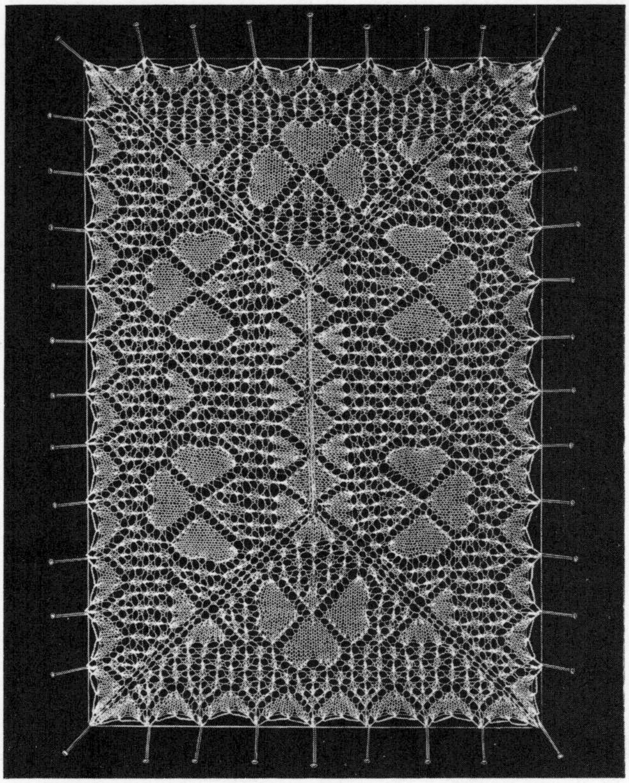

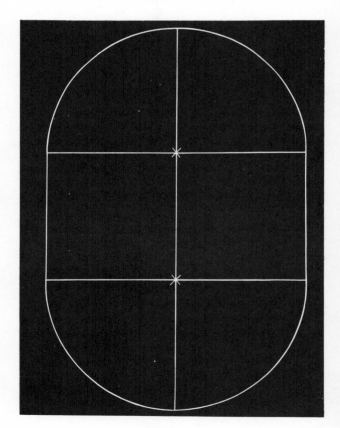

Fig. 15

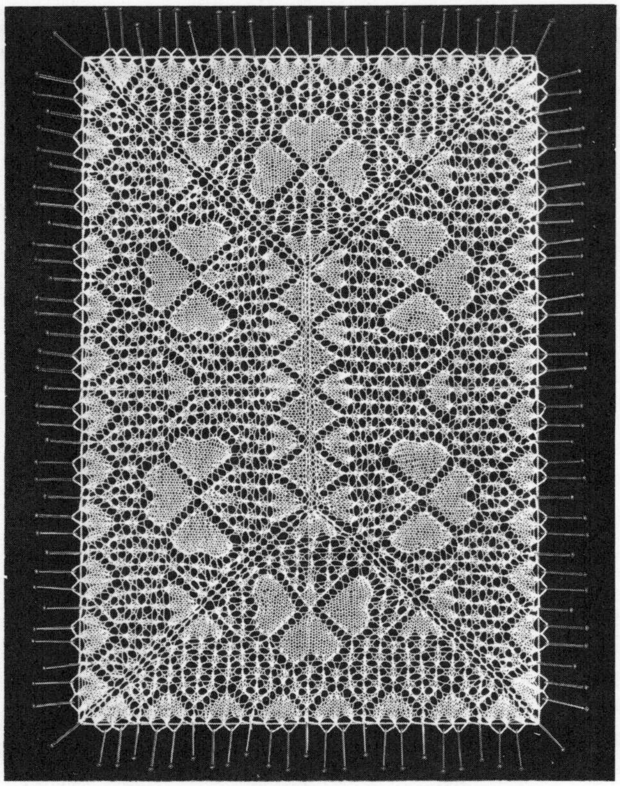

Fig. 16

Fig. 15.   Now pin down the two loops of chain which give the inside of the scallop with one pin only all along the four sides.

Fig. 16.   Place the remaining loops of chain, each with one pin, about ¼ in. outside the drawn line thus forming a little scallop as seen on the photo.

Fig. 17.   This shows a diagram for the pinning-out of an oval design.

IRONING OF ARTICLES IN COTTON OR LINEN THREAD

Leave the lace cloth pinned out, till completely dry. Then remove the pins and press carefully, without pulling, to give the thread the final smooth finish. A clean dry cloth should be placed on to the lace before applying the iron.

IRONING OF LACE IN WOOL

When the pinned-out lace shawl is half dry, place a clean dry cloth on to it and then iron gently. Now leave the lace piece stretched on the board till completely dry before removing the pins.

NOTICE

If the work does not stretch to the suggested size, through the tension being too slack or too tight, the measurements can easily be altered by making either a smaller or larger drawing and adjusting the marks accordingly. Always stretch to capacity.

Fig. 17

CHART INSTRUCTIONS IN ENGLISH

Charts are given as an alternative to written instructions for knitters who may find it rather trying to follow the long lines of printed directions.

The chart signs are evolved by the designer in such a way that they symbolise, in their form, the stitch or action they represent, thus giving already the outline of the pattern side of the finished lace fabric. A knitter used to chart reading can see at a glance how a pattern is developed, a fact which eliminates the endless counting of stitches and reduces the possibilities of errors. Once familiar with the symbols which, being so few, can be memorised easily, the knitter will be amazed to find how much more quickly she can work from a chart than from written instructions.

It is, of course, left to the reader to decide which method of following a pattern she prefers, but the chart is quite indispensable for those who may one day try their skill as designers of new patterns.

GENERAL RULES FOR CHART READERS

Every line on the chart is read from right to left as the knitting of a row, or round, proceeds in the same direction, each needle being knitted from the right to the left, too.

Empty squares on the chart have no meaning but are necessary to give a clear picture of the pattern, also to simplify the reading of the chart.

For designs worked on two needles, every chart line signifies a section of the front or pattern row, and is marked with a number. All rows of which the numbers are missing are back rows and worked purl.

For designs knitted on four needles or a circular pin, every chart line presents a section of one pattern round and is marked with a number. Every round of which the number is missing, knit plain.

Where part of a chart line is embraced by a bracket, the number of repetitions of this section is given below the chart. Chart lines marked by a double arrow are also repeated, as stated in the relevant instructions.

Whenever in doubt compare with the fully written working instructions of the pattern concerned. The knitter is, of course, expected to have read first the BASIC INSTRUCTIONS of this book, in which also a paragraph concerning the working of Yo.2 should be carefully studied.

The casting-on and the finishing of a design should always be taken from the written directions.

Notice: When working the 'Rose of England' or the 'Balmoral' follow the KEY OF CHART which is printed specially for these two designs. Some of the symbols have a different meaning than those given above, since these patterns were not designed for this book but are reprints of leaflets which are not any more available but still in great demand.

KEY FOR CHART

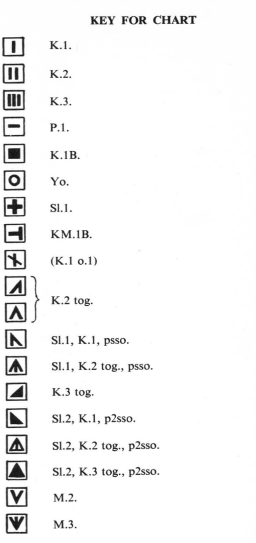

X This sign in front of a chart line means: knit first stitch of the round plain, adding the same to the previous round. Then proceed by knitting the marked pattern round.

XX Do as explained above but move two stitches instead of one.

L This sign in front of a round means: do not knit last stitch of previous plain round but use it as first stitch for marked pattern round.

LL Do as explained above with two stitches.

— The brace on top of the last chart line indicates **the number of stitches taken together by one double crochet.**

The figures stand for the number of chain combining these groups of stitches.

23

STRICKSCHRIFT—ANWEISUNGEN IN DEUTSCH

ALLGEMEINE ANWEISUNGEN ZUM LESEN DER STRICKSCHRIFT

Alle Zeilen der Strickschrift werden von rechts nach links gelesen. Die leeren Kästchen in der Strickschrift haben keine Bedeutung.

Für Modelle, welche mit Hilfe von zwei Stricknadeln gearbeitet sind, jede Zeile der Strickschrift vertritt einen Mustersatz einer Musterreihe und ist mit einer Nummer versehen. Alle Zwischenreihen, die nicht nummeriert sind, werden links gestrickt.

Für Modelle, welche in der Runde gestrickt sind, jede nummerierte Zeile der Strickschrift ist ein Mustersatz einer Runde. Jede nicht bezeichnete Runde wird rechts gestrickt.

Die Teile der Strickschrift, welche mit einer Klammer oder einem Pfeil bezeichnet sind, werden in einer bestimmten Weise wiederholt. Die Anzahl dieser Wiederholungen des Mustersatzes ist in der schriftlichen Erklärung neben oder unter der Strickschrift gegeben und mit Hilfe der folgenden Übersetzungen leicht zu folgen.

Die Maschenanzahl, welche nötig ist um die Modelle zu beginnen, kann von der schriftlichen Anweisung unter 'Casting-on' d.h. anschlagen, genommen werden.

Materials—Material.

Crochet Cotton—Häkelgarn.

Knitting Pins, Knitting Needles—Stricknadeln.

Circular Pin (Needle)—Strickring.

Crochet Hook—Häkelnadel.

Measurements—Masse.

4 inches (ins.)—sind beiläufig 10 cm.

Casting-On—Anschlagen von Maschen.

Casting-off—Abketten der Maschen.

Crocheting-Off—Abhäkeln.

Finishing—Fertigstellen.

Washing—Waschen.

Stretching—Spannen.

Knit (Knit plain)—Rechts stricken.

Purl—Links stricken.

Stitch (Stitches)—Strickmasche (Strickmaschen).

Chain—Luftmasche.

Double Crochet—Feste Masche (Häkelmasche).

Row—Musterreihe.

Round—Musterrunde.

Repeat—Wiederholen.

Once—Einmal.

Twice—Zweimal.

Times (3 times, 4 times, etc.)—Mal (3 mal, 4 mal usw.).

Part—Teil.

Section—Abschnitt.

ZEICHENERKLÄRUNG

Eine Masche rechts stricken.

Zwei Maschen rechts stricken.

Drei Maschen rechts stricken.

Eine Masche links stricken.

Eine Masche rechts verschränkt stricken, d.h. die Masche von ihrer Mitte nach hinten abstricken.

Einmal umschlagen.
Sind mehrere Umschläge nebeneinander, so werden diese in der folgenden Reihe oder Runde abwechselnd rechts und links abgestrickt.

Eine Masche abheben.

Aus einer Masche zwei Maschen stricken, und zwar eine Masche rechts, und eine Masche rechts verschränkt stricken.

Zwei Maschen gekreuzt abstricken, d.h. zuerst den Faden wie zum Rechtsstricken durch die zweite und dann durch die erste Masche holen bevor man beide Maschen von der Nadel gleiten lässt.

Zwei Maschen rechts zusammenstricken.

Eine Masche abheben, die nächste Masche rechts stricken und dann die abgehobene Masche überziehen.

Eine Masche abheben, die zwei folgenden Maschen rechts zusammenstricken und dann die abgehobene Masche überziehen.

Drei Maschen recht zusammen stricken.

Zwei Maschen abheben, eine Masche abstricken und dann die zwei abgehobenen Maschen überziehen.

Zwei Maschen abheben, zwei Maschen rechts zusammenstricken und dann die zwei abgehobenen Maschen überziehen.

Zwei Maschen abheben, drei Maschen rechts zusammenstricken und dann die zwei abgehobenen Maschen überziehen.

Aus einer Masche zwei Maschen stricken, und zwar eine Masche links und eine Masche rechts.

Aus einer Masche drei Maschen stricken, und zwar eine Masche rechts, eine Masche links und eine Masche rechts.

X Dieses Zeichen vor einer Musterrunde bedeutet, dass die erste Masche noch auf die vorhergehende Nadel gestrickt wird bevor man anfängt die gegebene Musterrunde zu arbeiten. Bei den anderen Nadeln verschiebt sich der Anfang genau so.

XX Zwei solche Zeichen bedeuten, dass sich der Anfang der Runde um zwei Maschen verschiebt wie oben erklärt.

L Dieses Zeichen vor einer Musterrunde bedeutet, dass die letzte Masche der vorhergehenden Runde nicht abgestrickt sondern als erste Masche der neuen, bezeichneten Runde gebraucht wird. Bei den andern Nadeln verschiebt sich der Anfang genau so.

LL Zwei soche Zeichen bedeuten, dass sich der Anfang der Runde um zwei Maschen verschiebt wie oben erklärt.

— Diese kleinen Klammern über der letzten Zeile der Strickschrift geben die Anzahl der Strickmaschen welche mit einer festen Masche zusammengehäkelt werden. Die Zahlen zwischen den Klammern geben die Anzahl der Luftmaschen, welche nötig sind für den Bogen von einer festen Masche zur anderen.

BEACHTEN SIE:

Besondere Beachtung muss dem Arbeiten der Entwürfe „Rose of England" und „Balmoral" gegeben werden. Die Zeichen der Strickschrift sind etwas verschieden von den oben gegebenen Erklärungen, und eine besondere Zeichenerklärung ist diesen beiden Mustern zugeteilt. Beide Decken wurden nicht für dieses Buch entworfen, sondern sind Nachdrucke von Musterbögen, die als solche nicht mehr erhältlich sind, sich aber einer grossen Nachfrage erfreuen.

Chart Instructions in French

EXPLICATIONS FRANÇAISES DES CARTES

Vous lisez chaque rang de la carte de droite à gauche, c'est à dire dans le même sens que vous travaillez. Les carreaux vides de la carte n'ont aucune signification, mais ils simplifient la lecture de la carte.

Pour les modèles exécutés sur deux aiguilles, chaque rang de la carte représente une partie d'un rang du motif (c'est à dire de l'endroit du travail), et il est marqué d'un numéro. Tous les rangs dont les numéros manquent sont des rangs de l'envers du travail et sont tricotés à l'envers.

Pour les modèles exécutés sur quatre aiguilles (à deux pointes) ou sur une aiguille circulaire, chaque rang de la carte représente une partie d'un rang du motif et il est marqué d'un numéro; chaque rang dont le numéro manque est tricoté à l'endroit.

Lorsqu'une partie d'un rang de la carte est mise entre crochets le chiffre au-dessous des crochets indique combien de fois il faut répéter cette partie. Le chiffre qui se trouve à côté de, ou au-dessous d'un rang de la carte marqué de deux flèches, indique combien de fois il faut répéter ce rang.

Knit plain (knit)—Tricoter à l'endroit.

Purl—Tricoter à l'envers.

Stitch (stitches)—Maille (mailles).

Chain—Point de chaînette.

Double-Crochet—Double-Crochet.

Row—Rang.

Round—Tour.

Repeat—Répéter.

Times—Fois.

Part—Partie.

Casting-on—Monter les mailles.

Finishing—Rabattre les mailles.

Stretching—Tension du travail fini.

I Une maille à l'endroit.

II 2 mailles à l'endroit.

III 3 mailles à l'endroit.

— Une maille à l'envers.

■ Une maille à l'endroit prise par derrière.

O Passer la laine devant le travail: c'est à dire, faire un jeté simple.

Quelquefois vous faites deux jetés de suite: au rang suivant vous tricotez le premier jeté à l'endroit, le deuxième à l'envers.

✚ Une maille glissée en la prenant à l'endroit.

⊣ Tricotez deux fois une maille, en prenant d'abord la maille sur le dessus, puis sur le dessous, avant de dégager l'aiguille.

⊁ Tricoter une maille à l'endroit au-dessus de la maille suivante: c'est à dire: Mettre l'aiguille derrière la première maille et l'introduire dans la deuxième maille comme pour la tricoter à l'endroit. Tricoter à l'endroit cette deuxième maille sans la glisser de l'aiguille gauche; puis tricoter à l'endroit la première maille en laissant glisser de l'aiguille en même temps la deuxième maille. Ceci forme un torse.

◿ ◺ Deux mailles ensemble à l'endroit.

◥ Un surjet simple, c'est à dire, glisser une maille, une maille à l'endroit, rabattre la maille glissée.

▲ Une maille glissée, deux mailles ensemble à l'endroit, rabattre la maille glissée.

◢ 3 mailles ensemble à l'endroit.

◣ 2 mailles glissées, 1 maille à l'endroit, rabattre les 2 mailles glissées.

▲ Deux mailles glissées, deux mailles ensemble à l'endroit, rabattre les mailles glissées.

▲ 2 mailles glissées, 3 mailles ensemble à l'endroit, rabattre les mailles glissées.

V Faire une augmentation, c'est à dire tricoter une maille à l'endroit, une maille à l'envers dans la même maille.

V Faire deux augmentations, c'est à dire tricoter une maille à l'endroit, une maille à l'envers, puis une deuxième maille à l'endroit dans la même maille.

L Ce signe au début d'un tour veut dire: ne tricotez pas la dernière maille du tour précédent, mais servez-vous-en comme maille pour le tour indiqué dans la marche à suivre.

LL Faites comme indiqué précédemment mais avec 2 mailles.

X Ce symbole devant un rang de la carte signifie: tricoter à l'endroit la première maille du rang et ajouter cette maille au rang précédent. Puis continuer en tricotant le rang marqué.

XX Suivre les explications comme ci-dessus, mais ajouter deux mailles, au lieu d'une maille, au rang précédent.

—— Ce symbole indique combien de mailles il faut prendre ensemble pour faire un double-crochet.

5, 7 etc., ceci indique combien de points de chaînette il faut faire entre les groupes de mailles qui sont prises ensemble pour faire un double-crochet.

Note: quand vous faites la « Rose d'Angleterre » ou le « Balmoral », suivez le chapitre specialement imprimé pour exécuter ces 2 dessins. Quelques-uns des symboles ont un sens légèrement différent de ceux qui sont données ci-dessus, puisque ces modèles n'ont pas été dessinés pour ce livre. Ils sont des réimpressions d'imprimés introuvables maintenant, et très demandés par le public.

CHAPTER II

DESIGNS WORKED ON
TWO PINS

'Maidenhair' Design

LACE BY THE YARD

MATERIALS

Crochet Cotton No. 40 or 50, or Linen Thread No. 40 or 50.

Two knitting needles No. 14.

The amount of cotton or linen thread needed depends, of course, on the length of lace required. One ball of cotton or 1 oz. of linen thread will give about a yard of lace or insertion, and a great length of the small edging.

MEASUREMENTS

LACE—4 in. deep. Length of one pattern 1 in.

EDGING—1½ in. deep. Length of pattern 1 in.

INSERTION—3 in. deep. Length of one pattern 1 in.

Lace

Commence by casting-on 35 stitches, turn, work 1 row plain and then knit the first pattern row. Ignore asterisks when working lace.

Every row of which the number is missing work purl.

Take care of the working of Yo.2 explained in BASIC INSTRUCTIONS.

1st row—Sl.1, P.2, Sl.1, K.1, psso., Yo., Sl.1, K.2, tog., psso., Yo., K.1, Yo., Sl.1, K.1, psso., K.7, K.2 tog., Yo., K.1, Yo., Sl.1, K.2 tog., psso., Yo., K.2 tog., P.2*, Sl.1, K.1, psso., Yo.2, K.2 tog., K.1, Yo., (K.1B.) twice.

3rd row—Sl.1, P.2, Sl.1, K.1, psso., Yo., K.1B., Yo., K.3, Yo., Sl.1, K.1, psso., K.5, K.2 tog., Yo., K.3, Yo., K.1B., Yo., K.2 tog., P.2*, Sl.1, K.1, psso., Yo.2, K.2 tog., K.2, Yo., (K.1B.) twice.

5th row—Sl.1, P.2, K.1B., (Yo., Sl.1, K.2 tog., psso.) twice, Yo., K.1, Yo., Sl.1, K.1, psso., K.3, K.2 tog., Yo., K.1, (Yo., Sl.1, K.2 tog., psso.) twice, Yo., K.1B., P.2*, Sl.1, K.1, psso., Yo.2, K.2 tog., K.3, Yo., (K.1B.) twice.

7th row—Sl.1, P.2, (K.1B., Yo., K.3, Yo.) twice, Sl.1, K.1, psso., K.1, K.2 tog., (Yo., K.3, Yo., K.1B.) twice, P.2*, Sl.1, K.1, psso., Yo.2, K.2 tog., K.1, Yo., Sl.1, K.1, psso., K.1, Yo., (K.1B.) twice.

9th row—Sl.1, P.2, Sl.1, K.1, psso., (Yo., Sl.1, K.2 tog., psso.) 3 times, Yo., K.1B., Yo., Sl.1, K.2 tog., psso., Yo., K.1B., (Yo., Sl.1, K.2 tog., psso.) 3 times, Yo., K.2 tog., P.2*, Sl.1, K.1, psso., Yo.2, K.2 tog., K.2, K.2 tog., Yo., K.2 tog., K.1B.

11th row—Sl.1, P.2, Sl.1, K.1, psso., Yo., K.1B., Yo., K.2, K.2 tog., Yo., K.3, M.3, K.3, Yo., Sl.1, K.1, psso., K.2, Yo., K.1B., Yo., K.2 tog., P.2*, Sl.1, K.1, psso., Yo.2, K.2 tog., K.1, K.2 tog., Yo., K.2 tog., K.1B.

13th row—Sl.1, P.2, K.1B., (Yo., Sl.1, K.2 tog., psso.) twice, Yo., K.2 tog., K.3, M.3, K.3, Sl.1, K.1, psso., Yo., (Sl.1, K.2 tog., psso., Yo.) twice, K.1B., P.2*, Sl.1, K.1, psso., Yo.2, (K.2 tog.) twice, Yo., K.2 tog., K.1B.

15th row—Sl.1, P.2, K.1B., Yo., K.2, K.2 tog., Yo., K.2 tog., K.9, Sl.1, K.1, psso., Yo., Sl.1, K.1, psso., K.2, Yo., K.1B., P.2*, Sl.1, K.1, psso., Yo.2, K.3 tog., Yo., K.2 tog., K.1B.

16th row—Work purl.

Repeat rows 1 to 16 as many times as the length of your lace requires.

Edging

Commence by casting on 10 stitches and work according to the directions given for the knitting of the **Lace** but with the following alterations: each pattern row must start with 1 slip stitch and 2 purl stitches and is then worked from the * onward to the end of the row.

Insertion

Commence by casting on 29 stitches and then work according to the directions given for the knitting of the **Lace** but with the following alteration; each pattern row has to be worked from the beginning to the * and then one slip stitch is added to form the second selvedge edge of the **Insertion**.

FINISHING OFF THE LACE BY THE YARD

After washing and starching the lace pieces can be ironed into perfect shape while still damp.

Charts for the Design 'Maidenhair'   Every row of which the number is missing, knit purl.

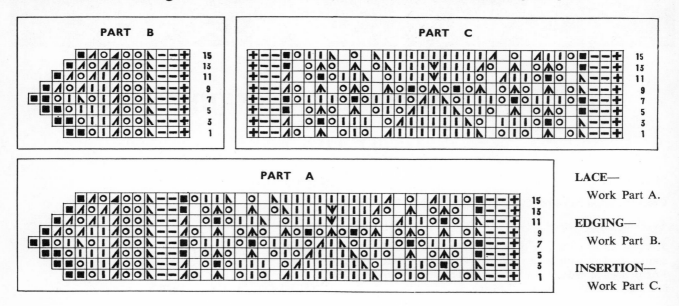

LACE—
Work Part A.

EDGING—
Work Part B.

INSERTION—
Work Part C.

Altar Lace

MATERIALS

Linen Thread No. 20, or Crochet Cotton No. 20.

Two knitting pins No. 14, 14 in. or 15 in. length, or 1 circular needle No. 14, 36 in. to 42 in. length.

Traditionally an altar lace should be worked in linen thread but of course, if not available, crochet cotton will have to be used. The amount of thread needed depends on the length of the altar lace. 1 oz. of linen thread (1 ball of cotton) will work about 7 in. lace, in the width of 13–14 in.

MEASUREMENTS

14 in. deep. Length: one double rose-leaf panel 6 in., one panel of the Cross design 7 in.

WORKING INSTRUCTIONS

The altar lace is composed of the double panel of rose leaves and the panel of the 'Cross' design. These panels have to be worked alternately, however long the lace is required, finishing always with the double panel of rose leaves. It is important that the order of these panels is not changed since the stitches on both sides of these panels interlock in a certain way.

The altar lace starts at the top edge and 47 cast-on stitches are needed to work one double panel of leaves (length 6 in.), 65 stitches are required for one panel of the 'Cross' design (length 7 in.). For the two selvedge edges at the very beginning and the very end of the altar lace 8 stitches are needed (4 stitches each edge).

Cast on, therefore, so many stitches as your panels require for the whole length of lace. If a long knitting needle seems to be too short to take all those stitches use a long circular needle, cast all stitches on to the same and knit to and fro using the two points like knitting pins.

In case the knitter finds such a length of stitches too difficult to work, a smaller amount of panels could be knitted and then stitched together. However, the first method suggested will give the more perfect result.

In the following instructions each row is composed of 4 stitches for the beginning, separated by a hyphen and 4 stitches at the end, after the second hyphen, giving the two selvedge edges on both sides of the whole length of the altar lace.

The part from * to *, the following stitch before the ** and the one more repeat of the part from * to * give the pattern of one double panel of rose leaves.

The section from † to † gives the pattern for the panel of the 'Cross' design.

Every row of which the number is missing knit purl.

1st row—Sl.1, P.2, (Yo., K.2 tog.) to the last 3 stitches, P.2, Sl.1.

3rd row—Sl.1, P.2, knit plain to the last 3 sts., P.2, Sl.1.

5th row, 7th row—as 3rd row.

9th row—Sl.1, P.2, K.1, - * (Yo., Sl.1, K.1 , psso., K.3, K.2 tog., Yo., K.1B.) twice, Yo., Sl.1, K.1, psso., K.3, K.2 tog., Yo., * K.1B., ** knit once more from * to *, † (K.1B., Yo., Sl.1, K.1, psso., K.3, K.2 tog., Yo.) 8 times, K.1B., †- K.1, P.2, Sl.1.

11th row—Sl.1, P.2, K.1, - * K.1, Yo., (Sl.1, K.1, psso., K.1, K.2 tog., Yo., K.3, Yo.) twice, Sl.1, K.1, psso., K.1, K.2 tog., Yo., K.1, * K.1, ** knit once more from * to *, † (K.2, Yo., Sl.1, K.1, psso., K.1, K.2 tog., Yo., K.1) 8 times, K.1, † - K.1, P.2, Sl.1.

13th row—Sl.1, P.2, K.1, - * K.2, (Yo., Sl.1, K.2 tog., psso., Yo., K.5) twice, Yo., Sl.1, K.2 tog., psso., Yo., K.2, * K.1, ** knit once more from * to *, † (K.3, Yo., Sl.1, K.2 tog., psso., Yo., K.2) 8 times, K.1, † - K.1, P.2, Sl.1.

15th row—Sl.1, P.2, K.1, - * K.2 tog., Yo., K.3, Yo., Sl.1, K.1, psso., K.1, K.2 tog., (Yo., K.1B.) 3 times, Yo., Sl.1, K.1, psso., K.1, K.2 tog., Yo., K.3, Yo., Sl.1, K.1, psso., * K.1, ** knit once more from * to *, † (K.1, K.2 tog., Yo., K.3, Yo., Sl.1, K.1, psso.) 8 times, K.1, † - K.1, P.2, Sl.1.

17th row—Sl.1, P.2, K.2 tog., - * Yo., K.5, Yo., Sl.1, K.2 tog., psso., Yo., K.3, Yo., K.1B., Yo., K.3, Yo., Sl.1, K.2 tog., psso., Yo., K.5, Yo., * Sl.1, K.2 tog., psso., ** knit once from * to *, † (Sl.1, K.2 tog, psso., Yo., K.5, Yo.) 8 times, Sl.1, K.2 tog., psso., † - Sl.1, K.1, psso., P.2, Sl.1.

19th row—Sl.1, P.2, K.1, - * K.6, (K.2 tog., Yo.) twice, K.1B., Yo., K.1, Yo., Sl.1, K.2 tog., psso., Yo., K.1, Yo., K.1B., (Yo., Sl.1, K.1, psso.) twice, K.6, * K.1, ** knit once more from * to *, † K.29, K.2 tog., Yo., K.3, Yo., Sl.1, K.1, psso., K.29, † - K.1, P.2, Sl.1.

21st row—Sl.1, P.2, K.1, - * K.4, K.3 tog., Yo., K.2 tog., K.1, Yo., K.1B., Yo., K.2, Yo., Sl.1, K.2 tog., psso., Yo., K.2, Yo., K.1B., Yo., K.1, Sl.1, K.1, psso., Yo., Sl.2, K.1, p2sso., K.4, * K.1, ** knit once from * to *, † K.28, (K.2 tog., Yo.,) twice, K.1, (Yo., Sl.1, K.1, psso.) twice, K.28, † - K.1, P.2, Sl.1.

23rd row—Sl.1, P.2, K.1, - * K.2, K.3 tog., Yo., K.2 tog., K.2, Yo., K.1B., Yo., K.3, Yo., Sl.1, K.2 tog., psso., Yo., K.3, Yo., K.1B., Yo., K.2, Sl.1, K.1, psso., Yo., Sl.2, K.1, p2sso., K.2, * K.1, ** knit once from * to *, † K.27, (K.2 tog., Yo.) twice, K.3, (Yo., Sl.1, K.1, psso.) twice, K.27, † - K.1, P.2, Sl.1.

25th row—Sl.1, P.2, K.1, - * K.3 tog., Yo., K.2 tog., K.3, Yo., K.1B., Yo., K.4, Yo., Sl.1, K.2 tog., psso., Yo., K.4, Yo., K.1B., Yo., K.3, Sl.1, K.1, psso., Yo., Sl.2, K.1, p2sso., * K.1, ** knit once from * to *, † K.5, Yo., Sl.1, K.1, psso., K.5, K.2 tog., Yo., K.12, (K.2 tog., Yo.) 3 times, K.1, (Yo., Sl.1, K.1, psso.) 3 times, K.12, Yo., Sl.1, K.1, psso., K.5, K.2 tog., Yo., K.5, † - K.1, P.2, Sl.1.

27th row—Sl.1, P.2, K.2 tog., - * Yo., K.2 tog., K.10, Yo., Sl.1, K.2 tog., psso., Yo., K.10, Sl.1, K.1, psso., Yo., * Sl.1, K.2 tog., psso., ** knit once from * to *, † Sl.1, K.1, psso., K.5, Yo., Sl.1, K.1, psso., K.3, K.2 tog., Yo., K.12, (K.2 tog., Yo.) 3 times, K.3, (Yo., Sl.1, K.1, psso.) 3 times, K.12, Yo., Sl.1, K.1 psso., K.3, K.2 tog., Yo., K.5, K.2 tog., † - Sl.1, K.1, psso., P.2, Sl.1.

29th row—Sl.1, P.2, K.1, - * K.2 tog., K.10, (Yo., K.1B.) 3 times, Yo., K.10, Sl.1, K.1, psso., * K.1, ** knit once from * to *, † K.2, Yo., Sl.1, K.1, psso., (Yo., Sl.1, K.1, psso., K.1) twice, K.2 tog., Yo., K.2, K.2 tog., Yo., K.8, (K.2 tog., Yo.) 4 times, K.1, (Yo., Sl.1, K.1, psso.) 4 times, K.7, Yo., Sl.1, K.1, psso., (Yo., Sl.1, K.1, psso., K.1) twice, K.2 tog., Yo., K.2, K.2 tog., Yo., K.3, † - K.1, P.2, Sl.1.

31st row—Sl.1, P.2, K.1, - * Sl.1, K.1, psso., K.7, K.2 tog., Yo., K.3, Yo., K.1B., Yo., K.3, Yo., Sl.1, K.1, psso., K.7, K.2 tog., * K.1, ** Knit once from * to *, † K.4, (Yo., Sl.1, K.1, psso., K.1) twice, (K.2 tog., Yo., K.1) twice, K.7, (K.2 tog., Yo.) 4 times, K.3, (Yo., Sl.1, K.1, psso.) 4 times, K.8, (Yo., Sl.1, K.1, psso., K.1) twice, (K.2 tog., Yo., K.1) twice, K.3, † - K.1, P.2, Sl.1.

33rd row—Sl.1, P.2, K.1, - * Sl.1, K.1, psso., K.5, (K.2 tog., Yo.) twice, K.1B., Yo., K.1, Yo., Sl.1, K.2 tog., psso., Yo., K.1, Yo., K.1B., (Yo., Sl.1, K.1, psso.) twice, K.5, K.2 tog., * K.1, ** knit once from * to *, † K.4, (Yo., Sl.1, K.1, psso., K.1) twice, (K.2 tog., Yo., K.1) twice, K.6, (K.2 tog., Yo.) 5 times, K.1, (Yo., Sl.1, K.1, psso.) 5 times, K.7, (Yo., Sl.1, K.1, psso., K.1) twice, (K.2 tog., Yo., K.1) twice, K.3, † - K.1, P.2, Sl.1.

35th row—Sl.1, P.2, K.1, - * Sl.1, K.1, psso., K.3, K.2 tog., Yo., K.2 tog., K.1, Yo., K.1B., Yo., K.2, Yo., Sl.1, K.2 tog., psso., Yo., K.2, Yo., K.1B., Yo., K.1, Sl.1, K.1, psso., Yo., Sl.1, K.1, psso., K.3, K.2 tog., * K.1, ** knit once from * to *, † K.3, (K.1, Yo., Sl.1, K.1, psso.) twice, Yo., K.1, K.2 tog., psso., Yo., K.3, Yo., Sl.1, K.1, psso., K.4, (K.2 tog., Yo.) 5 times, K.3, (Yo., Sl.1, K.1, psso.) 5 times, K.5, (K.1, Yo., Sl.1, K.1, psso.) twice, Yo., K.1, K.2 tog., psso., Yo., K.3, Yo., Sl.1, K.1, psso., K.2, † - K.1, P.2, Sl.1.

37th row—Sl.1, P.2, K.1, - * Sl.1, K.1, psso., K.1, K.2 tog., Yo., K.2 tog., K.2, Yo., K.1B., Yo., K.3, Yo., Sl.1, K.2 tog., psso., Yo., K.3, Yo., K.1B., Yo., K.2, Sl.1, K.1, psso., Yo., Sl.1, K.1, psso., K.1, K.2 tog., * K.1, ** knit once from * to *, † K.4, (Yo., Sl.1, K.1, psso., K.1) twice, K.2 tog., Yo., K.4, Yo., Sl.1, K.1, psso., K.2, (K.2 tog., Yo.) 6 times, K.1, (Yo., Sl.1, K.1, psso.) 6 times, K.5, (Yo., Sl.1, K.1, psso., K.1) twice, K.2 tog., Yo., K.4, Yo., Sl.1, K.1, psso., K.1, † - K.1, P.2, Sl.1.

39th row—Sl.1, P.2, K.1, - * Sl.1, K.2 tog., psso., Yo., K.2 tog., K.3, Yo., K.1B., Yo., K.4, Yo., Sl.1, K.2 tog., psso., Yo., K.4, Yo., K.1B., Yo., K.3, Sl.1, K.1, psso., Yo., Sl.1, K.2 tog., psso., * K.1, ** Knit once from * to *, † K.4, (Yo., Sl.1, K.1, psso., K.1) twice, K.2 tog., Yo., K.3, K.2 tog., Yo., K.4, (Yo., K.2 tog.) 5 times, Yo., Sl.1, K.2 tog., psso., Yo., (Sl.1, K.1, psso., Yo.) 5 times, K.6, (Yo., Sl.1, K.1, psso., K.1) twice, K.2 tog., Yo., K.3, K.2 tog., Yo., K.2, † - K.1, P.2, Sl.1.

41st row—Sl.1, P.2, K.2 tog., - * Yo., K.2 tog., K.10, Yo., Sl.1, K.2 tog., psso., Yo., K. 10, Sl.1, K.1, psso., Yo., * Sl.1, K.2 tog., psso., ** knit once from * to *, † Sl.1, K.1, psso., K.1, K.2 tog., Yo., K.3, Yo., Sl.1, K.1, psso., (K.1, K.2 tog., Yo., K.1) twice, K.4, (Yo., K.2 tog.) 4 times, Yo., Sl.1, K.2 tog., psso., Yo., K.1B., Yo., Sl.1, K.2 tog., psso., Yo., (Sl.1, K.1, psso., Yo.) 4 times, K.4, K.2 tog., Yo., K.3, Yo., Sl.1, K.1, psso., (K.1, K.2 tog., Yo., K.1) twice, K.1, K.2 tog., † - Sl.1, K.1, psso., P.2, Sl.1.

43rd row—same as 29th row up to first † and then continue: † K.5, K.2 tog., Yo., K.5, Yo., Sl.1, K.1, psso., K.7, (Yo., K.2 tog.) 3 times, (Yo., Sl.1, K.2 tog., psso., Yo., K.1B.) twice, Yo., Sl.1, K.2 tog., psso., (Yo., Sl.1, K.1, psso.) 3 times, Yo., K.7, K.2 tog., Yo., K.5, Yo., Sl.1, K.1, psso., K.5, † - K.1, P.2, Sl.1.

45th row—same as 31st row up to first † K.4, K.2 tog., Yo., K.7, Yo., Sl.1, K.1, psso., K.6, (Yo., K.2 tog.) twice, (Yo., Sl.1, K.2 tog., psso., Yo., K.1B.) 3 times, Yo., Sl.1, K.2 tog., psso., (Yo., Sl.1, K.1, psso.) twice, Yo., K.6, K.2 tog., Yo., K.7, Yo., Sl.1, K.1, psso., K.4, † - K.1, P.2, Sl.1.

47th row—as 33rd row up to first † K.3, K.2 tog., Yo., K.9, Yo., Sl.1, K.1, psso., K.5, Yo., K.2 tog., (Yo., Sl.1, K.2 tog., psso., Yo., K.1B.) 4 times, Yo., Sl.1, K.2 tog., psso., Yo., Sl.1, K.1, psso., Yo., K.5, K.2 tog., Yo., K.9, Yo., Sl.1, K.1, psso., K.3, † - K.1, P.2, Sl.1.

49th row—as 35th row up to first † K.21, (Yo., Sl.1, K.2 tog., psso., Yo., K.1B.) 5 times, Yo., Sl.1, K.2 tog., psso., Yo., K.21, † - K.1, P.2, Sl.1.

51st row—as 37th row to first † K.19, (Yo., Sl.1, K.2 tog., psso., Yo., K.1B.) 6 times, Yo., Sl.1, K.2 tog., psso., Yo., K.19, † - K.1, P.2, Sl.1.

53rd row—as 39th row to first † K.17, (Yo., Sl.1, K.2 tog., psso., Yo., K.1B.) 7 times, Yo., Sl.1, K.2 tog., psso., Yo., K.17, † - K.1, P.2, Sl.1.

55th row—as 41st row to first † Sl.1, K.1, psso., K.14, (Yo., Sl.1, K.2 tog., psso., Yo., K.1B.) 3 times, Yo., Sl.1, K.2 tog., psso., Yo., K.5, (Yo., Sl.1, K.2 tog., psso., Yo., K.1B.) 3 times, Yo., Sl.1, K.2 tog., psso., Yo., K.14, K.2 tog., † - Sl.1, K.1, psso., P.2, Sl.1.

57th row—as 29th row to first † K.13, (Yo., Sl.1, K.2 tog., psso., Yo., K.1B.) 3 times, Yo., Sl.1, K.2 tog., psso., Yo., K.9,

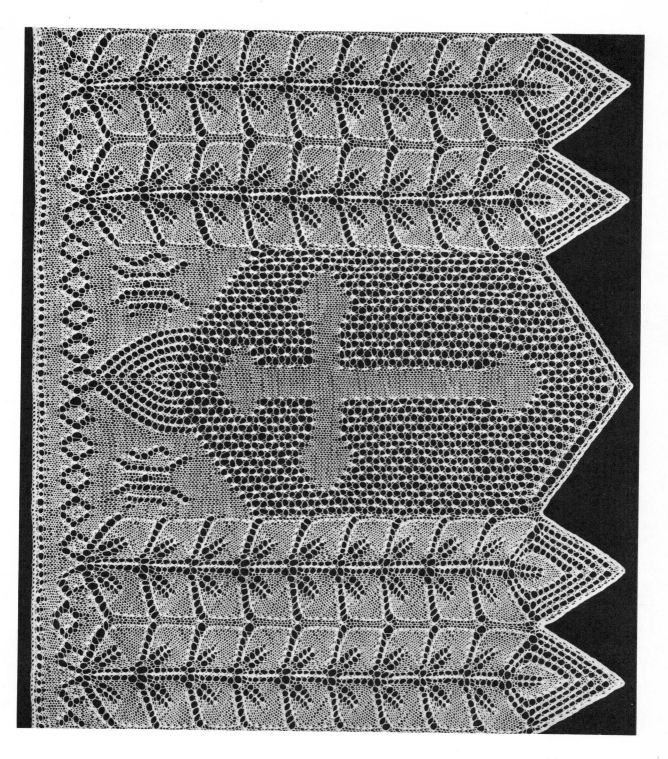

Altar Lace

(Yo., Sl.1, K.2 tog., psso., Yo., K.1B.) 3 times, Yo., Sl.1, K.2 tog., psso., Yo., K.13, † - K.1, P.2, Sl.1.

59th row—as 31st row to first † K.11, (Yo., Sl.1, K.2 tog., psso., Yo., K.1B.) 3 times, Yo., Sl.1, K.2 tog., psso., Yo., K.13, (Yo., Sl.1, K.2 tog., psso., Yo., K.1B.) 3 times, Yo. Sl.1, K.2 tog., psso., Yo., K.11, † - K.1, P.2, Sl.1.

61st row—as 33rd row to first † K.9, (Yo., Sl.1, K.2 tog., psso., Yo., K.1B.) 3 times, Yo., Sl.1, K.2 tog., psso., Yo., K.17, (Yo., Sl.1, K.2 tog., psso., Yo., K1.B.) 3 times, Yo., Sl.1, K.2 tog., psso., Yo., K.9, † - K.1, P.2, Sl.1.

63rd row—as 35th row to first † K.7, (Yo., Sl.1, K.2 tog., psso., Yo., K.1B.) 4 times, Yo., K.2 tog., K.15, Sl.1, K.1, psso., (Yo., K.1B., Yo., Sl.1, K.2 tog., psso.) 4 times, Yo., K.7, † - K.1, P.2, Sl.1.

65th row—as 37th row to first † K.5, (Yo , Sl.1, K.2 tog., psso., Yo., K.1B.) 4 times, Yo., Sl.1, K.2 tog., psso., Yo., K.17, (Yo., Sl.1, K.2 tog., psso., Yo., K.1B.) 4 times, Yo., Sl.1, K.2 tog., psso., Yo., K.5, † - K.1, P.2, Sl.1.

67th row—as 39th row to first † K.3, (Yo., Sl.1, K.2 tog., psso., Yo., K.1B.) 5 times, Yo., Sl.1, K.2 tog., psso., Yo., K.13, (Yo., Sl.1, K.2 tog., psso., Yo., K.1B.) 5 times, Yo., Sl.1, K.2 tog., psso., Yo., K.3, † - K.1, P.2, Sl.1.

69th row—as 41st row to first † Sl.1, K.1, psso., (Yo., Sl.1, K.2 tog., psso., Yo., K.1B.) 6 times, Yo., Sl.1, K.2 tog., psso., Yo., K.9, (Yo., Sl.1, K.2 tog., psso., Yo., K.1B.) 6 times, Yo., Sl.1, K.2 tog., psso., Yo., K.2 tog., † - Sl.1, K.1, psso., P.2, Sl.1.

71st row—as 29th row to first † Sl.1, K.1, psso., (Yo., K.1B., Yo., Sl.1, K.2 tog., psso.) 6 times, Yo., K.1B., Yo., K.2 tog., K.7, Sl.1, K.1, psso., (Yo., K.1B., Yo., Sl.1, K.2 tog., psso.) 6 times, Yo., K.1B., Yo., K.2 tog., † - K.1, P.2, Sl.1.

73rd row—as 31st row to first † K.1, (Yo., Sl.1, K.2 tog., psso., Yo., K.1B.) 6 times, Yo., Sl.1, K.2 tog., psso., Yo., K.9, (Yo., Sl.1, K.2 tog., psso., Yo., K.1B.) 6 times, Yo., Sl.1, K.2 tog., psso., Yo., K.1, † - K.1, P.2, Sl.1.

75th row—as 33rd row to first † and continue as 71st row from † to the end.

77th row—as 35th row to first † and continue as 73rd row from † to end.

79th row—as 37th row to first † and continue as 71st row from † to end.

81st row—as 39th row to first † K.1, (Yo., Sl.1, K.2 tog., psso., Yo., K.1B.) twice, Yo., Sl.1, K.2 tog., psso., Yo., K.5, (Yo., Sl.1, K.2 tog., psso., Yo., K.1B.) twice, Yo., Sl.1, K.2 tog., psso., Yo., K.9, (Yo., Sl.1, K.2 tog., psso., Yo., K.1B.) twice, Yo., Sl.1, K.2 tog., psso., Yo., K.5, (Yo., Sl.1, K.2 tog., psso., Yo., K.1B.) twice, Yo., Sl.1, K.2 tog., psso., Yo., K.1, † - K.1, P.2, Sl.1.

83rd row—as 41st row to first † (Sl.1, K.2 tog., psso., Yo., K.1B., Yo.) twice, Sl.1, K.2 tog., psso., Yo., K.9, (Yo., Sl.1, K.2 tog., psso., Yo., K.1B.) twice, Yo., K.2 tog., K.7, Sl.1, K.1, psso., (Yo., K.1B., Yo., Sl.1, K.2 tog., psso.) twice, Yo., K.9, (Yo., Sl.1, K.2 tog., psso., Yo., K.1B.) twice, Yo., Sl.1, K.2 tog., psso., † - Sl.1, K.1, psso., P.2, Sl.1.

85th row—as 29th row to first † K.1, Yo., Sl.1, K.2 tog., psso., Yo., K.1B., Yo., Sl.1, K.2 tog., psso., Yo., K.49, Yo., Sl.1, K.2 tog., psso., Yo., K.1B., Yo., Sl.1, K.2 tog., psso., Yo., K.1, † - K.1, P.2, Sl.1.

87th row—as 31st row to first † Sl.1, K.1, psso., Yo., K.1B., Yo., Sl.1, K.2 tog., psso., Yo., K.53, Yo., Sl.1, K.2 tog., psso., Yo., K.1B., Yo., K.2 tog., † - K.1, P.2, Sl.1.

89th row—as 33rd row to first † K.1, Yo., Sl.1, K.2 tog., psso., Yo., K.1B., Yo., K.2 tog., K.51, Sl.1, K.1, psso., Yo., K.1B., Yo., Sl.1, K.2 tog., psso., Yo., K.1, † - K.1, P.2, Sl.1.

91st row—as 35th row to first † and continue as 87th row to the end.

93rd row—as 37th row to first † and continue as 85th row to the end.

95th row—39th row to first † Sl.1, K.1, psso., (Yo., K.1B., Yo., Sl.1, K.2 tog., psso.) twice, Yo., K.9, (Yo., Sl.1, K.2 tog., psso., Yo., K.1B.) twice, Yo., K.2 tog., K.7, Sl.1, K.1, psso., (Yo., K.1B., Yo., Sl.1, K.2 tog., psso.) twice, Yo., K.9, (Yo., Sl.1, K.2 tog., psso., Yo., K.1B.) twice, Yo., K.2 tog., † - K.1, P.2, Sl.1.

97th row—as 41st row to first † Sl.1, K.1, psso., (Yo., Sl.1, K.2 tog., psso., Yo., K.1B.) twice, Yo., Sl.1, K.2 tog., psso., Yo., K.5, (Yo., Sl.1, K.2 tog., psso., Yo., K.1B.) twice, Yo., Sl.1, K.2 tog., psso., Yo., K.9, (Yo., Sl.1, K.2 tog., psso., Yo., K.1B.) twice, Yo., Sl.1, K.2 tog., psso., Yo., K.5, (Yo., Sl.1, K.2 tog., psso., Yo., K.1B.) twice, Yo., Sl.1, K.2 tog., psso., Yo., K.2 tog., † - Sl.1, K.1, psso., P.2, Sl.1.

99th row—as 29th row to first † and continue as 71st row to the end.

101st row—as 31st row to first † and continue as 73rd row to the end.

103rd row—as 33rd row to first † and continue as 71st row to the end.

105th row—as 35th row to first † continue as 73rd row to the end.

107th row—as 37th row to first † continue as 71st row to the end.

109th row—as 39th row to first † continue as 73rd row to the end.

111th row—as 41st row to first † (Sl.1, K.2 tog., psso., Yo., K.1B., Yo.) 7 times, K.2 tog., K.7, Sl.1, K.1, psso., (Yo., K.1B., Yo., Sl.1, K.2 tog., psso.) 7 times, † - Sl.1, K.1, psso., P.2, Sl.1.

113th row—as 29th row to first † continue as 73rd row to the end.

115th row—as 31st row to first † continue as 71st row to the end.

117th row—as 33rd row to first † continue as 73rd row to the end.

119th row—as 35th row to first † continue as 71st row to the end.

121st row—as 37th row to first † continue as 73rd row to the end.

123rd row—as 39th row to first † continue as 71st row to the end.

125th row—as 41st row to first † continue as 69th row to the end.

127th row to 139th row are exactly the same as 99th row to 111th row.

141st row—same as 29th row to first † continue as 73rd row to the end.

143rd row—Sl.1, P.2, K.1, - * Sl.1, K.1, psso., K.7, (K.2 tog., Yo.) twice, K.3, (Yo., Sl.1, K.1, psso.) twice, K.7, K.2 tog., * K.1, ** knit once from * to *, † Sl.1, K.1, psso., (Yo., K.1B., Yo., Sl.1, K.2 tog., psso.) 6 times, Yo., K.13, (Yo., Sl.1, K.2, tog., psso., Yo., K.1B.) 6 times, Yo., K.2 tog., † - K.1, P.2, Sl.1.

145th row—Sl.1, P.2, K.1, - * Sl.1, K.1, psso., K.5, (K.2 tog., Yo.) twice, K.2, Yo., K.1B., Yo., K.2, (Yo., Sl.1, K.1, psso.) twice, K.5, K.2 tog., * K.1, ** knit once from * to *, † K.1, (Yo., Sl.1, K.2 tog., psso., Yo., K.1B.) 5 times, Yo., Sl.1, K.2 tog., psso., Yo., K.17, (Yo., Sl.1, K.2 tog., psso., Yo., K.1B.) 5 times, Yo., Sl.1, K.2 tog., psso., Yo., K.1, † - K.1, P.2, Sl.1.

147th row—Sl.1, K.1, psso., P.1, K.1, - * Sl.1, K.1, psso., K.3, (K.2 tog., Yo.) twice, K.2, Yo., K.1B., Yo., K.2, (Sl.1, K.1, psso., Yo.) twice, Sl.1, K.1, psso., K.3, K.2 tog., * K.1, ** knit once from * to *, † Sl.1, K.1, psso., (Yo., K.1B., Yo., Sl.1, K.2 tog., psso.) 5 times, Yo., K.1B., Yo., K.2 tog., K.15, Sl.1, K.1, psso., (Yo., K.1B., Yo., Sl.1, K.2 tog., psso.) 5 times, Yo., K.1B., Yo., K.2 tog., † - K.1, P.1, K.2 tog.

149th row—Sl.1, K.1, psso., K.1, - * Sl.1, K.1, psso., K.1, (K.2 tog., Yo.) twice, K.2 tog., K.3, Yo., K.1B., Yo., K.3, (Sl.1, K.1, psso., Yo.) twice, Sl.1, K.1, psso., K.1, K.2 tog., * K.1, ** knit once from * to *, † K.5, (Yo., Sl.1, K.2 tog., psso., Yo., K.1B.) 4 times, Yo., Sl.1, K.2 tog., psso., Yo., K.17, (Yo., Sl.1, K.2 tog., psso., Yo., K.1B.) 4 times, Yo., Sl.1, K.2 tog., psso., Yo., K.5, † - K.1, K.2 tog.

151st row—Sl.1, K.1, psso., - * Sl.1, K.2 tog., psso., Yo., K.1B., (Yo., Sl.1, K.1, psso.) twice, K.3, Yo., K.1B., Yo., K.3, (K.2 tog., Yo.) twice, K.1B., Yo., Sl.1, K.2 tog., psso., * M.2, ** knit once from * to *, † K.3, Yo., Sl.1, K.1, psso., K.2, (Yo., Sl.1, K.2 tog., psso., Yo., K.1B.) 4 times, Yo., Sl.1, K.2 tog., psso., Yo., K.13, (Yo., Sl.1, K.2 tog., psso., Yo., K.1B.) 4 times, Yo., Sl.1, K.2 tog., psso., Yo., K.2, K.2 tog., Yo., K.3, † - K.2 tog.

WORKING OF THE SCALLOPS OF THE VARIOUS PANELS

From row 153 onwards the scallops of the various panels are finished separately one after the other.

1. Take on to a spare needle the first 25 stitches which belong to the first 'single leaf panel' and work to and fro, knitting according to the following instructions:

153rd row—(K.1B.) twice, Yo., K.1B., (Yo., Sl.1, K.1, psso.) 3 times, K.7, (K.2 tog., Yo.) 3 times, K.1B., Yo., (K.1B.) twice.

155th row—K.1B., (Sl.1, K.1, psso., Yo.) 4 times, Sl.1, K.1, psso., K.5, K.2 tog., (Yo., K.2 tog.) 4 times, K.1B.

157th row—K.1B., (Sl.1, K.1, psso., Yo.) 4 times, Sl.1, K.1, psso., K.3, K.2 tog., (Yo., K.2 tog.) 4 times, K.1B.

159th row—K.1B., (Sl.1, K.1, psso., Yo.) 4 times, Sl.1, K.1, psso., K.1, K.2 tog., (Yo., K.2 tog.) 4 times, K.1B.

161st row—K.1B., (Sl.1, K.1, psso., Yo.) 4 times, Sl.1, K.2 tog., psso., (Yo., K.2 tog.) 4 times, K.1B.

163rd row—K.1B., (Sl.1, K.1, psso., Yo.) 3 times, Sl.1, K.1, psso., K.1, K.2 tog., (Yo., K.2 tog.) 3 times, K.1B.

165th row—K.1B., (Sl.1, K.1, psso., Yo.) 3 times, Sl.1, K.2 tog., psso., (Yo., K.2 tog.) 3 times, K.1B.

167th row—K.1B., (Sl.1, K.1, psso., Yo.) twice, Sl.1, K.1, psso., K.1, K.2 tog., (Yo., K.2 tog.) twice, K.1B.

169th row—K.1B., (Sl.1, K.1, psso., Yo.) twice, Sl.1, K.2 tog., psso., (Yo., K.2 tog.) twice, K.1B.

171st row—K.1B., Sl.1, K.1, psso., Yo., Sl.1, K.1, psso., K.1, K.2 tog., Yo., K.2 tog., K.1B.

173rd row—K.1B., Sl.1, K.1, psso., Yo., Sl.1, K.2 tog., psso., Yo., K.2 tog., K.1B.

175th row—K.1B., Sl.1, K.1, psso., K.1, K.2 tog., K.1B.

177th row—Sl.2, K.3 tog., p2sso.

Break off and secure thread carefully.

Chart for Altar Lace

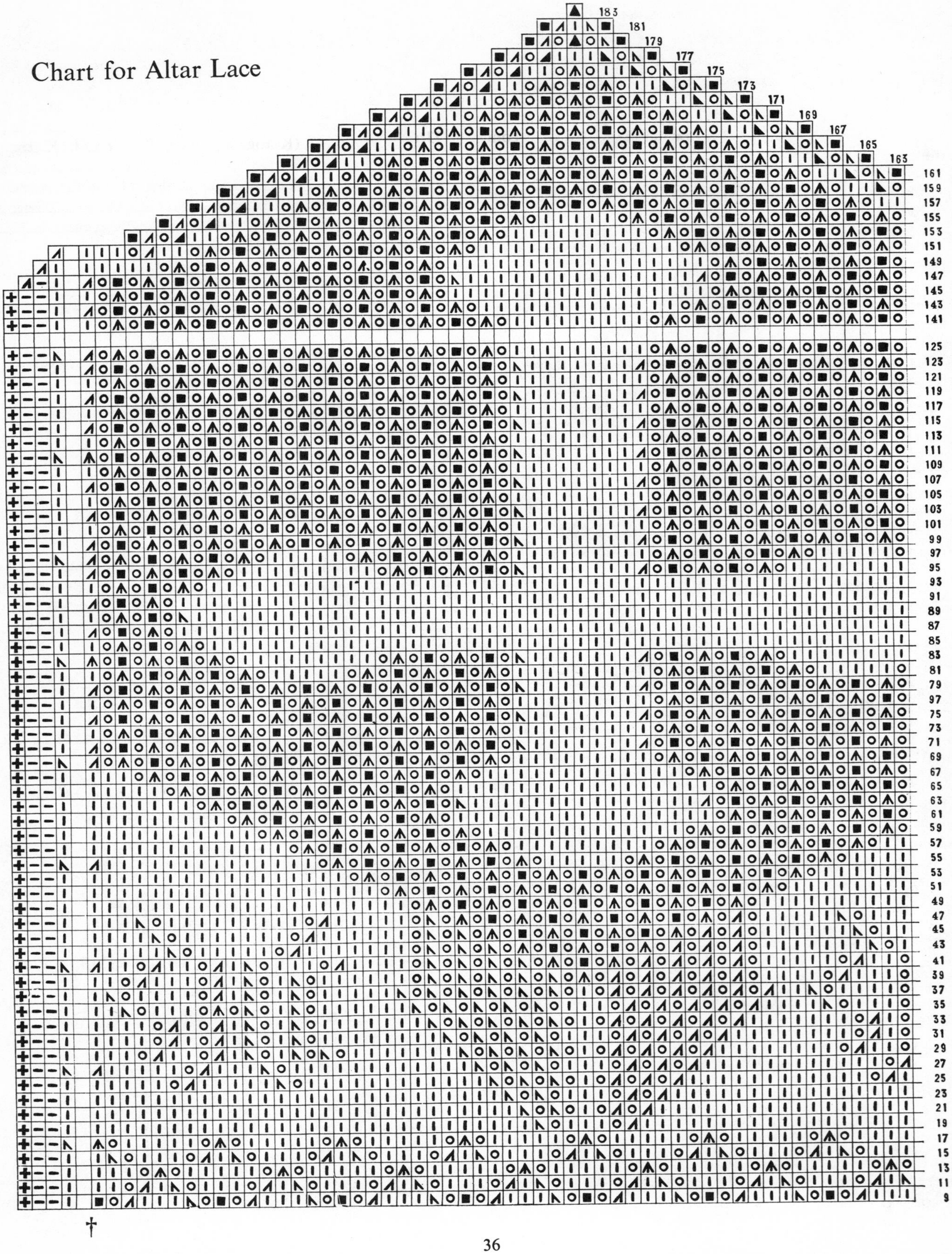

Chart for Altar Lace

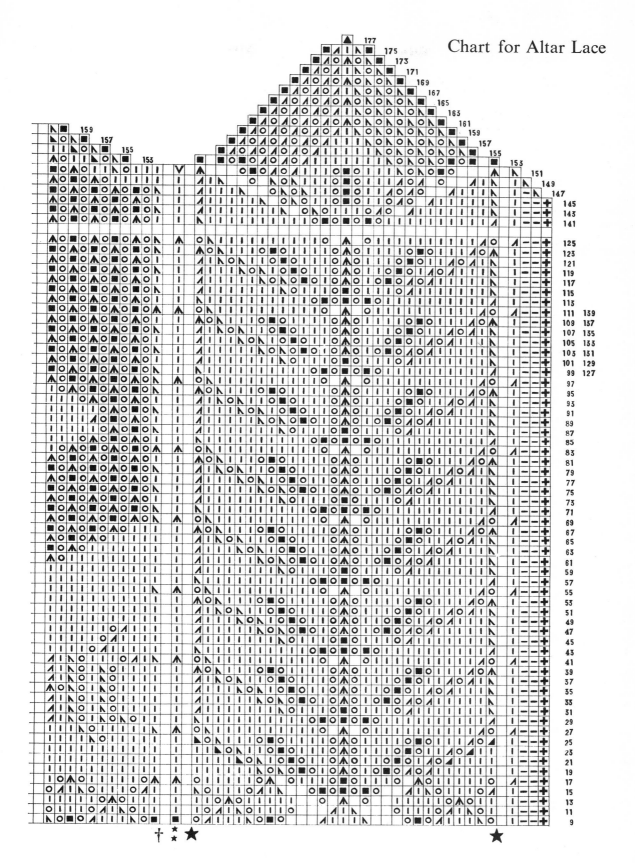

37

2. Take now on to your spare needle the next 25 stitches belonging to the second 'single leaf panel' and knit to and fro, working according to the instructions given for the finishing of the first 'single leaf panel' (rows 153 to 177).

3. Now take on to a spare needle the next 63 stitches belonging to the panel of the 'Cross' and knit according to the following directions:

153rd row—K.1B., Sl.1, K.1, psso., Yo., Sl.2, K.1, p2sso., K.2, (Yo., Sl.1, K.2 tog., psso., Yo., K.1B.) 4 times, Yo., Sl.1, K.2 tog., psso., Yo., K.9, (Yo., Sl.1, K.2 tog., psso., Yo., K.1B.) 4 times, Yo., Sl.1, K.2 tog., psso., Yo., K.2, K.3 tog., Yo., K.2 tog., K.1B.

155th row—K.1B., Sl.1, K.1, psso., Yo., Sl.2, K.1, p2sso., K.2, (Yo., Sl.1, K.2 tog., psso., Yo., K.1B.) 4 times, Yo., Sl.1, K.2 tog., psso., Yo., K.5, (Yo., Sl.1, K.2 tog., psso., Yo., K.1B.) 4 times, Yo., Sl.1, K.2 tog., psso., Yo., K.2, K.3 tog., Yo., K.2 tog., K.1B.

157th row—K.1B., Sl.1, K.1, psso., Yo., Sl.2, K.1, p2sso., K.2, (Yo., Sl.1, K.2 tog., psso., Yo., K.1B.) 9 times, Yo., Sl.1, K.2 tog., psso., Yo., K.2, K.3 tog., Yo., K.2 tog., K.1B.

159th row—K.1B., Sl.1, K.1, psso., Yo., Sl.2, K.1, p2sso., K.2, (Yo., Sl.1, K.2 tog., psso., Yo., K.1B.) 8 times, Yo., Sl.1, K.2 tog., psso., Yo., K.2, K.3 tog., Yo., K.2 tog., K.1B.

161st row—as row 159 but knit the part within the bracket 7 times only.

163rd row—as row 159 but knit the part within the bracket 6 times only.

165th row—as row 159 but the part within the bracket 5 times.

167th row—as row 159 but part within the bracket 4 times only.

169th row—as row 159 but part within the bracket 3 times only.

171st row—as row 159 but part within the bracket twice only.

173rd row—K.1B., Sl.1, K.1, psso., Yo., Sl.2, K.1, p2sso., K.2, Yo., Sl.1, K.2 tog., psso., Yo., K.1B., Yo., Sl.1, K.2 tog., psso., Yo., K.2, K.3 tog., Yo., K.2 tog., K.1B.

175th row—K.1B., Sl.1, K.1, psso., Yo., Sl.2, K.1, p2sso., K.2, Yo., Sl.1, K.2 tog., psso., Yo., K.2, K.3 tog., Yo., K.2 tog., K.1B.

177th row—K.1B., Sl.1, K.1, psso., Yo., Sl.2, K.1, p2sso., K.3, K.3 tog., Yo., K.2 tog., K.1B.

179th row—K.1B., Sl.1, K.1, psso., Yo., Sl.2, K.3 tog., p2sso., Yo., K.2 tog., K.1B.

181st row—K.1B., Sl.1, K.1, psso., K.1, K.2 tog., K.1B.

183rd row—Sl.2, K.3 tog., p2sso.

Break off thread, slip through the last stitch and secure invisibly.

FINISHING OF ALTAR LACE

It is most important that all threads which are left when working the points of the various panels are really secured invisibly. If well done it will look like one continuous edge. One can, of course, also work a row of double crochet into all the stitches into the bottom edge of the lace working 2 d.c. into 1st. This gives a very firm finish to the lace.

The altar lace could be pinned out to measurements, but starching and ironing is also sufficient since it is a perfectly flat piece of lace. Take care of the various points when ironing. The two points of the double rose leaf panel are shorter than the point of the panel of the 'Cross'.

Chart for Altar Lace

(See pages 36 and 37)

Work according to the written instructions up to and inclusive of row 8 and then proceed with row 9 of the Chart.

Remember that from row 153 onwards the points of the panels are finished separately by knitting to and fro a certain amount of stitches. See written instructions.

Since the Chart is too large for one page, each chart line is continued on the opposite page. To facilitate the reading the numbers of the lines are given once more before the continuation of the corresponding line.

Every row of which the number is missing knit purl.

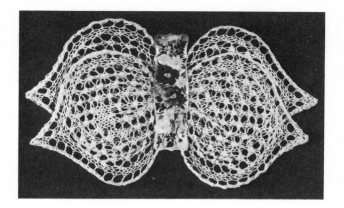

'Fritillary' Design

DRESS TRIMMING

MATERIALS

One ball of Crochet Cotton No. 20, or 1 oz. of Linen Thread No. 20 is sufficient for numerous trimmings, 2 knitting needles No. 13.

MEASUREMENTS

About 7 in. from point to point. This size could easily be altered by using finer or thicker needles.

CASTING-ON

Commence by casting on 9 stitches, work 1 plain and 1 purl row and then knit first pattern row of PART A.

Every row of which the number is missing work purl.

PART A

1st row—(K.1B.) twice, Yo., K.2, Yo., K.1B., Yo., K.2, Yo., (K.1B.) twice.

3rd row—(K.1B.) twice, Yo., K.2, Yo., K.1B., Yo., Sl.1, K.2 tog., psso., Yo., K.1B., Yo., K.2, Yo., (K.1B.) twice.

5th row—(K.1B.) twice, Yo., K.2, (Yo., K.1B., Yo., Sl.1, K.2 tog., psso.) twice, Yo., K.1B., Yo., K.2, Yo., (K.1B.) twice.

7th row—(K.1B.) twice, Yo., K.2, (Yo., K.1B., Yo., Sl.1, K.2 tog., psso.) 3 times, Yo., K.1B., Yo., K.2, Yo., (K.1B.) twice.

Now proceed with PART B1.

PART B1

9th row—(K.1B.) twice, Yo., K.2, (Yo., K.1B., Yo., Sl.1, K.2 tog., psso.) 4 times, Yo., K.1B., Yo., K.2, Yo., (K.1B.) twice.

11th row—K.1B., Sl.1, K.1, psso., Yo., K.2, (Yo., Sl.1, K.2 tog., psso., Yo., K.1B.) 4 times, Yo., Sl.1, K.2 tog., psso., Yo., K.2, Yo., K.2 tog., K.1B.

13th row—K.1B., Sl.1, K.1, psso., Yo., K.1, Sl.1, K.1, psso., (Yo., K.1B., Yo., Sl.1, K.2 tog., psso.) 4 times, Yo., K.1B., Yo., K.2 tog., K.1, Yo., K.2 tog., K.1B.

15th row—same as 11th row.

17th row—same as 13th row.

19th row—same as 11th row.

Now proceed with PART C.

PART C

21st row—K.1B., Sl.1, K.1, psso., Yo., K.1, Sl.2, K.1, p2sso., (Yo., Sl.1, K.2 tog., psso., Yo., K.1B.) 3 times, Yo., Sl.1, K.2 tog., psso., Yo., K.3 tog., K.1, Yo., K.2 tog., K.1B.

23rd row—K.1B., Sl.1, K.1, psso., Yo., K.1, Sl.2, K.1, p2sso., Yo., (Sl.1, K.2 tog., psso., Yo., K.1B., Yo.) twice, Sl.1, K.2 tog., psso., Yo., K.3 tog., K.1, Yo., K.2 tog., K.1B.

25th row—K.1B., Sl.1, K.1, psso., Yo., K.1, Sl.2, K.1, p2sso., Yo., Sl.1, K.2 tog., psso., Yo., K.1B., Yo., Sl.1, K.2 tog., psso., Yo., K.3 tog., K.1, Yo., K.2 tog., K.1B.

27th row—K.1B., Sl.1, K.1, psso., Yo., K.1, Sl.2, K.1, p2sso., Yo., Sl.1, K.2 tog., psso., Yo., K.3 tog., K.1, Yo., K.2 tog., K.1B.

29th row—K.1B., Sl.1, K.1, psso., Yo., K.1, Sl.1, K.1, psso., K.1, K.2 tog., K.1, Yo., K.2 tog., K.1B.

31st row—K.1B., Sl.1, K.1, psso., Yo., K.1, Sl.1, K.2 tog., psso., K.1, Yo., K.2 tog., K.1B.

33rd row—K.1B., Sl.1, K.1, psso., Yo., Sl.1, K.2 tog., psso., Yo., K.2 tog., K.1B.

35th row—K.1B., Sl.1, K.1, psso., K.1, K.2 tog., K.1B.

37th row—Sl.2, K.3 tog., p2sso.

Break off the thread and then take great care to secure thread invisibly.

Now take on to your needle the 9 stitches of the cast-on end of the finished wing and work as follows: Knit PART A, PART B1 up to and inclusive row 13, then work PART B2.

PART B2

15th row—K.1B., Sl.1, K.1, psso., Yo., K.2, Yo., Sl.1, K.2 tog., psso., Yo., K.1B., Yo., Sl.1, K.2 tog., psso., Yo., K.5, Yo., Sl.1, K.2 tog., psso., Yo., K.1B., Yo., Sl.1, K.2 tog., psso., Yo., K.2, Yo., K.2 tog., K.1B.

17th row—K.1B., Sl.1, K.1, psso., Yo., K.1, Sl.1, K.1, psso., Yo., K.1B., Yo., Sl.1, K.2 tog., psso., Yo., K.9, Yo., Sl.1, K.2 tog., psso., Yo., K.1B., Yo., K.2 tog., K.1, Yo., K.2 tog., K.1B.

19th row—same as 15th row.

Now proceed with PART C, finishing it carefully the same way as already explained.

This piece of lace is worked once more to give the dress trimming the appearance of a four-winged butterfly.

Wash, starch and iron carefully and pin together with a suitable brooch.

This dress trimming can, of course, be varied by working the first two wings both plain or both spotted.

Chart for 'Fritillary' Design

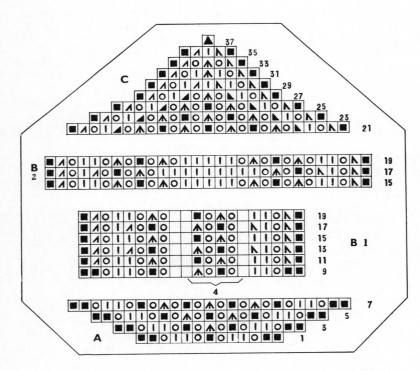

Work PART A, PART B1 and PART C.

Work PART A, PART B1 row 13 inclusive, PART B2, and PART C.

Every chart line is one pattern row, but knit the section within the brackets 4 times.

Every row of which the number is missing work purl.

'Diamond' Design

YOKE FOR
NIGHTGOWN
OR BLOUSE

(Note: this design calls for four needles but was put into this section because of its character.)

MATERIALS

One ball of Crochet Cotton No. 40, or 1 oz. of Linen Thread No. 40.

Four double pointed knitting needles No. 14, length 9 in., or one circular needle No. 14, length 16 in.

One steel crochet hook No. 5.

MEASUREMENTS

2½ in. to 3 in. deep—inner edge 8 in. square.
The design can easily be adapted to other measurements.

CASTING-ON

Commence by casting-on 304 stitches on to 3 needles having 76 stitches each on the first and second needles, and 152 on the third needle. By help of this arrangement one side of the yoke will be worked on the first needle, one on the second and two sides will be worked on the third needle.

Every round of which the number is missing knit plain.

Take care of the working of Yo.2 as explained in BASIC INSTRUCTIONS.

Work two rounds plain and then proceed with the third pattern round.

Knit each section from [to] 4 times in one round
Work each part from * to * 4 times in each section

3rd round—[Yo., Sl.1, K.2 tog., psso., * (Yo.2, Sl.1, K.2 tog., psso.) 6 times, * Yo., K.1B.]

4th round—Knit plain but work a K.1, P.1 into Yo.2 of previous round.

5th round—[Yo., K.2, * K.18, * K.1, Yo., K.1B.]

7th round—[Yo., K.1, Yo., K.2, * K.18, * K.1, Yo., K.1, Yo., K.1B.]

9th round—[(Yo., Sl.1, K.2 tog., psso.) twice, * (Yo., Sl.1, K.2 tog., psso.) 6 times, * Yo., Sl.1, K.2 tog., psso., Yo., K.1B.]

11th round—[Yo., K.3, Yo., M.2, * (Yo., K.3, Yo., K.1B.) twice, Yo., K.3, Yo., M.2, * Yo., K.3, Yo., K.1B.]

13th round—[Yo., K.1, Yo., Sl.1, K.2 tog., psso., Yo., (K.1 o.1), * (K.1 o.1) (Yo., Sl.1, K.2 tog., psso.) 5 times, Yo., (K.1 o.1) * (K.1 o.1), Yo., Sl.1, K.2 tog., psso., Yo., K.1, Yo., K.1B.]

15th round—[Yo., K.2, K.2 tog., Yo., (K.1 o.1) twice, * (K.1 o.1), Yo., Sl.1, K.1, psso., K.2, Yo., K.1B., Yo., K.2, K.2 tog., Yo., (K.1 o.1) twice, * (K.1 o.1), Yo., Sl.1, K.1, psso., K.2, Yo., K.1B.]

17th round—[Yo., K.1, Yo., Sl.1, K.2 tog., psso., Yo., (K.1 o.1) twice, * (K.1 o.1) twice, (Yo., Sl.1, K.2 tog., psso.) 3 times, Yo., (K.1 o.1) twice, * (K.1 o.1) twice, Yo., Sl.1, K.2 tog., psso., Yo., K.1, Yo., K.1B.]

19th round—[Yo., K.2, K.2 tog., Yo., Sl.1, K.1, psso., (K.1 o.1) twice, * (K.1 o.1), K.2 tog., Yo., Sl.1, K.1, psso., K.1, K.2 tog., Yo., Sl.1, K.1, psso., (K.1 o.1) twice, * (K.1 o.1), K.2 tog., Yo., Sl.1, K.1, psso., K.2, Yo., K.1B.]

21st round—[Yo., K.1, Yo., Sl.1, K.2 tog., psso., Yo., K.1, Yo., Sl.1, K.1, psso., (K.1 o.1), * (K.1 o.1), K.2 tog., Yo., K.1, Yo., Sl.1, K.2 tog., psso., Yo., K.1, Yo., Sl.1, K.1, psso., (K.1 o.1), * (K.1 o.1), K.2 tog., Yo., K.1, Yo., Sl.1, K.2 tog., psso., Yo., K.1, Yo., K.1B.]

23rd round—[Yo., K.3, Yo., K.1B., Yo., K.3, Yo., Sl.1, K.1, psso., (K.1 o.1), * K.2 tog., Yo., K.3, Yo., K.1B., Yo., K.3, Yo., Sl.1, K.1, psso., (K.1 o.1), * K.2 tog., (Yo., K.3, Yo., K.1B.) twice.]

25th round—[Yo., K.1, (Yo., Sl.1, K.2 tog., psso.) 3 times, Yo., K.1, Yo., Sl.1, K.1, psso., * K.2 tog., Yo., K.1, (Yo., Sl.1, K.2 tog., psso.) 3 times, Yo., K.1, Yo., Sl.1, K.1, psso., * K.2 tog., Yo., K.1, (Yo., Sl.1, K.2 tog., psso.) 3 times, Yo., K.1, Yo., K.1B.]

27th round—[(Yo., K.3, Yo., K.1B.) twice, Yo., K.3, Yo., K.2 tog., * (Yo., K.3, Yo., K.1B.) twice, Yo., K.3, Yo., K.2 tog., * (Yo., K.3, Yo., K.1B.) 3 times.]

29th round—[Yo., K.1, Yo., Sl.1, K.2 tog., psso., (Yo.2, Sl.1, K.2 tog., psso.) 5 times, * (Yo.2, Sl.1, K.2 tog., psso.) 6 times, * (Yo.2, Sl.1, K.2 tog., psso.) 5 times, Yo., K.1, Yo., K.1B.]

30th round—Knit plain but work K.1, P.1 into Yo.2 of previous round.

31st round—[Yo., K.19, * K.18, * K.18, Yo., K.1B.]

33rd round—[K.20, * K.18, * K.19, Yo., K.1B., Yo.]

35th round—(Yo.2, Sl.1, K.2 tog., psso.) all round.

36th round—Knit plain but work K.1, P.1 into Yo.2 of previous round.

37th round—Knit plain.

After last round of plain cast off all stitches fairly loosely so that the edge stretches easily to the necessary measurements.

To give the inside edge a firmer finish it is advisable to work one round of d.c. making one d.c. into one cast-on stitch.

Wash and starch the lace, lay it flat on an ironing board and stretch it gently into shape. When almost dry iron carefully.

Adaptation of Pattern

The pattern of the yoke is made up of a certain number of sections called side section and the corners. With altering the number of side sections the pattern can be adapted to a different size. The corners and the depth of the lace remain the same.

One side section is in the instructions the part from * to * and requires 18 cast-on stitches measuring about 2 in. If more side sections are added the lace increases accordingly.

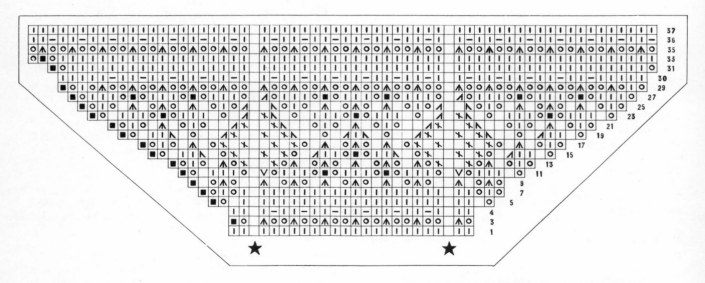

Chart for Yoke

Every chart line to be knitted 4 times in one round.

Work the part from * to * 4 times in each section.

Take care of the working of Yo.2 as explained in BASIC INSTRUCTIONS.

Every round of which the number is missing knit plain.

'Grand Slam' Design

TEA CLOTH FOR BRIDGE PARTY

This cloth is worked in single motifs of four different designs: Club, Diamond, Heart and Spade and one motif of a lace ground pattern. These motifs are joined together as explained in the following working instructions and their number and arrangement can vary according to the individual taste of the knitter and the required size of the cloth.

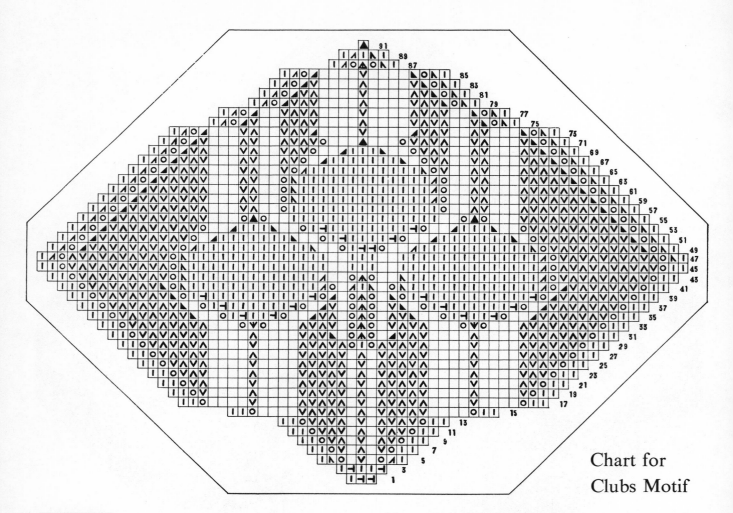

Chart for Clubs Motif

MATERIALS

Eight motifs of this design can be worked from one ball of Crochet Cotton No. 50 or 60, or 1 oz. of Linen Thread No. 50 or 60.

Two knitting needles No. 13.

One steel crochet hook No. 4 or 5.

MEASUREMENTS

Each motif is 5½ in. square.

Motif for Club

Commence by casting on 3 stitches, turn and work 1 row purl. Now knit first pattern row.

Every row of which the number is missing work purl.

1st row—(KM.1B.) twice, K.1.

3rd row—KM.1B., K.2, KM.1B., K.1.

5th row—K.1, K.2 tog., Yo., M.2, Yo., Sl.1, K.1, psso., K.1.

7th row—K.2, Yo., M.2, K.2 tog., M.2, Yo., K.2.

9th row—K.2, Yo., (M.2, K.2 tog.) twice, M.2, Yo., K.2.

11th row—K.2, Yo., (M.2, K.2 tog.) 3 times, M.2, Yo., K.2.

13th row—K.2, Yo., (M.2, K.2 tog.) 4 times, M.2, Yo., K.2.

15th row—K.2, Yo., (M.2, K.2 tog.) 5 times, M.2, Yo., K.2.

17th row—K.2, Yo., (M.2, K.2 tog.) 6 times, M.2, Yo., K.2.

19th row—K.2, Yo., (M.2, K.2 tog.) 7 times, M.2, Yo., K.2.

21st row—K.2, Yo., (M.2, K.2 tog.) 8 times, M.2, Yo., K.2.

23rd row—K.2, Yo., (M.2, K.2 tog.) 9 times, M.2, Yo., K.2.

25th row—K.2, Yo., (M.2, K.2 tog.) 10 times, M.2, Yo., K.2.

27th row—K.2, Yo., (M.2, K.2 tog.) 11 times, M.2, Yo., K.2.

29th row—K.2, Yo., (M.2, K.2 tog.) 6 times, Yo., K.1, Yo., (K.2 tog., M.2) 6 times, Yo., K.2.

31st row—K.2, Yo., (M.2, K.2 tog.) 5 times, M.2, K.3 tog., Yo., Sl.1, K.2 tog., psso., Yo., Sl.2, K.1, p2sso., (M.2, K.2 tog.) 5 times, M.2, Yo., K.2.

33rd row—K.2, Yo., (M.2, K.2 tog.) 4 times, Yo., M.3, Yo., (K.2 tog., M.2) twice, Yo., Sl.1, K.2 tog., psso., Yo., (M.2, K.2 tog.) twice, Yo., M.3, Yo., (K.2 tog., M.2) 4 times, Yo., K.2.

35th row—K.2, Yo., (M.2, K.2 tog.) 3 times, M.2, K.3 tog., Yo., KM.1B., K.2, KM.1B., K.1, Yo., Sl.2, K.1, p2sso., M.2, K.2 tog., Yo., Sl.1, K.2 tog., psso., Yo., K.2 tog., M.2, K.3 tog., Yo., KM.1B., K.2, KM.1B., K.1, Yo., Sl.2, K.1, p2sso., (M.2, K.2 tog.) 3 times, M.2, Yo., K.2.

37th row—K.2, Yo., (M.2, K.2 tog.) 3 times, * M.2, K.3 tog., Yo., KM.1B., K.6, KM.1B., K.1, Yo., Sl.2, K.1, p2sso., M.2, * Yo., Sl.1, K.2 tog., psso., Yo., knit once more from * to *, (K.2 tog., M.2) 3 times, Yo., K.2.

39th row—K.2, Yo., (M.2, K.2 tog.) 3 times, M.2, * K.3 tog., Yo., KM.1B., K.10, KM.1B., K.1, Yo., Sl.2, K.1, p2sso., *, Yo., Sl.1, K.2 tog., psso., Yo., knit once more from * to *, (M.2, K.2 tog.) 3 times, M.2, Yo., K.2.

41st row—K.2, Yo., (M.2, K.2 tog.) 3 times, M.2, K.3 tog., Yo., K.2 tog., K.13, Sl.1, K.1, psso., Yo., Sl.1, K.1, psso., K.1, K.2 tog., Yo., K.2 tog., K.13, Sl.1, K.1, psso., Yo., Sl.2, K.1, p2sso., (M.2, K.2 tog.) 3 times, M.2, Yo., K.2.

43rd row—K.2, Yo., (M.2, K.2 tog.) 4 times, M.2, Yo., K.2 tog., K.13, Sl.1, K.1, psso., Yo., Sl.1, K.2 tog., psso., Yo., K.2 tog., K.13, Sl.1, K.1, psso., Yo., (M.2, K.2 tog.) 4 times, M.2, Yo., K.2.

45th row—K.2, Yo., (M.2, K.2 tog.) 5 times, Yo., K.2 tog., K.31, Sl.1, K.1, psso., Yo., (K.2 tog., M.2) 5 times, Yo., K.2.

47th row—K.1, Sl.1, K.1, psso., Yo., (K.2 tog., M.2) 5 times, Yo., K.2 tog., K.31, Sl.1, K.1, psso., Yo., (M.2, K.2 tog.) 5 times, Yo., K.2 tog., K.1.

49th row—K.1, Sl.1, K.1, psso., Yo., Sl.2, K.1, p2sso., (M.2, K.2 tog.) 4 times, M.2, Yo., Sl.1, K.1, psso., K.11, K.2 tog., Yo., (KM.1B.) twice, K.1, Yo., Sl.1, K.1, psso., K.11, K.2 tog., Yo., (M.2, K.2 tog.) 4 times, M.2, K.3 tog., Yo., K.2 tog., K.1.

51st row—K.1, Sl.1, K.1, psso., Yo., Sl.2, K.1, p2sso., (M.2, K.2 tog.) 4 times, M.2, Yo., Sl.2, K.1, p2sso., K.7, K.3 tog., Yo., KM.1B., K.4, KM.1B., K.1, Yo., Sl.2, K.1, p2sso., K.7, K.3 tog., Yo., (M.2, K.2 tog.) 4 times, M.2, K.3 tog., Yo., K.2 tog., K.1.

53rd row—K.1, Sl.1, K.1, psso., Yo., Sl.2, K.1, p2sso., (M.2, K.2 tog.) 4 times, M.2, Yo., Sl.2, K.1, p2sso., K.3, K.3 tog., Yo., KM.1B., K.8, KM.1B., K.1, Yo., Sl.2, K.1, p2sso., K.3, K.3 tog., Yo., (M.2, K.2 tog.) 4 times, M.2, K.3 tog., Yo., K.2 tog., K.1.

55th row—K.1, Sl.1, K.1, psso., Yo., Sl.2, K.1, p2sso., (M.2, K.2 tog.) 4 times, M.2, Yo., Sl.2, K.3 tog., p2sso., Yo., K.15, Yo., Sl.2, K.3 tog., p2sso., Yo., (M.2, K.2 tog.) 4 times, M.2, K.3 tog., Yo., K.2 tog., K.1.

57th row—K.1, Sl.1, K.1, psso., Yo., Sl.2, K.1, p2sso., (M.2, K.2 tog.) 5 times, Yo., K.15, Yo., (K.2 tog., M.2) 5 times, K.3 tog., Yo., K.2 tog., K.1.

59th row—K.1, Sl.1, K.1, psso., Yo., Sl.2, K.1, p2sso., (M.2, K.2 tog.) 4 times, M.2, Yo., K.2 tog., K.13, Sl.1, K.1, psso., Yo., (M.2, K.2 tog.) 4 times, M.2, K.3 tog., Yo., K.2 tog., K.1.

61st row—K.1, Sl.1, K.1, psso., Yo., Sl.2, K.1, p2sso., (M.2, K.2 tog.) 4 times, Yo., K.2 tog., K.13, Sl.1, K.1, psso., Yo., (K.2 tog., M.2) 4 times, K.3 tog., Yo., K.2 tog., K.1.

63rd row—K.1, Sl.1, K.1, psso., Yo., Sl.2, K.1, p2sso., (M.2, K.2 tog.) 3 times, M.2, Yo., K.2 tog., K.13, Sl.1, K.1, psso., Yo., (M.2, K.2 tog.) 3 times, M.2, K.3 tog., Yo., K.2 tog., K.1.

65th row—K.1, Sl.1, K.1, psso., Yo., Sl.2, K.1, p2sso., (M.2, K.2 tog.) 3 times, M.2, Yo., Sl.1, K.1, psso., K.11, K.2 tog., Yo., (M.2, K.2 tog.) 3 times, M.2, K.3 tog., Yo., K.2 tog., K.1.

67th row—K.1, Sl.1, K.1, psso., Yo., Sl.2, K.1, p2sso., (M.2, K.2 tog.) 3 times, M.2, Yo., Sl.2, K.1, p2sso., K.7, K.3 tog., Yo., (M.2, K.2 tog.) 3 times, M.2, K.3 tog., Yo., K.2 tog., K.1.

69th row—K.1, Sl.1, K.1, psso., Yo., Sl.2, K.1, p2sso., (M.2, K.2 tog.) 3 times, M.2, Yo., Sl.2, K.1, p2sso., K.3, K.3 tog., Yo., (M.2, K.2 tog.) 3 times, M.2, K.3 tog., Yo., K.2 tog., K.1.

71st row—K.1, Sl.1, K.1, psso., Yo., Sl.2, K.1, p2sso., (M.2, K.2 tog.) 3 times, M.2, Yo., Sl.2, K.3 tog., p2sso., Yo., (M.2, K.2 tog.) 3 times, M.2, K.3 tog., Yo., K.2 tog., K.1.

73rd row—K.1, Sl.1, K.1, psso., Yo., Sl.2, K.1, p2sso., (M.2, K.2 tog.) twice, (M.2, K.3 tog.) twice, (M.2, K.2 tog.) twice, M.2, K.3 tog., Yo., K.2 tog., K.1.

75th row—K.1, Sl.1, K.1, psso., Yo., Sl.2, K.1, p2sso., (M.2, K.2 tog.) 5 times, M.2, K.3 tog., Yo., K.2 tog., K.1.

77th row—K.1, Sl.1, K.1, psso., Yo., Sl.2, K.1, p2sso., (M.2, K.2 tog.) 4 times, M.2, K.3 tog., Yo., K.2 tog., K.1.

79th row—K.1, Sl.1, K.1, psso., Yo., Sl.2, K.1, p2sso., (M.2, K.2 tog.) 3 times, M.2, K.3 tog., Yo., K.2 tog., K.1.

81st row—K.1, Sl.1, K.1, psso., Yo., Sl.2, K.1, p2sso., (M.2, K.2 tog.) twice, M.2, K.3 tog., Yo., K.2 tog., K.1.

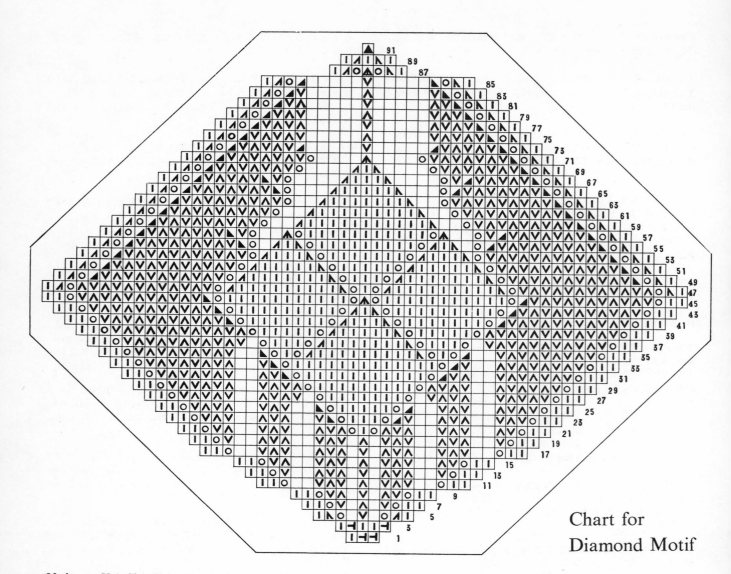

Chart for Diamond Motif

83rd row—K.1, Sl.1, K.1, psso., Yo., Sl.2, K.1, p2sso., M.2, K.2 tog., M.2, K.3 tog., Yo., K.2 tog., K.1.

85th row—K.1, Sl.1, K.1, psso., Yo., Sl.2, K.1, p2sso., M.2, K.3 tog., Yo., K.2 tog., K.1.

87th row—K.1, Sl.1, K.1, psso., Yo., Sl.2, K.2 tog., p2sso., Yo., K.2 tog., K.1.

89th row—K.1, Sl.1, K.1, psso., K.1, K.2 tog., K.1.

91st row—Sl.2, K.3 tog., p2sso.

Break off thread, slip through the last stitch and make sure to secure invisibly.

Thread cast-on end into a needle and draw together the 3 cast-on stitches into a point, so that it looks the same as the finishing point of the motif.

Motif for Diamond

Commence and work according to instructions of MOTIF FOR CLUB up to row 19 inclusive, then continue as follows:

21st row—K.2, Yo., (M.2, K.2 tog.) 4 times, Yo., K.1, Yo., (K.2 tog., M.2) 4 times, Yo., K.2.

23rd row—K.2, Yo., (M.2, K.2 tog.) 3 times, M.2, K.3 tog., Yo., K.3, Yo., Sl.2, K.1, p2sso., (M.2, K.2 tog.) 3 times, M.2, Yo., K.2.

25th row—K.2, Yo., (M.2, K.2 tog.) 3 times, M.2, K.3 tog., Yo., K.5, Yo., Sl.2, K.1, p2sso., (M.2, K.2 tog.) 3 times, M.2, Yo., K.2.

27th row—K.2, Yo., (M.2, K.2 tog.) 4 times, M.2, Yo., K.7, Yo., (M.2, K.2 tog.) 4 times, M.2, Yo., K.2.

46

29th row—K.2, Yo., (M.2, K.2 tog.) 5 times, Yo., K.9, Yo., (K.2 tog., M.2) 5 times, Yo., K.2.

31st row—K.2, Yo., (M.2, K.2 tog.) 4 times, M.2, K.3 tog., Yo., K.11, Yo., Sl.2, K.1, p2sso., (M.2, K.2 tog.) 4 times, M.2, Yo., K.2.

33rd row—K.2, Yo., (M.2, K.2 tog.) 4 times, M.2, K.3 tog., Yo., K.13, Yo., Sl.2, K.1, p2sso., (M.2, K.2 tog.) 4 times, M.2, Yo., K.2.

35th row—K.2, Yo., (M.2, K.2 tog.) 4 times, M.2, K.3 tog., Yo., K.1, Yo., Sl.1, K.1, psso., K.9, K.2 tog., Yo., K.1, Yo., Sl.2, K.1, p2sso., (M.2, K.2 tog.) 4 times, M.2, Yo., K.2.

37th row—K.2, Yo., (M.2, K.2 tog.) 5 times, M.2, Yo., K.3, Yo., Sl.1, K.1, psso., K.7, K.2 tog., Yo., K.3, Yo., (M.2, K.2 tog.) 5 times, M.2, Yo., K.2.

39th row—K.2, Yo., (M.2, K.2 tog.) 6 times, Yo., K.5, Yo., Sl.1, K.1, psso., K.5, K.2 tog., Yo., K.5, Yo., (K.2 tog., M.2) 6 times, Yo., K.2.

41st row—K.2, Yo., (M.2, K.2 tog.) 5 times, M.2, K.3 tog., Yo., K.7, Yo., Sl.1, K.1, psso., K.3, K.2 tog., Yo., K.7, Yo., Sl.2, K.1, p2sso., (M.2, K.2 tog.) 5 times, M.2, Yo., K.2.

43rd row—K.2, Yo., (M.2, K.2 tog.) 5 times, M.2, K.3 tog., Yo., K.9, Yo., Sl.1, K.1, psso., K.1, K.2 tog., Yo., K.9, Yo., Sl.2, K.1, p2sso., (M.2, K.2 tog.) 5 times, M.2, Yo., K.2.

45th row—K.2, Yo., (M.2, K.2 tog.) 5 times, M.2, K.3 tog., Yo., K.11, Yo., Sl.1, K.2 tog., psso., Yo., K.11, Yo., Sl.2, K.1, p2sso., (M.2, K.2 tog.) 5 times, M.2, Yo., K.2.

47th row—K.1, Sl.1, K.1, psso., Yo., (K.2 tog., M.2) 6 times, Yo., Sl.1, K.1, psso., K.9, K.2 tog., Yo., K.1, Yo., Sl.1, K.1, psso., K.9, K.2 tog., Yo., (M.2, K.2 tog.) 6 times, Yo., K.2 tog., K.1.

49th row—K.1, Sl.1, K.1, psso., Yo., Sl.2, K.1, p2sso., (M.2, K.2 tog.) 5 times, M.2, Yo., Sl.1, K.1, psso., K.7, K.2 tog., Yo., K.3, Yo., Sl.1, K.1, psso., K.7, K.2 tog., Yo., (M.2, K.2 tog.) 5 times, M.2, K.3 tog., Yo., K.2 tog., K.1.

51st row—K.1, Sl.1, K.1, psso., Yo., Sl.2, K.1, p2sso., (M.2, K.2 tog.) 5 times, M.2, Yo., Sl.1, K.1, psso., K.5, K.2 tog., Yo., K.5. Yo., Sl.1, K.1, psso., K.5, K.2 tog., Yo., (M.2, K.2 tog.) 5 times, M.2, K.3 tog., Yo., K.2 tog., K.1.

53rd row—K.1, Sl.1, K.1, psso., Yo., Sl.2, K.1, p2sso., (M.2, K.2 tog.) 5 times, M.2, Yo., Sl.1, K.1, psso., K.3, K.2 tog., Yo., K.7, Yo., Sl.1, K.1, psso., K.3, K.2 tog., Yo., (M.2, K.2 tog.) 5 times, M.2, K.3 tog., Yo., K.2 tog., K.1.

55th row—K.1, Sl.1, K.1, psso., * Yo., Sl.2, K.1, p2sso., (M.2, K.2 tog.) 4 times, M.2, K.3 tog., Yo., * Sl.1, K.1, psso., K.1, K.2 tog., Yo., K.9, Yo., Sl.1, K.1, psso., K.1, K.2 tog., knit once more from * to *, K.2 tog., K.1.

57th row—K.1, Sl.1, K.1, psso., Yo., * Sl.2, K.1, p2sso., (M.2, K.2 tog.) 3 times, M.2, K.3 tog., * M.2, Yo., Sl.1, K.2 tog., psso., Yo., K.11, Yo., Sl.1, K.2 tog., psso., Yo., M.2, knit once more from * to *, Yo., K.2 tog., K.1.

59th row—K.1, Sl.1, K.1, psso., Yo., Sl.2, K.1, p2sso., (M.2, K.2 tog.) 4 times, M.2, Yo., Sl.1, K.1, psso., K.11, K.2 tog., Yo., (M.2, K.2 tog.) 4 times, M.2, K.3 tog., Yo., K.2 tog., K.1.

61st row—K.1, Sl.1, K.1, psso., Yo., Sl.2, K.1, p2sso., (M.2, K.2 tog.) 4 times, M.2, Yo., Sl.1, K.1, psso., K.9, K.2 tog., Yo., (M.2, K.2 tog.) 4 times, M.2, K.3 tog., Yo., K.2 tog., K.1.

63rd row—K.1, Sl.1, K.1, psso., Yo., Sl.2, K.1, p2sso., (M.2, K.2 tog.) 4 times, M.2, Yo., Sl.1, K.1, psso., K.7, K.2 tog., Yo., (M.2, K.2 tog.) 4 times, M.2, K.3 tog., Yo., K.2 tog., K.1.

65th row—K.1, Sl.1, K.1, psso., * Yo., Sl.2, K.1, p2sso., (M.2, K.2 tog.) 3 times, M.2, K.3 tog., Yo., * Sl.1, K.1, psso., K.5, K.2 tog., knit once more from * to *, K.2 tog., K.1.

67th row—K.1, Sl.1, K.1, psso., Yo., * Sl.2, K.1, p2sso., (M.2, K.2 tog.) twice, M.2, K.3 tog., * M.2, Yo., Sl.1, K.1, psso., K.3, K.2 tog., Yo., M.2, knit once more from * to *, Yo., K.2 tog., K.1.

69th row—K.1, Sl.1, K.1, psso., Yo., Sl.2, K.1, p2sso., (M.2, K.2 tog.) 3 times, M.2, Yo., Sl.1, K.1, psso., K.1, K.2 tog., Yo., (M.2, K.2 tog.) 3 times, M.2, K.3 tog., Yo., K.2 tog., K.1.

71st row—K.1, Sl.1, K.1, psso., Yo., Sl.2, K.1, p2sso., (M.2, K.2 tog.) 3 times, M.2, Yo., Sl. 1, K.2 tog., psso., Yo., (M.2, K.2 tog.) 3 times, M.2, K.3 tog., Yo., K.2 tog., K.1.

Rows 73 to 91 inclusive and the final finish are the same as given in directions for working the CLUB MOTIF.

Motif for Heart

Commence and work according to instructions of MOTIF FOR DIAMOND up to row 27 inclusive, then continue as follows:

29th row—K.2, Yo., (M.2, K.2 tog.) 3 times, M.2, K.3 tog., Yo., KM.1B., K.6, KM.1B., K.1, Yo., Sl.2, K.1, p2sso., (M.2, K.2 tog.) 3 times, M.2, Yo., K.2.

31st row—K.2, Yo., (M.2, K.2 tog.) 3 times, M.2, K.3 tog., Yo., KM.1B., K.10, KM.1B., K.1, Yo., Sl.2, K.1, p2sso., (M.2, K.2 tog.) 3 times, M.2, Yo., K.2.

33rd row—K.2, Yo., (M.2, K.2 tog.) 3 times, M.2, K.3 tog., Yo., KM.1B., K.14, KM.1B., K.1, Yo., Sl.2, K.1, p2sso., (M.2, K.2 tog.) 3 times, M.2, Yo., K.2.

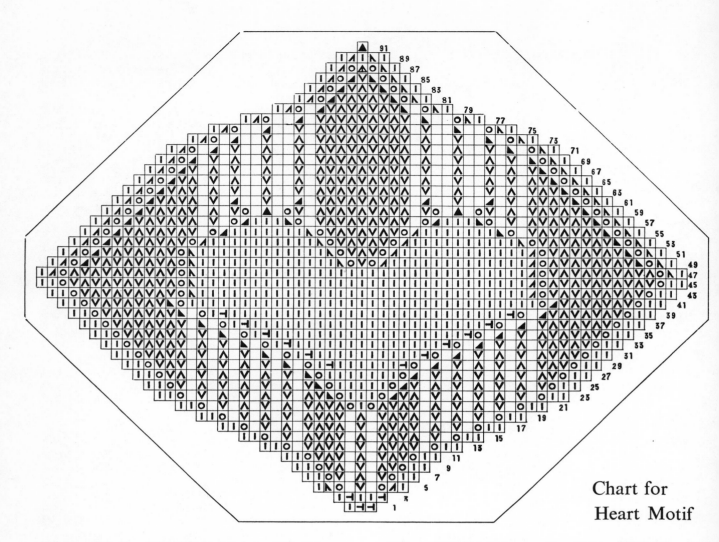

Chart for Heart Motif

35th row—K.2, Yo., (M.2, K.2 tog.) 3 times, M.2, K.3 tog., Yo., KM.1B., K.18, KM.1B., K.1, Yo., Sl.2, K.1, p2sso., (M.2, K.2 tog.) 3 times, M.2, Yo., K.2.

37th row—K.2, Yo., (M.2, K.2 tog.) 3 times, M.2, K.3 tog., Yo., KM.1B., K.22, KM.1B., K.1, Yo., Sl.2, K.1, p2sso., (M.2, K.2 tog.) 3 times, M.2, Yo., K.2.

39th row—K.2, Yo., (M.2, K.2 tog.) 3 times, M.2, K.3 tog., Yo., KM.1B., K.26, KM.1B., K.1, Yo., Sl.2, K.1, p2sso., (M.2, K.2 tog.) 3 times, M.2, Yo., K.2.

41st row—K.2, Yo., (M.2, K.2 tog.) 3 times, M.2, K.3 tog., Yo., K.33, Yo., Sl.2, K.1, p2sso., (M.2, K.2 tog.) 3 times, M.2, Yo., K.2.

43rd row—K.2, Yo., (M.2, K.2 tog.) 4 times, M.2, Yo., K.2 tog., K.31, Sl.1, K.1, psso., Yo., (M.2, K.2 tog.) 4 times, M.2, Yo., K.2.

45th row—K.2, Yo., (M.2, K.2 tog.) 5 times, Yo., K.2 tog., K.31, Sl.1, K.1, psso., Yo., (K.2 tog., M.2) 5 times, Yo., K.2.

47th row—K.1, Sl.1, K.1, psso., Yo., (K.2 tog., M.2) 5 times, Yo., K.2 tog., K.31, Sl.1, K.1, psso., Yo., (M.2, K.2 tog.) 5 times, Yo., K.2 tog., K.1.

49th row—K.1, Sl.1, K.1, psso., Yo., Sl.2, K.1, p2sso., (M.2, K.2 tog.) 4 times, Yo., K.2 tog., K.13, K.2 tog., Yo., M.2, Yo., Sl.1, K.1, psso., K.13, Sl.1, K.1, psso., Yo., (K.2 tog., M.2) 4 times, K.3 tog., Yo., K.2 tog., K.1.

51st row—K.1, Sl.1, K.1, psso., Yo., Sl.2, K.1, p2sso., (M.2, K.2 tog.) 3 times, M.2, Yo., K.2 tog., K.12, K.2 tog., Yo., M.2, Yo., Sl.1, K.1, psso., K.12, Sl.1, K.1, psso., Yo., (M.2, K.2 tog.) 3 times, M.2, K.3 tog., Yo., K.2. tog., K.1.

53rd row—K.1, Sl.1, K.1, psso., Yo., Sl.2, K.1, p2sso., (M.2, K.2 tog.) 3 times, M.2, * Yo., Sl.1, K.1, psso., K.10, K.2 tog., Yo., * (M.2, K.2 tog.) twice, M.2, knit once more from * to *, (M.2, K.2 tog.) 3 times, M.2, K.3 tog., Yo., K.2 tog., K.1.

55th row—K.1, Sl.1, K.1, psso., Yo., Sl.2, K.1, p2sso., (M.2, K.2 tog.) 3 times, M.2, Yo., Sl.2, K.1, p2sso., K.7, K.2 tog., Yo., (M.2, K.2 tog.) 3 times, M.2, Yo., Sl.1, K.1, psso., K.7,

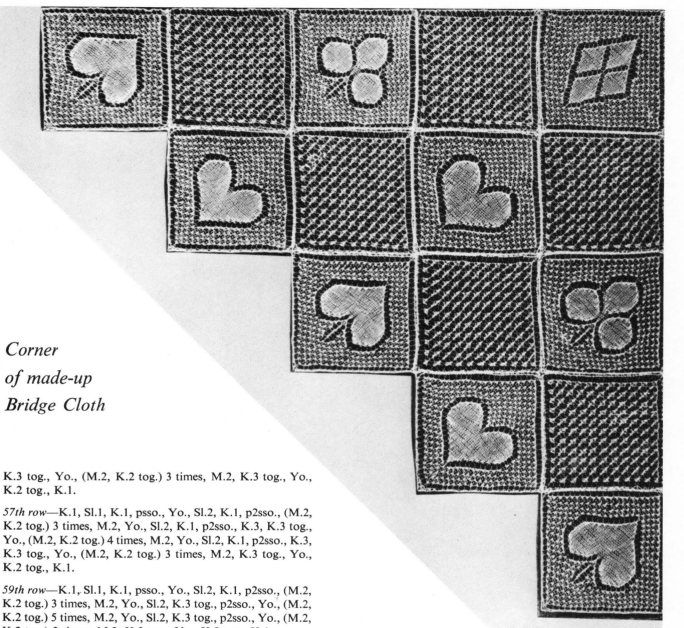

Corner

of made-up

Bridge Cloth

K.3 tog., Yo., (M.2, K.2 tog.) 3 times, M.2, K.3 tog., Yo., K.2 tog., K.1.

57th row—K.1, Sl.1, K.1, psso., Yo., Sl.2, K.1, p2sso., (M.2, K.2 tog.) 3 times, M.2, Yo., Sl.2, K.1, p2sso., K.3, K.3 tog., Yo., (M.2, K.2 tog.) 4 times, M.2, Yo., Sl.2, K.1, p2sso., K.3, K.3 tog., Yo., (M.2, K.2 tog.) 3 times, M.2, K.3 tog., Yo., K.2 tog., K.1.

59th row—K.1, Sl.1, K.1, psso., Yo., Sl.2, K.1, p2sso., (M.2, K.2 tog.) 3 times, M.2, Yo., Sl.2, K.3 tog., p2sso., Yo., (M.2, K.2 tog.) 5 times, M.2, Yo., Sl.2, K.3 tog., p2sso., Yo., (M.2, K.2 tog.) 3 times, M.2, K.3 tog., Yo., K.2 tog., K.1.

61st row—K.1, Sl.1, K.1, psso., Yo., Sl.2, K.1, p2sso., (M.2, K.2 tog.) twice, (M.2, K.3 tog.) twice, (M.2, K.2 tog.) 4 times, (M.2, K.3 tog.) twice, (M.2, K.2 tog.) twice, M.2, K.3 tog., Yo., K.2 tog., K.1.

63rd row—K.1, Sl.1, K.1, psso., Yo., Sl.2, K.1, p2sso., (M.2, K.2 tog.) 11 times, M.2, K.3 tog., Yo., K.2 tog., K.1.

65th row—same as row 63 but knit the section in brackets only 10 times.

67th row—same as row 63 but knit the section in brackets only 9 times.

69th row—same as row 63 but knit section in brackets only 8 times.

71st row—same as row 63 but knit the section in brackets only 7 times.

73rd row—same as row 63 but knit the section in brackets only 6 times.

Rows 75 to 91 inclusive and the final finish are the same as given in the directions for working the CLUB MOTIF.

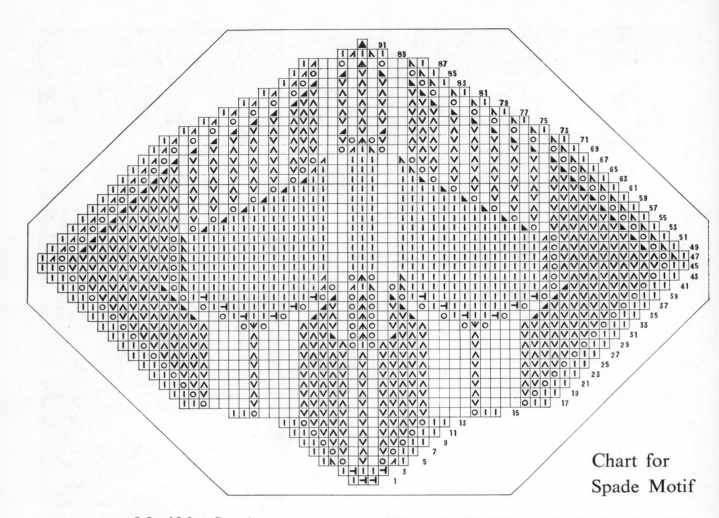

Chart for Spade Motif

Motif for Spade

Commence and work according to instructions of MOTIF FOR CLUB up to row 47 inclusive, then continue as follows:

49th row—K.1, Sl.1, K.1, psso., Yo., Sl.2, K.1, p2sso., (M.2, K.2 tog.) 4 times, Yo., K.2 tog., K.31, Sl.1, K.1, psso., Yo., (K.2 tog., M.2) 4 times, K.3 tog., Yo., K.2 tog., K.1.

51st row—K.1, Sl.1, K.1, psso., Yo., Sl.2, K.1, p2sso., (M.2, K.2 tog.) 3 times, M.2, Yo., K.2 tog., K.31, Sl.1, K.1, psso., Yo., (M.2, K.2 tog.) 3 times, M.2, K.3 tog., Yo., K.2 tog., K.1.

53rd row—K.1, Sl.1, K.1, psso., Yo., Sl.2, K.1, p2sso., (M.2, K.2 tog.) 3 times, M.2, Yo., Sl.2, K.1, p2sso., K.27, K.3 tog., Yo., (M.2, K.2 tog.) 3 times, M.2, K.3 tog., Yo., K.2 tog., K.1.

55th row—K.1, Sl.1, K.1, psso., Yo., Sl.2, K.1, p2sso., (M.2, K.2 tog.) 3 times, M.2, Yo., Sl.2, K.1, p2sso., K.23, K.3 tog., Yo., (M.2, K.2 tog.) 3 times, M.2, K.3 tog., Yo., K.2 tog., K.1.

57th row—K.1, Sl.1, K.1, psso., Yo., Sl.2, K.1, p2sso., (M.2, K.2 tog.) 3 times, M.2, Yo., Sl.2, K.1, p2sso., K.19, K.3 tog., Yo., (M.2, K.2 tog.) 3 times, M.2, K.3 tog., Yo., K.2 tog., K.1.

59th row—K.1, Sl.1, K.1, psso., Yo., Sl.2, K.1, p2sso., (M.2, K.2 tog.) 3 times, M.2, Yo., Sl.2, K.1, p2sso., K.15, K.3 tog., Yo., (M.2, K.2 tog.) 3 times, M.2, K.3 tog., Yo., K.2 tog., K.1.

61st row—K.1, Sl.1, K.1, psso., Yo., Sl.2, K.1, p2sso., (M.2, K.2 tog.) 3 times, M.2, Yo., Sl.2, K.1, p2sso., K.11, K.3 tog., Yo., (M.2, K.2 tog.) 3 times, M.2, K.3 tog., Yo., K.2 tog., K.1.

63rd row—K.1, Sl.1, K.1, psso., Yo., Sl.2, K.1, p2sso., (M.2, K.2 tog.) 3 times, M.2, Yo., Sl.2, K.1, p2sso., K.7, K.3 tog., Yo., (M.2, K.2 tog.) 3 times, M.2, K.3 tog., Yo., K.2 tog., K.1.

65th row—K.1, Sl.1, K.1, psso., Yo., Sl.2, K.1, p2sso., (M.2, K.2 tog.) 3 times, M.2, Yo., Sl.1, K.1, psso., K.5, K.2 tog., Yo., (M.2, K.2 tog.) 3 times, M.2, K.3 tog., Yo., K.2 tog., K.1.

67th row—K.1, Sl.1, K.1, psso., Yo., Sl.2, K.1, p2sso., (M.2, K.2 tog.) 3 times, M.2, Yo., Sl.1, K.1, psso., K.3, K.2 tog., Yo., (M.2, K.2 tog.) 3 times, M.2, K.3 tog., Yo., K.2 tog., K.1.

69th row—K.1, Sl.1, K.1, psso., Yo., Sl.2, K.1, p2sso., (M.2, K.2 tog.) 3 times, M.2, Yo., Sl.1, K.1, psso., K.1, K.2 tog., Yo., (M.2, K.2 tog.) 3 times, M.2, K.3 tog., Yo., K.2 tog., K.1.

71st row—K.1, Sl.1, K.1, psso., Yo., Sl.2, K.1, p2sso., (M.2, K.2 tog.) 3 times, M.2, Yo., Sl.1, K.2 tog., psso., Yo., (M.2, K.2 tog.) 3 times, M.2, K.3 tog., Yo., K.2 tog., K.1.

Rows 73 to 91 inclusive and the final finish are the same as given in directions for working the CLUB MOTIF.

Motif for Lace Ground Pattern

Commence by casting on 3 stitches, turn and work 1 row purl. Now knit first pattern row of PART A.

Every row of which the number is missing work purl.

PART A

1st row—(KM.1B.) twice, K.1.

3rd row—KM.1B., K.2, KM.1B., K.1.

5th row—K.1, K.2 tog., Yo., K.1, Yo., Sl.1, K.1, psso., K.1.

7th row—K.2, Yo., K.3, Yo., K.2.

9th row—K.2, Yo., K.1, Yo., Sl.1, K.2 tog., psso., Yo., K.1, Yo., K.2.

11th row—K.2, Yo., K.3, Yo., K.1B., Yo., K.3, Yo., K.2.

13th row—K.2, Yo., K.1, (Yo., Sl.1, K.2 tog., psso.) 3 times, Yo., K.1, Yo., K.2.

15th row—K.2, (Yo., K.3, Yo., K.1B.) twice, Yo., K.3, Yo., K.2.

17th row—same as 13th row but knit the section within the brackets 5 times.

19th row—same as row 15 but work the section within the brackets 3 times.

Now proceed with PART B.

PART B

21st row—K.2., Yo., K.1, Yo., * (Sl.1, K.2 tog., psso., Yo.) twice, * rep. twice more from * to *, Sl.1, K.2 tog., psso., Yo., K.1, Yo., K.2.

23rd row—K.2, Yo., K.3, * Yo., K.1B., Yo., K.3, * rep. twice more from * to *, Yo., K.1B., Yo., K.3, Yo., K.2.

25th row—K.2, Yo., K.1, Yo., Sl.1, K.2 tog., psso., * (Yo., Sl.1, K.2 tog., psso.) twice, * rep. twice more from * to *, (Yo., Sl.1, K.2 tog., psso.) twice, Yo., K.1, Yo., K.2.

27th row—K.2, Yo., K.3, Yo., K.1B., Yo., * K.3, Yo., K.1B., Yo., * rep. twice more from * to *, K.3, Yo., K.1B., Yo., K.3, Yo., K.2.

29th row to 35th row—same as 21st row to 27th row but knit the section within the asterisks 5 times.

Proceed with PART C.

PART C

37th row to 43rd row—same as 21st row to 27th row but knit the section within the asterisks 7 times.

45th row—K.2, Yo., K.1, (Yo., Sl.1, K.2 tog., psso.) 19 times, Yo., K.1, Yo., K.2.

47th row—K.2, (Yo., K.3, Yo., K.1B.) 10 times, Yo., K.3, Yo., K.2.

49th row—K.1, Sl.1, K.1, psso., (Yo., Sl.1, K.2 tog., psso.) 21 times, Yo., K.2 tog., K.1.

51st row—K.1, Sl.1, K.1, psso., Yo., Sl.1, K.1, psso., K.2, Yo., K.1B., Yo., * K.3, Yo., K.1B., Yo., * rep. 6 times more from * to *, K.3, Yo., K.1B., Yo., K.2, K.2 tog., Yo., K.2 tog., K.1.

53rd row—K.1, Sl.1, K.1, psso., Yo., (Sl.1, K.2 tog., psso., Yo.) twice, * (Sl.1, K.2 tog., psso., Yo.) twice,* rep. 6 times more from * to *, (Sl.1, K.2 tog., psso., Yo.) 3 times, K.2 tog., K.1.

55th row—K.1, Sl.1, K.1, psso., Yo., Sl.1, K.1, psso., K.2, * Yo., K.1B., Yo., K.3, * rep. 6 times more from * to *, Yo., K.1B., Yo., K.2, K.2 tog., Yo., K.2 tog., K.1.

57th row—K.1, Sl.1, K.1, psso., Yo., Sl.1, K.2 tog., psso., * (Yo., Sl.1, K.2 tog., psso.) twice, * rep. 6 times more from * to *, (Yo., Sl.1, K.2 tog., psso.) twice, Yo., K.2 tog., K.1.

Now proceed with PART D.

PART D

59th row to 65th row—same as 51st row to 57th row but knit the section within the asterisks only 5 times.

67th row to 73rd row—same as 51st row to 57th row but knit the section within the asterisks only 3 times.

Proceed with PART E.

PART E

75th row—K.1, Sl.1, K.1, psso., Yo., Sl.1, K.1, psso., (K.2, Yo., K.1B., Yo., K.1) 3 times, K.1, K.2 tog., Yo., K.2 tog., K.1.

77th row—K.1, Sl.1, K.1, psso., (Yo., Sl.1, K.2 tog., psso.) 7 times, Yo., K.2 tog., K.1.

79th row—same as 75th row but knit the section within the bracket only twice.

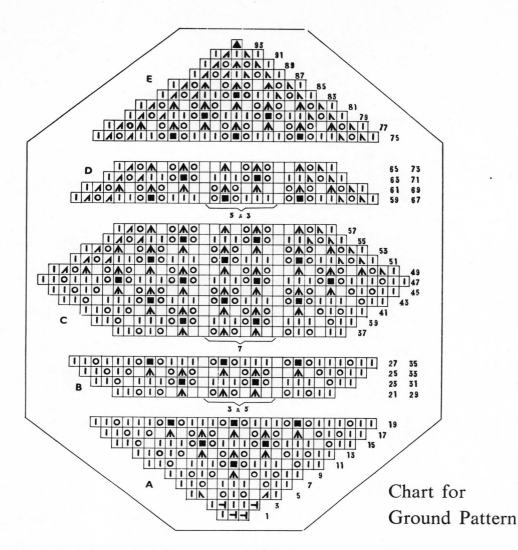

Chart for Ground Pattern

81st row—same as 77th row but knit the section within the bracket only 5 times.

83rd row—same as 75th row but knit the section within the bracket only once.

85th row—same as 77th row but knit the section within the bracket only 3 times.

87th row—K.1, Sl.1, K.1, psso., Yo., Sl.1, K.1, psso., K.1, K.2 tog., Yo., K.2 tog., K.1.

89th row—K.1, Sl.1, K.1, psso., Yo., Sl.1, K.2 tog., psso., Yo., K.2 tog., K.1.

91st row—K.1, Sl.1, K.1, psso., K.1, K.2 tog., K.1.

93rd row—Sl.2, K.3 tog., p2sso.

Break off thread, slip through the last stitch and make sure to secure invisibly.

Thread cast-on end into a needle and draw together the 3 cast-on stitches into a point, so that it looks the same as the finishing point of the Motif.

FINISHING OF THE BRIDGE CLOTH

The squares can now be joined together either by overcasting stitches (sewing together the end stitches of the various motives) or with help of a crochet hook.

The washed and starched lace cloth can either be ironed out to its shape or pinned out by making a paper pattern consisting of as many squares as the cloth is composed of. Since all the squares are of the same size, either method of finishing will give a perfect result.

CHART INSTRUCTIONS

Club, Diamond, Heart and Spade: every chart line to be knitted once in one row.

Every row of which the number is missing work purl.

Motif for Ground Pattern: Every chart line to be knitted once in one row but work the section within the bracket as many times as stated below. When two numbers are given the first refers to the first set of numbers beside the chart, the second to the second set. Every row of which the number is missing work purl.

CHAPTER III

DESIGNS WORKED IN WOOL

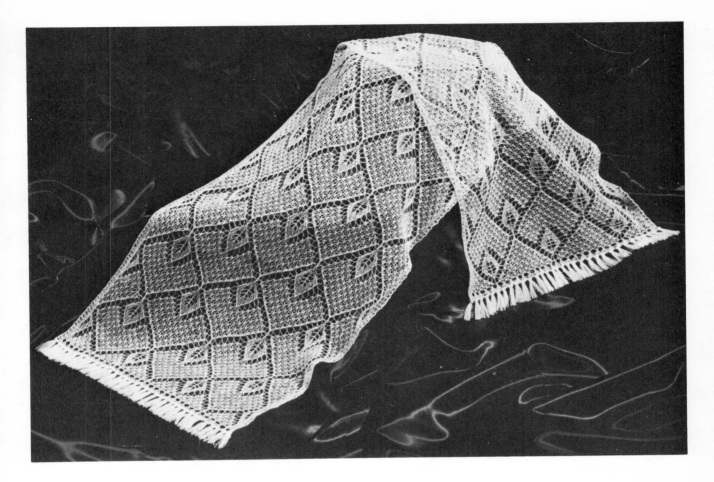

'Arabesque' Design

SCARF

MATERIALS

One oz. 1-ply wool, or 2 oz. 2-ply wool.

Two knitting pins No. 10.

MEASUREMENTS

Length 42 in. Width 13 in.

The design can easily be adapted to other measurements as shown in paragraph ADAPTATION OF PATTERN.

CASTING-ON

Commence by casting on 97 stitches and then knit the first pattern row of PART A.

Notice: Every row of which the number is missing knit purl.

PART A

1st row—Sl.1, P.2, knit to the last 3 stitches, P.2, Sl.1.

3rd row—Sl.1, P.2, K.2 tog., * (Yo., Sl.1, K.2 tog., psso.) 9 times, Yo., ** Sl.1, K.2 tog., psso., * rep. once more from * to *, rep. once more from * to **, Sl.1, K.1, psso., P.2, Sl.1, Pay special attention to next row.

4th row—Knit purl but work 2 stitches, that is K.1, P.1, into all Yo. of previous pattern round.

5th row—Sl.1, P.2, M.2, * (K.2 tog., M.2) 4 times, K.2 tog., Yo., K.1, Yo., (K.2 tog., M.2) 4 times, K.2 tog., ** M.2, * rep. once more from * to *, rep. once more from * to **, M.2, P.2, Sl.1.

Now proceed with PART B.

PART B

7th row—Sl.1, P.2, K.2 tog., * (M.2, K.2 tog.) 3 times, M.2, K.3 tog., Yo., K.3, Yo., Sl.2, K.1, p2sso., (M.2, K.2 tog.) 3 times, M.2, ** K.2 tog., * rep. once more from * to *, rep. once more from * to **, K.2 tog., P.2, Sl.1.

9th row—Sl.1, P.2, M.2, * (K.2 tog., M.2) 3 times, K.3 tog., Yo., K.5, Yo., Sl.2, K.1, p2sso., (M.2, K.2 tog.) 3 times, ** M.2, * rep. once more from * to *, rep. once more from * to **, M.2, P.2, Sl.1.

11th row—Sl.1, P.2, K.2 tog., * (M.2, K.2 tog.) twice, M.2, K.3 tog., Yo., K.2 tog., K.1, Yo., K.1B., Yo., K.1, Sl.1, K.1, psso., Yo., Sl.2, K.1, p2sso., (M.2, K.2 tog.) twice, M.2, ** K.2 tog., * rep. once more from * to *, rep. once more from * to **, K.2 tog., P.2, Sl.1.

13th row—Sl.1, P.2, M.2, * (K.2 tog., M.2) twice, K.3 tog., Yo., K.2 tog., K.2, Yo., K.1B., Yo., K.2, Sl.1, K.1, psso., Yo., Sl.2, K.1, p2sso., (M.2, K.2 tog.) twice, ** M.2, * rep. once more from * to *, rep. once more from * to **, M.2, P.2, Sl.1.

15th row—Sl.1, P.2, K.2 tog., * M.2, K.2 tog., M.2, K.3 tog., Yo., M.2, Yo., Sl.1, K.1, psso., K.2, Yo., K.1B., Yo., K.2, K.2 tog., Yo., M.2, Yo., Sl.2, K.1, p2sso., M.2, K.2 tog., M.2, ** K.2 tog., * rep. once more from * to *, rep. once from * to **, K.2 tog., P.2, Sl.1.

17th row—Sl.1, P.2, M.2, * K.2 tog., M.2, K.3 tog., Yo., M.2, K.2 tog., M.2, Yo., Sl.1, K.1, psso., K.5, K.2 tog., Yo., M.2, K.2 tog., M.2, Yo., Sl.2, K.1, p2sso., M.2, K.2 tog., ** M.2, * rep. once more from * to *, rep. once from * to **, M.2, P.2, Sl.1.

19th row—Sl.1, P.2, K.2 tog., * M.2, K.3 tog., Yo., (M.2, K.2 tog.) twice, M.2, Yo., Sl.1, K.1, psso., K.3, K.2 tog., Yo., (M.2, K.2 tog.) twice, M.2, Yo., Sl.2, K.1, p2sso., M.2, ** K.2 tog., * rep. once more from * to *, rep. once from * to **, K.2 tog., P.2, Sl.1.

21st row—Sl.1, P.2, M.2, * K.3 tog., Yo., (M.2, K.2 tog.) 3 times, M.2, Yo., Sl.1, K.1, psso., K.1, K.2 tog., Yo., (M.2, K.2 tog.) 3 times, M.2, Yo., Sl.2, K.1, p2sso., ** M.2, * rep. once more from * to *, rep. once from * to **, M.2, P.2, Sl.1.

23rd row—Sl.1, P.2, K.3 tog., * Yo., (M.2, K.2 tog.) 4 times, M.2, Sl.1, K.2 tog., psso., (M.2, K.2 tog.) 4 times, M.2, Yo., ** Sl.2, K.2 tog., p2sso., * rep. once more from * to *, rep. once from * to **, Sl.2, K.1, p2sso., P.2, Sl.1.

25th row—Sl.1, P.2, K.2 tog., * Yo., (K.2 tog., M.2) 9 times, K.2 tog., Yo., ** Sl.1, K.2 tog., psso., * rep. once more from * to *, rep. once from * to **, Sl.1, K.1, psso., P.2, Sl.1.

27th row—Sl.1, P.2, K.1, * K.1, Yo., Sl.2, K.1, p2sso., (M.2, K.2 tog.) 7 times, M.2, K.3 tog., Yo., K.1, ** K.1, * rep. once more from * to *, rep. once from * to **, K.1, P.2, Sl.1.

29th row—Sl.1, P.2, K.1, * K.2, Yo., Sl.2, K.1, p2sso., (M.2, K.2 tog.) 6 times, M.2, K.3 tog., Yo., K.2, ** K.1, * rep. once more from * to *, rep. once from * to **, K.1, P.2, Sl.1.

31st row—Sl.1, P.2, K.1B., * Yo., K.1, Sl.1, K.1, psso., Yo., Sl.2, K.1, p2sso., (M.2, K.2 tog.) 5 times, M.2, K.3 tog., Yo., K.2 tog., K.1, Yo., ** K.1B., * rep. once more from * to *, rep. once from * to **, K.1B., P.2, Sl.1.

33rd row—Sl.1, P.2, K.1B., * Yo., K.2, Sl.1, K.1, psso., Yo., Sl.2, K.1, p2sso., (M.2, K.2 tog.) 4 times, M.2, K.3 tog., Yo., K.2 tog., K.2, Yo., ** K.1B., * rep. once more from * to *, rep. once from * to **, K.1B., P.2, Sl.1.

35th row—Sl.1, P.2, K.1B., * Yo., K.2, K.2 tog., Yo., M.2, Yo., Sl.2, K.1, p2sso., (M.2, K.2 tog.) 3 times, M.2, K.3 tog., Yo., M.2, Yo., Sl.1, K.1, psso., K.2, Yo., ** K.1B., * rep. once more from * to *, rep. once from * to **, K.1B., P.2, Sl.1.

37th row—Sl.1, P.2, K.1, * K.2, K.2 tog., Yo., M.2, K.2 tog., M.2, Yo., Sl.2, K.1, p2sso., (M.2, K.2 tog.) twice, M.2, K.3 tog., Yo., M.2, K.2 tog., M.2, Yo., Sl.1, K.1, psso., K.2, ** K.1, * rep. once more from * to *, rep. once from * to **, K.1, P.2, Sl.1.

39th row—Sl.1, P.2, K.1, * K.1, K.2 tog., Yo., (M.2, K.2 tog.) twice, M.2, Yo., Sl.2, K.1, p2sso., M.2, K.2 tog., M.2, K.3 tog., Yo., (M.2, K.2 tog.) twice, M.2, Yo., Sl.1, K.1, psso., K.1, ** K.1, * rep. once more from * to *, rep. once from * to **, K.1, P.2, Sl.1.

41st row—Sl.1, P.2, K.1, * K.2 tog., Yo., (M.2, K.2 tog.) 3 times, M.2, Yo., Sl.2, K.1, p2sso., M.2, K.3 tog., Yo., (M.2, K.2 tog.) 3 times, M.2, Yo., Sl.1, K.1, psso., ** K.1, * rep. once more from * to *, rep. once from * to **, K.1, P.2, Sl.1.

43rd row—Sl.1, P.2, K.2 tog., * (M.2, K.2 tog.) 4 times, M.2, Yo., Sl.2, K.2 tog., p2sso., Yo., (M.2, K.2 tog.) 4 times, M.2, ** Sl.1, K.2 tog., psso., * rep. once more from * to *, rep. once from * to **, Sl.1, K.1, psso., P.2, Sl.1.

45th row—Sl.1, P.2, M.2, * (K.2 tog., M.2) 4 times, K.2 tog., Yo., Sl.1, K.2 tog., psso., Yo., (K.2 tog., M.2) 4 times, K.2 tog., ** M.2, * rep. once more from * to *, rep. once from * to **, M.2, P.2, Sl.1.

After finishing purl row 46, work PART B rows 7 to 45 inclusive 7 times more, and then knit PART B another time but only to row 43 inclusive. Now proceed with PART C.

PART C

45th row—Sl.1, P.2, K.1, * (K.2 tog., M.2) 5 times, K.1, (M.2, K.2 tog.) 5 times, ** M.2, * rep. once more from * to *, rep. once from * to **, K.1, P.2, Sl.1.

47th row—Sl.1, P.2, Yo., * (Sl.1, K.2 tog., psso., Yo.) 10 times, Sl.1, K.2 tog., psso., ** Yo., * rep. once more from * to *, rep. once from * to **, Yo., P.2, Sl.1.

Pay special attention to next row.

48th row—Knit purl but work 2 stitches, that is K.1, P.1, into all Yo. of previous pattern row.

49th row—Sl.1, P.2, knit to the last 3 stitches, P.2, Sl.1.

50th row—turn and cast off.

Break off wool and secure end invisibly.

STRETCHING AND FINISHING OF SCARF

Prepare paper pattern by drawing an oblong 13 in. by 42 in. Take the lace scarf which has been washed and pin down the corners first. Then pin out the scarf along the edges in regular spaces.

Finish by treating the lace according to BASIC INSTRUCTIONS.

The scarf could also be fringed in a similar fashion to the stole, only a shorter fringe will be more suitable. Cut a cardboard about 2½ in. wide, wind round required wool and cut along one edge. Then take about 6 strands of the cut wool, fold into half, draw folded end with help of crochet hook through the hole of edge, draw cut ends through the loop and pull tight. Complete fringe by working one tassel into each hole and cut evenly.

Adaptation of Pattern

The pattern is made up of the selvedge edge on each side and a middle panel, the latter being composed of the section within the asterisks. If the number of middle sections is altered the width of the lace scarf alters accordingly.

The selvedge edges on the right and left measure together 1 in., and 8 stitches are needed for the start. One middle section requires 30 stitches and measures 4 in. It is therefore possible to cast on as many times 30 stitches as the width of the scarf to be worked requires, remembering that an extra inch will be added by the edges on each side. **Notice:** the last repeat of the middle section will require only 29 cast-on stitches.

The length of the pattern is governed by the repetition of PART B, one repeat measuring 4½ in. PARTS A and C which form the borders on the top and bottom measure together 1 in.

In this manner scarves of various sizes can be worked, and the pattern is quite suitable for knitting even a large stole.

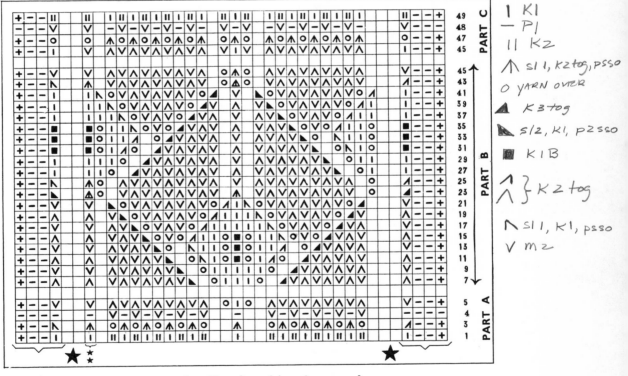

Chart for Design 'Arabesque'

Work PART A, PART B 8 times and a 9th time up to and inclusive row 43. Then work PART C.

Every chart line to be knitted once in one row but work the section from * to * 3 times but notice: when knitting the section from * to * for the 3rd time leave out the last stitch marked with ** and add immediately the 4 stitches forming the end selvedge edge. Every row of which the number is missing work purl.

'La Traviata' Design

STOLE

MATERIALS

Five oz. 1-ply wool, or about 7 oz. very fine 2-ply wool.

Two knitting pins No. 9 or 10.

MEASUREMENTS

Length 83 in., width 32 in. The design can easily be adapted to other measurements as given in paragraph ADAPTATION OF PATTERN.

CASTING-ON

Commence by casting-on 234 stitches, turn and work 1 row purl. Now knit first pattern row of PART A bottom edge. **Notice:** the first and last stitch of every pattern row could also be slipped knitwise to obtain a chain edge if desired.

Every row of which the number is missing work purl, but great care must be taken of the knitting of Yo.2 as explained in BASIC INSTRUCTIONS.

PART A

1st row—P.3, knit to last 3 stitches, P.3.

3rd row—P.3, K.2 tog., Yo.2, Sl.1, K.1, psso., * (K.2 tog., Yo.2, Sl.1, K.1, psso.) 11 times, * rep. 4 times more from * to *, K.2 tog., Yo.2, Sl.1, K.1, psso., P.3.

5th row—P.3, K.2, K.2 tog., Yo., * (Yo., Sl.1, K.1, psso., K.2 tog., Yo.) 11 times, * rep. 4 times more from * to *, Yo., Sl.1, K.1, psso., K.2, P.3.

7th row—same as 3rd row.

9th row—same as 5th row.

Proceed with PART B.

PART B

11th row—P.3, K.2 tog., Yo.2, Sl.1, K.1, psso., * (K.2 tog., Yo.2, Sl.1, K.1, psso.) 4 times, K.2 tog., Yo.2, Sl.2, K.1, p2sso., Yo., K.2 tog., Yo., K.3 tog., Yo.2, Sl.1, K.1, psso., (K.2 tog., Yo.2, Sl.1, K.1, psso.) 4 times, * rep. 4 times more from * to *, K.2 tog., Yo.2, Sl.1, K.1, psso., P.3.

13th row—P.3, K.2, K.2 tog., Yo., * (Yo., Sl.1, K.1, psso., K.2 tog., Yo.) 4 times, Yo., Sl.1, K.1, psso., K.2, Yo., Sl.1, K.2 tog., psso., Yo., K.2, K.2 tog., Yo., (Yo., Sl.1, K.1, psso., K.2 tog., Yo.) 4 times, * rep. 4 times more from * to *, Yo., Sl.1, K.1, psso., K.2, P.3.

15th row—P.3, K.2 tog., Yo.2, Sl.1, K.1, psso., * (K.2 tog., Yo.2, Sl.1, K.1, psso.) 5 times, Yo., K.3, Yo., (K.2 tog., Yo.2, Sl.1, K.1, psso.) 5 times, * rep. 4 times more from * to *, K.2 tog., Yo.2, Sl.1, K.1, psso., P.3.

17th row—P.3, K.2, K.2 tog., Yo., * (Yo., Sl.1, K.1, psso., K.2 tog., Yo.) 5 times, K.1, (KM.1B) twice, K.2, Yo., K.2, K.2 tog., Yo., (Yo., Sl.1, K.1, psso., K.2 tog., Yo.) 4 times, * rep. 4 times more from * to *, Yo., Sl.1, K.1, psso., K.2, P.3.

19th row—P.3, K.2 tog., Yo.2, Sl.1, K.1, psso., * (K.2 tog., Yo.2, Sl.1, K.1, psso.) 4 times, K.3 tog., Yo., K.2 tog., K.1, (KM.1B) twice, K.2, Sl.1, K.1, psso., Yo., (K.2 tog., Yo.2, Sl.1, K.1, psso.) 5 times, * rep. 4 times more from * to *, K.2 tog., Yo.2, Sl.1, K.1, psso., P.3.

21st row—P.3, K.2, K.2 tog., Yo., * (Yo., Sl.1, K.1, psso., K.2 tog., Yo.) 3 times, Yo., Sl.1, K.1, psso., K.3 tog., Yo., K.2 tog., K.2, (KM.1B) twice, K.3, Sl.1, K.1, psso., Yo., K.2, K.2 tog., Yo., (Yo., Sl.1, K.1, psso., K.2 tog., Yo.) 4 times, * rep. 4 times more from * to *, Yo., Sl.1, K.1, psso., K.2, P.3.

23rd row—P.3, K.2 tog., Yo.2, Sl.1, K.1, psso., * (K.2 tog., Yo.2, Sl.1, K.1, psso.) 3 times, K.3 tog., Yo., K.2 tog., K.3, (KM.1B.) twice, K.4, Sl.1, K.1, psso., Yo., (K.2 tog., Yo.2, Sl.1, K.1, psso.) 5 times, * rep. 4 times more from * to *, K.2 tog., Yo.2, Sl.1, K.1, psso., P.3.

25th row—P.3, K.2, K.2 tog., Yo., * (Yo., Sl.1, K.1, psso., K.2 tog., Yo.) twice, Yo., Sl.1, K.1, psso., K.3 tog., Yo., K.2 tog., K.4, (KM.1B.) twice, K.5, Sl.1, K.1, psso., Yo., K.2, K.2 tog., Yo., (Yo., Sl.1, K.1, psso., K.2 tog., Yo.) 4 times, * rep. 4 times more from * to *, Yo., Sl.1, K.1, psso., K.2, P.3.

27th row—P.3, K.2 tog., Yo.2, Sl.1, K.1, psso., * (K.2 tog., Yo.2, Sl.1, K.1, psso.) twice, K.3 tog., Yo., K.2 tog., K.13, Sl.1, K.1, psso., Yo., (K.2 tog., Yo.2, Sl.1, K.1, psso.) 5 times, * rep. 4 times more from * to *, K.2 tog., Yo.2, Sl.1, K.1, psso., P.3.

29th row—P.3, K.2, K.2 tog., Yo., * Yo., Sl.1, K.1, psso., K.2 tog., Yo.2, Sl.1, K.1, psso., K.3 tog., Yo., K.2 tog., K.13, Sl.1, K.1, psso., Yo., K.2, K.2 tog., Yo., (Yo., Sl.1, K.1, psso., K.2 tog., Yo.) 4 times, * rep. 4 times more from * to *, Yo., Sl.1, K.1, psso., K.2, P.3.

31st row—P.3, K.2 tog., Yo.2, Sl.1, K.1, psso., * K.2 tog., Yo.2, Sl.1, K.1, psso., K.3 tog., Yo., K.2 tog., K.11, K.3 tog., Yo.2, K.1, (K.2 tog., Yo.2, Sl.1, K.1, psso.) twice, K.4, (K.2 tog., Yo.2, Sl.1, K.1, psso.) twice, * rep. 4 times more from * to *, K.2 tog., Yo.2, Sl.1, K.1, psso., P.3.

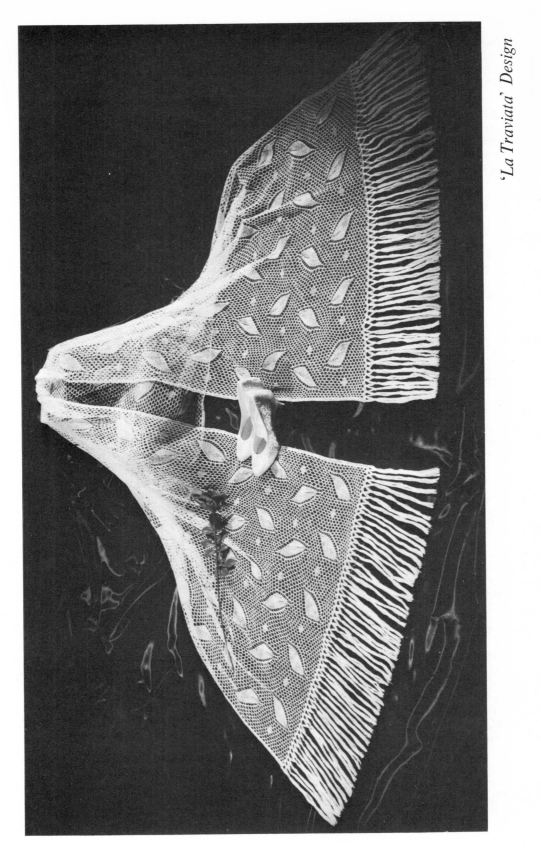

33rd row—P.3, K.2, K.2 tog., Yo., * Yo., Sl.1, K.1, psso., K.1, K.2 tog., Yo., K.2 tog., K.9, K.3 tog., Yo.2, K.1, (K.2 tog., Yo.2, Sl.1, K.1, psso.) twice, K.8, K.2 tog., Yo.2, Sl.1, K.1, psso., K.2 tog., Yo., * rep. 4 times more from * to *, Yo., Sl.1, K.1, psso., K.2, P.3.

35th row—P.3, K.2 tog., Yo.2, Sl.1, K.1, psso., * K.2 tog., Yo.2, Sl.1, K.1, psso., Yo., K.2 tog., K.7, K.3 tog., Yo.2, K.1, (K.2 tog., Yo.2, Sl.1, K.1, psso.) 3 times, K.4, (K.2 tog., Yo.2, Sl.1, K.1, psso.) twice, * rep. 4 times more from * to *, K.2 tog., Yo.2, Sl.1, K.1, psso., P.3.

37th row—P.3, K.2, K.2 tog., Yo., * Yo., Sl.1, K.1, psso., K.2, Yo., K.2 tog., K.5, K.3 tog., Yo.2, K.1, K.2 tog., Yo., (Yo., Sl.1, K.1, psso., K.2 tog., Yo.) 6 times, * rep. 4 times more from * to *, Yo., Sl.1, K.1, psso., K.2, P.3.

39th row—P.3, K.2 tog., Yo.2, Sl.1, K.1, psso., * K.2 tog., Yo.2, Sl.1, K.1, psso., Yo., K.2 tog., K.3, K.3 tog., Yo.2, K.1, (K.2 tog., Yo.2, Sl.1, K.1, psso.) 7 times, * rep. 4 times more from * to *, K.2 tog., Yo.2, Sl.1, K.1, psso., P.3.

41st row—P.3, K.2, K.2 tog., Yo., * Yo., Sl.1, K.1, psso., K.2, Yo., K.2 tog., K.1, K.3 tog., Yo.2, K.1, K.2 tog., Yo., (Yo., Sl.1, K.1, psso., K.2 tog., Yo.) 7 times, * rep. 4 times more from * to *, Yo., Sl.1, K.1, psso., K.2, P.3.

43rd row—P.3, K.2 tog., Yo.2, Sl.1, K.1, psso., * K.2 tog., Yo.2, Sl.1, K.1, psso., Yo., (K.2 tog.) twice, Yo.2, K.1, (K.2 tog., Yo.2, Sl.1, K.1, psso.) 8 times, * rep. 4 times more from * to *, K.2 tog., Yo.2, Sl.1, K.1, psso., P.3.

45th row—P.3, K.2, K.2 tog., Yo., * Yo., Sl.1, K.1, psso., K.2, Yo.2, K.3 tog., Yo.2, K.1, K.2 tog., Yo., (Yo., Sl.1, K.1, psso., K.2 tog., Yo.) 8 times, * rep. 4 times more from * to *, Yo., Sl.1, K.1, psso., K.2, P.3.

47th row—P.3, K.2 tog., Yo.2, Sl.1, K.1, psso., * K.2 tog., Yo.2, Sl.2, K.1, p2sso., K.2 tog., Yo.2, K.1, (K.2 tog., Yo.2, Sl.1, K.1, psso.) 9 times, * rep. 4 times more from * to *, K.2 tog., Yo.2, Sl.1, K.1, psso., P.3.

49th row—P.3, K.2, K.2 tog., Yo., * (Yo., Sl.1, K.1, psso., K.2 tog., Yo.) 11 times, * rep. 4 times more from * to *, Yo., Sl.1, K.1, psso., K.2, P.3.

51st row—P.3, K.2 tog., Yo.2, Sl.1, K.1, psso., * (K.2 tog., Yo.2, Sl.1, K.1, psso.) 4 times, K.2 tog., Yo.2, Sl.2, K.1, p2sso., Yo., K.2 tog., Yo., K.3 tog., Yo.2, Sl.1, K.1, psso., (K.2 tog., Yo.2, Sl.1, K.1, psso.) 4 times, * rep. 4 times more from * to *, K.2 tog., Yo.2, Sl.1, K.1, psso., P.3.

53rd row—P.3, K.2, K.2 tog., Yo., * (Yo., Sl.1, K.1, psso., K.2 tog., Yo.) 4 times, Yo., Sl.1, K.1, psso., K.2, Yo., Sl.1, K.2 tog., psso., Yo., K.2, K.2 tog., Yo., (Yo., Sl.1, K.1, psso., K.2 tog., Yo.) 4 times, * rep. 4 times more from * to *, Yo., Sl.1, K.1, psso., K.2, P.3.

55th row—P.3, K.2 tog., Yo.2, Sl.1, K.1, psso., * (K.2 tog., Yo.2, Sl.1, K.1, psso.) 5 times, Yo., K.3, Yo., (K.2 tog., Yo.2, Sl.1, K.1, psso.) 5 times,* rep. 4 times more from * to *, K.2 tog., Yo.2, Sl.1, K.1, psso., P.3.

57th row—P.3, K.2, K.2 tog., Yo., * (Yo., Sl.1, K.1, psso., K.2 tog., Yo.,) 4 times, Yo., Sl.1, K.1, psso., K.2, Yo., K.1, (KM.1B.) twice, K.2, (Yo., Sl.1, K.1, psso., K.2 tog., Yo.), 5 times, * rep. 4 times more from * to *, Yo., Sl.1, K.1, psso., K.2, P.3.

59th row—P.3, K.2 tog., Yo.2, Sl.1, K.1, psso., * (K.2 tog., Yo.2, Sl.1, K.1, psso.) 5 times, Yo., K.2 tog., K.1, (KM.1B.) twice, K.2, Sl.1, K.1, psso., Yo., Sl.2, K.1, p2sso., (K.2 tog., Yo.2, Sl.1, K.1, psso.) 4 times, * rep. 4 times more from * to *, K.2 tog., Yo.2, Sl.1, K.1, psso., P.3.

61st row—P.3, K.2, K.2 tog., Yo., * (Yo., Sl.1, K.1, psso., K.2 tog., Yo.) 4 times, Yo., Sl.1, K.1, psso., K.2, Yo., K.2 tog., K.2, (KM.1B.) twice, K.3, Sl.1, K.1, psso., Yo., Sl.2, K.1, p2sso., K.2 tog., Yo., (Yo., Sl.1, K.1, psso., K.2 tog., Yo.) 3 times, * rep. 4 times more from * to *, Yo., Sl.1, K.1, psso., K.2, P.3.

63rd row—P.3, K.2 tog., Yo.2, Sl.1, K.1, psso., * (K.2 tog., Yo.2, Sl.1, K.1, psso.) 5 times, Yo., K.2 tog., K.3, (KM.1B.) twice, K.4, Sl.1, K.1, psso., Yo., Sl.2, K.1, p2sso., (K.2 tog., Yo.2, Sl.1, K.1, psso.) 3 times, * rep. 4 times more from * to *, K.2 tog., Yo.2, Sl.1, K.1, psso. P.3.

65th row—P.3, K.2, K.2 tog., Yo., * (Yo., Sl.1, K.1, psso., K.2 tog., Yo.) 4 times, Yo., Sl.1, K.1, psso., K.2, Yo., K.2 tog., K.4, (KM.1B.) twice, K.5, Sl.1, K.1, psso., Yo., Sl.2, K.1, p2sso., K.2 tog., Yo., (Yo., Sl.1, K.1, psso., K.2 tog., Yo.) twice, * rep. 4 times more from * to *, Yo., Sl.1, K.1, psso., K.2, P.3.

67th row—P.3, K.2 tog., Yo.2, Sl.1, K.1, psso., * (K.2 tog., Yo.2, Sl.1, K.1, psso.) 5 times, Yo., K.2 tog., K.13, Sl.1, K.1, psso., Yo., Sl.2, K.1, p2sso., (K.2 tog., Yo.2, Sl.1, K.1, psso.) twice, * rep. 4 times more from * to *, K.2 tog., Yo.2, Sl.1, K.1, psso., P.3.

69th row—P.3, K.2, K.2 tog., Yo., * (Yo., Sl.1, K.1, psso., K.2 tog., Yo.) 4 times, Yo., Sl.1, K.1, psso., K.2, Yo., K.2 tog., K.13, Sl.1, K.1, psso., Yo., Sl.2, K.1, p2sso., K.2 tog., Yo.2, Sl.1, K.1, psso., K.2 tog., Yo., * rep. 4 times more from * to *, Yo., Sl.1, K.1, psso., K.2, P.3.

71st row—P.3, K.2 tog., Yo.2, Sl.1, K.1, psso., * (K.2 tog., Yo.2, Sl.1, K.1, psso.) twice, K.4, (K.2 tog., Yo.2, Sl.1 K.1, psso.) twice, K.1, Yo.2, Sl.2, K.1, p2sso., K.11, Sl.1, K.1, psso., Yo., Sl.2, K.1, p2sso., K.2 tog., Yo.2, Sl.1, K.1, psso., * rep. 4 times more from * to *, K.2 tog., Yo.2, Sl.1, K.1, psso., P.3.

73rd row—P.3, K.2, K.2 tog., Yo., * Yo., Sl.1, K.1, psso., K.2 tog., Yo.2, Sl.1, K.1, psso., K.8, (K.2 tog., Yo.2, Sl.1,

K.1, psso.) twice, K.1, Yo.2, Sl.2, K.1, p2sso., K.9, Sl.1, K.1, psso., Yo., Sl.1, K.1, psso., K.1, K.2 tog., Yo., * rep. 4 times more from * to *, Yo., Sl.1, K.1, psso., K.2, P.3.

75th row—P.3, K.2 tog., Yo.2, Sl.1, K.1, psso., * (K.2 tog., Yo.2, Sl.1, K.1, psso.) twice, K.4, (K.2 tog., Yo.2, Sl.1, K.1, psso.) 3 times, K.1, Yo.2, Sl.2, K.1, p2sso., K.7, Sl.1, K.1, psso., Yo., K.2 tog., Yo.2, Sl.1, K.1, psso., * rep. 4 times more from * to *, K.2 tog., Yo.2, Sl.1, K.1, psso., P.3.

77th row—P.3, K.2, K.2 tog., Yo., * (Yo., Sl.1, K.1, psso., K.2 tog., Yo.) 6 times, Yo., Sl.1, K.1, psso., K.1, Yo.2, Sl.2, K.1, p2sso., K.5, Sl.1, K.1, psso., Yo., K.2, K.2 tog., Yo., * rep. 4 times more from * to *, Yo., Sl.1, K.1, psso., K.2, P.3.

79th row—P.3, K.2 tog., Yo.2, Sl.1, K.1, psso., * (K.2 tog., Yo.2, Sl.1, K.1, psso.) 7 times, K.1, Yo.2, Sl.2, K.1, p2sso., K.3, Sl.1, K.1, psso., Yo., K.2 tog., Yo.2, Sl.1, K.1, psso., * rep. 4 times more from * to *, K.2 tog., Yo.2, Sl.1, K.1, psso., P.3.

81st row—P.3, K.2, K.2 tog., Yo., * (Yo., Sl.1, K.1, psso., K.2 tog., Yo.) 7 times, Yo., Sl.1, K.1, psso., K.1, Yo.2, Sl.2, K.1, p2sso., K.1, Sl.1, K.1, psso., Yo., K.2, K.2 tog., Yo., * rep. 4 times more from * to *, Yo., Sl.1, K.1, psso., K.2, P.3.

83rd row—P.3, K.2 tog., Yo.2, Sl.1, K.1, psso., * (K.2 tog., Yo.2, Sl.1, K.1, psso.) 8 times, K.1, Yo.2, (Sl.1, K.1, psso.) twice, Yo., K.2 tog., Yo.2, Sl.1, K.1, psso., * rep. 4 times more from * to *, K.2 tog., Yo.2, Sl.1, K.1, psso., P.3.

85th row—P.3, K.2, K.2 tog., Yo., * (Yo., Sl.1, K.1, psso., K.2 tog., Yo.) 8 times, Yo., Sl.1, K.1, psso., K.1, Yo.2, Sl.2, K.1, p2sso., Yo., K.2, K.2 tog., Yo., * rep. 4 times more from * to *, Yo., Sl.1, K.1, psso., K.2, P.3.

87th row—P.3, K.2 tog., Yo.2, Sl.1, K.1, psso., * (K.2 tog., Yo.2, Sl.1, K.1, psso.) 9 times, K.1, Yo.2, Sl.1, K.1, psso., K.3 tog., Yo.2, Sl.1, K.1, psso., * rep. 4 times more from * to *, K.2 tog., Yo.2, Sl.1, K.1, psso., P.3.

89th row—same as 49th row.

After finishing purl row 90 work PART B rows 11 to 89 inclusive 8 times more, and then proceed with PART C, top edge.

PART C

91st row—same as 3rd row of bottom edge.

93rd row—same as 5th row.

95th row—same as 3rd row.

97th row—same as 5th row.

99th row—same as 3rd row.

101st row—same as 1st row.

102nd row—work purl.

After last row cast off all stitches fairly loosely so that the edge stretches easily to the necessary measurements. At the end break off wool and secure invisibly.

Stretching and Finishing of Stole

Prepare paper pattern by drawing an oblong 32 in. by 83 in. Take the lace stole which has been washed and pin down the corners first. Then pin out the stole along the edges in regular spaces. Finish by treating the lace according to BASIC INSTRUCTIONS.

To give a perfect appearance the stole should be trimmed along the bottom and top edge with a fairly long fringe. Cut a piece of cardboard 6 to 8 in. wide, wind round the required wool and cut along one edge. Then take about 6 strands of the cut wool, fold into half, draw folded end with help of a thick crochet hook through the first hole of the edge, draw cut ends through the loop and pull tight. This makes the first knot. Work in the same way one tassel into each hole along the two edges. The fringe can be made even more attractive and durable by giving it a second row of knots about 1 in. apart from the first row. When working this second row, divide the bunches of wool that hang from the knots of the first row, take half a bunch from the right and half from the left and knot them together, so that the knots come between those of the rows above. Finish by cutting them evenly.

Adaptation of Pattern

The pattern is made up of the two side edges and a middle panel, the latter being composed of the section within the asterisks. If the number of middle sections is altered, the width of the stole alters accordingly.

The two side edges measure together 2 in. and 14 stitches are needed for the start. One middle section requires 44 cast-on stitches and measures about 6 in. in width. It is, therefore, possible to cast on as many times 44 stitches as the width of the stole requires, remembering that an extra 2 in. are added by the edges on each side.

The length of the pattern is governed by the repetition of PART B, one repeat measuring about 9 in. PARTS A and C which form the borders at the top and the bottom measure together 2 in.

Chart for Design 'La Traviata'

Every chart line is one pattern row, but knit the section between the asterisks 5 times.

Every row of which the number is missing work purl but take great care of Yo.2 as explained in BASIC INSTRUCTIONS.

Casting-on and PART A, rows 1 to 9 inclusive, see written instructions. Proceed with PART B working rows 11 to 89 inclusive 9 times. Now knit PART C as given in the written instructions.

PART B

89 87 85 83 81 79 77 75 73 71 69 67 65 63 61 59 57 55 53 51 49 47 45 43 41 39 37 35 33 31 29 27 25 23 21 19 17 15 13 11

'Maple Garland' Design
CHRISTENING SHAWL FOR JANE

MATERIALS

Six oz. of 1-ply wool, or 9 oz. of 2-ply wool.

Four double pointed knitting needles No. 9.

One circular knitting needle No. 9, length 24 in.

One circular knitting needle No. 9, length 36 in. or 42 in.

One steel crochet hook No. 2.

MEASUREMENTS

56 in. square. If a smaller size is required use needles No. 10. For a larger size needles No. 8.

CASTING-ON

Commence by casting on 8 stitches (either method) having 2 stitches on the first, 2 stitches on the second and 4 stitches on the third needle. By help of this arrangement one quarter of a round will be worked on the first needle, one quarter on the second needle, and two quarters on the third needle. Now knit one round into the back of all stitches, and then start to work the first pattern round of PART A.

Every round of which the number is missing knit plain.

PART A

Knit each section from [to] 4 times in one round

1st round—[(Yo., K.1B.) twice.]

3rd round—[Yo., K.3, Yo., K.1B.]

5th round—[Yo., K.5, Yo., K.1B.]

7th round—[(Yo., K.3, Yo., K.1B.) twice.]

9th round—[Yo., K.2, (KM.1B.) twice, K.2, (KM.1B.) twice, K.3, Yo., K.1B.]

11th round—[Yo., K.4, (KM.1B.) twice, K.4, (KM.1B.) twice, K.5, Yo., K.1B.]

13th round—[Yo., K.2 tog., K.4, (KM.1B.) twice, K.6, (KM.1B.) twice, K.5, Sl.1, K.1, psso., Yo., K.1B.]

15th round—[Yo., K.2 tog., K.23, Sl.1, K.1, psso., Yo., K.1B.]

17th round—[Yo., K.2 tog., K.23, Sl.1, K.1, psso., Yo., K.1B.]

19th round—[Yo., M.2, Yo., Sl.1, K.1, psso., K.3, K.2 tog., Yo., Sl.1, K.1, psso., K.7, K.2 tog., Yo., Sl.1, K.1, psso., K.3, K.2 tog., Yo., M.2, Yo., K.1B.]

21st round—[Yo., M.2, K.2 tog., M.2, Yo., Sl.1, K.1, psso., K.1, K.2 tog., Yo., M.2, Yo., Sl.1, K.1, psso., K.5, K.2 tog., Yo., M.2, Yo., Sl.1, K.1, psso., K.1, K.2 tog., Yo., M.2, K.2 tog., M.2, Yo., K.1B.]

23rd round—[Yo., (M.2, K.2 tog.) twice, M.2, Sl.1, K.2 tog., psso., M.2, K.2 tog., M.2, Yo., Sl.1, K.1, psso., K.3, K.2 tog., Yo., M.2, K.2 tog., M.2, Sl.1, K.2 tog., psso., (M.2, K.2 tog.) twice, M.2, Yo., K.1B.]

25th round—[Yo., (M.2, K.2 tog.) 5 times, M.2, Yo., Sl.1, K.1, psso., K.1, K.2 tog., Yo., (M.2, K.2 tog.) 5 times, M.2, Yo., K.1B.]

27th round—[Yo., (M.2, K.2 tog.) 6 times, M.2, Sl.1, K.2 tog., psso., (M.2, K.2 tog.) 6 times, M.2, Yo., K.1B.]

29th round—[Yo., (M.2, K.2 tog.) 14 times, M.2, Yo., K.1B.]

31st round—[Yo., (M.2, K.2 tog.) 15 times, M.2, Yo., K.1B.]

Now proceed with PART B.

PART B

Knit each section from [to] 4 times in one round

33rd round—[Yo., M.2, (K.2 tog., M.2) 16 times, Yo., K.1B.]

The following rounds 35 to 95 are the same as round 33 but the section within the round brackets increases in each of the following pattern rounds by one more repeat.

For instance:

35th round—[Yo., M.2, (K.2 tog., M.2) 17 times, Yo., K.1B.]

Thus working until the last round of this part which will read:

95th round—[Yo., M.2, (K.2 tog., M.2) 47 times, Yo., K.1B.]

Now proceed with PART C.

PART C

Knit each section from [to] 4 times in one round

97th round—[Yo., M.2, * (K.2 tog., M.2) 8 times, * rep. 5 times more from * to *, Yo., K.1B.]

99th round—[Yo., M.2, K.2 tog., * (M.2, K.2 tog.) 8 times, * rep. 5 times more from * to *, M.2, Yo., K.1B.]

101st round—[Yo., M.2, K.2 tog., Yo., K.1B., * Yo., (K.2 tog., M.2) 7 times, K.2 tog., Yo., K.1B., * rep. 5 times more from * to *, Yo., K.2 tog., M.2, Yo., K.1B.]

103rd round—[Yo., M.2, K.3 tog., Yo., K.2, * K.1, Yo., Sl.2, K.1, p2sso., (M.2, K.2 tog.) 5 times, M.2, K.3 tog., Yo., K.2, * rep. 5 times more from * to *, K.1, Yo., Sl.2, K.1, p2sso., M.2, Yo., K.1B.]

105th round—[Yo., M.2, K.3 tog., Yo., K.3, * K.2, Yo., Sl.2, K.1, p2sso., (M.2, K.2 tog.) 4 times, M.2, K.3 tog., Yo., K.3, * rep. 5 times more from * to *, K.2, Yo., Sl.2, K.1, p2sso., M.2, Yo., K.1B.]

107th round—[Yo., M.2, K.3 tog., M.2, Yo., Sl.1, K.1, psso., K.1, * K.2 tog., Yo., M.2, Sl.2, K.1, p2sso., (M.2, K.2 tog.) 3 times, M.2, K.3 tog., M.2, Yo., Sl.1, K.1, psso., K.1, * rep. 5 times more from * to *, K.2 tog., Yo., M.2, Sl.2, K.1, p2sso., M.2, Yo., K.1B.]

109th round—[Yo., (M.2 K.2 tog.) twice, M.2, Yo., Sl.1, K.2 tog., psso., * Yo., (M.2, K.2 tog.) 6 times, M.2, Yo., Sl.1, K.2 tog., psso., * rep. 5 times more from * to *, Yo., (M.2, K.2 tog.) twice, M.2, Yo., K.1B.]

111th round—[Yo., (M.2, K.2 tog.) 3 times, M.2, K.1, * (M.2, K.2 tog.) 7 times, M.2, K.1, * rep. 5 times more from * to *, (M.2, K.2 tog.) 3 times, M.2, Yo., K.1B.]

Rounds 113 up to 127 inclusive are the same as rounds 97 to 111 inclusive but knit the part from * to * 7 times in every section.

Now proceed with **PART D**.

PART D

Knit each section from [to] 4 times in one round

129th round—[Yo., K.1B., * Yo., (K.2 tog., M.2) 7 times, K.2 tog., Yo., K.1B., * rep. 7 times more from * to *, Yo., K.1B.]

131st round—[Yo., K.2, * K.1, Yo., Sl.2, K.1, p2sso., (M.2, K.2 tog.) 5 times, M.2, K.3 tog., Yo., K.2, * rep. 7 times more from * to *, K.1, Yo., K.1B.]

133rd round—[Yo., K.3, * K.2, Yo., Sl.2, K.1, p2sso., (M.2, K.2 tog.) 4 times, M.2, K.3 tog., Yo., K.3, * rep. 7 times more from * to *, K.2, Yo., K.1B.]

135th round—[Yo., K.3, Yo., K.1B., * Yo., K.3, Yo., Sl.2, K.1, p2sso., (M.2, K.2 tog.) 3 times, M.2, K.3 tog., Yo., K.3, Yo., K.1B., * rep. 7 times more from * to *, Yo., K.3, Yo., K.1B.]

137th round—[Yo., K.2, (KM.1B.) twice, K.2, * (KM.1B.) twice, K.3, Yo., Sl.2, K.1, p2sso., (M.2, K.2 tog.) twice, M.2, K.3 tog., Yo., K.2, (KM.1B.) twice, K.2, * rep. 7 times more from * to *, (KM.1B.) twice, K.3, Yo., K.1B.]

139th round—[Yo., K.4, (KM.1B.) twice, K.3, * K.1, (KM.1B.) twice, K.5, Yo., Sl.2, K.1, p2sso., M.2, K.2 tog., M.2, K.3 tog., Yo., K.4, (KM.1B.) twice, K.3, * rep. 7 times more from * to *, K.1, (KM.1B.) twice, K.5, Yo., K.1B.]

141st round—[Yo., K.2 tog., K.4, (KM.1B.) twice, K.4, * K.2, (KM.1B.) twice, K.5, Sl.1, K.1, psso., Yo., Sl.2, K.1, p2sso., M.2, K.3 tog., Yo., K.2 tog., K.4, (KM.1B.) twice, K.4, * rep. 7 times more from * to *, K.2, (KM.1B.) twice, K.5, Sl.1, K.1, psso., Yo., K.1B.]

143rd round—[Yo., K.2 tog., K.12, * K.11, Sl.1, K.1, psso., Yo., Sl.2, K.2 tog., p2sso., Yo., K.2 tog., K.12, * rep. 7 times more from * to *, K.11, Sl.1, K.1, psso., Yo., K.1B.]

145th round—[Yo., K.2 tog., K.12, * K.11, Sl.1, K.1, psso., Yo., K.1B., Yo., K.2 tog., K.12, * rep. 7 times more from * to *, K.11, Sl.1, K.1, psso., Yo., K.1B.]

147th round—[Yo., M.2, Yo., Sl.1, K.1, psso., K.3, K.2 tog., Yo., Sl.1, K.1, psso., K.4, * K.3, K.2 tog., Yo., Sl.1, K.1, psso., K.3, K.2 tog., Yo., Sl.1, K.2 tog., psso., Yo., Sl.1, K.1, psso., K.3, K.2 tog., Yo., Sl.1, K.1, psso., K.4, * rep. 7 times more from * to *, K.3, K.2 tog., Yo., Sl.1, K.1, psso., K.3, K.2 tog., Yo., M.2, Yo., K.1B.]

149th round—[Yo., M.2, K.2 tog., M.2, Yo., Sl.1, K.1, psso., K.1, K.2 tog., Yo., M.2, Yo., Sl.1, K.1, psso., K.3, * K.2, K.2 tog., Yo., M.2, Yo., Sl.1, K.1, psso., K.1, K.2 tog., Yo., Sl.1, K.2 tog., psso., Yo., Sl.1, K.1, psso., K.1, K.2 tog., Yo., M.2, Yo., Sl.1, K.1, psso., K.3, * rep. 7 times more from * to *, K.2, K.2 tog., Yo., M.2, Yo., Sl.1, K.1, psso., K.1, K.2 tog., Yo., M.2, K.2 tog., M.2, Yo., K.1B.]

151st round—[Yo., (M.2, K.2 tog.) twice, M.2, Sl.1, K.2 tog., psso., M.2, K.2 tog., M.2, Yo., Sl.1, K.1, psso., K.2, * K.1, K.2 tog., Yo., M.2, K.2 tog., M.2, Sl.1, K.2 tog., psso., M.2, K.1, M.2, Sl.1, K.2 tog., psso., M.2, K.2 tog., M.2, Yo., Sl.1, K.1, psso., K.2, * rep. 7 times more from * to *, K.1, K.2 tog., Yo., M.2, K.2 tog., M.2, Sl.1, K.2 tog., psso., (M.2, K.2 tog.) twice, M.2, Yo., K.1B.]

153rd round—[Yo., (M.2, K.2 tog.) 5 times, M.2, Yo., Sl.1, K.1, psso., K.1, * K.2 tog., Yo., (M.2, K.2 tog.) 6 times, M.2, Yo., Sl.1, K.1, psso., K.1, * rep 7 times more from * to *, K.2 tog., Yo., (M.2, K.2 tog.) 5 times, M.2, Yo., K.1B.]

155th round—[Yo., (M.2, K.2 tog.) 6 times, M.2, Sl.1, K.2 tog., psso., * (M.2, K.2 tog.) 7 times, M.2, Sl.1, K.2 tog., psso., * rep. 7 times more from * to *, (M.2, K.2 tog.) 6 times, M.2, Yo., K.1B.]

157th round—[Yo., (M.2, K.2 tog.) 78 times, M.2, Yo., K.1B.]

159th round—[Yo., (M.2, K.2 tog.) 79 times, M.2, Yo., K.1B.]

Now return to instructions of PART C.

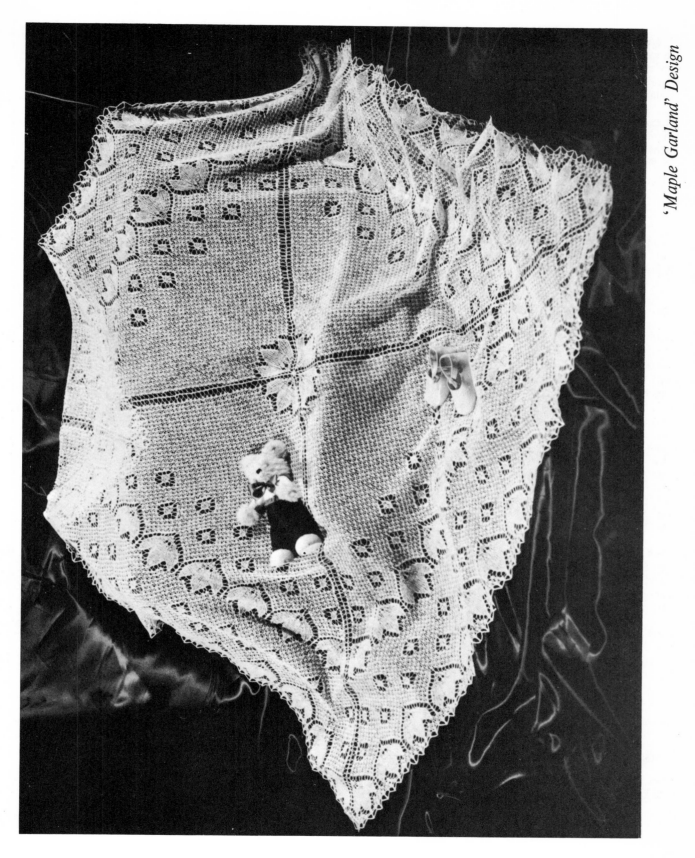

'Maple Garland' Design

Work rounds 97 to 111 but knit the part from * to * 10 times in every section. This brings the rounds from 161 to 175 inclusive. Then knit once more PART C but working the part from * to * 11 times in every section. This brings the rounds from 177 to 191 inclusive.

Return now to instructions of PART D but working only the rounds 129 to 145 inclusive, knitting the part from * to * 12 times in every section. This brings the rounds from 193 to 209. Then proceed with PART E.

PART E

Knit each section from [to] 4 times in one round

211th round—[M.2, Yo., Sl.1, K.1, psso., K.3, K.2 tog., Yo., Sl.1, K.1, psso., K.4, * K.3, K.2 tog., Yo., Sl.1, K.1, psso., K.3, K.2 tog., Yo., Sl.1, K.2 tog., psso., Yo., Sl.1, K.1, psso., K.3, K.2 tog., Yo., Sl.1, K.1, psso., K.4, * rep. 11 times more from * to *, K.3, K.2 tog., Yo., Sl.1, K.1, psso., K.3, K.2 tog., Yo., M.2, Yo., K.1B., Yo.]

213th round—[K.2 tog., M.2, Yo., Sl.1, K.1, psso., K.1, K.2 tog., Yo., M.2, Yo., Sl.1, K.1, psso., K.3, * K.2, K.2 tog., Yo., M.2, Yo., Sl.1, K.1, psso., K.1, K.2 tog., Yo., Sl.1, K.2 tog., psso., Yo., Sl.1, K.1, psso., K.1, K.2 tog., Yo., M.2, Yo., Sl.1, K.1, psso., K.3, * rep. 11 times more from * to *, K.2, K.2 tog., Yo., M.2, Yo., Sl.1, K.1, psso., K.1, K.2 tog., Yo., M.2, K.2 tog., Yo., K.3, Yo.]

215th round—[Sl.2, K.1, p2sso., M.2, Sl.1, K.2 tog., psso., M.2, K.2 tog., M.2, Yo., Sl.1, K.1, psso., K.2, * K.1, K.2 tog., Yo., M.2, K.2 tog., M.2, Sl.1, K.2 tog., psso., M.2, K.1, M.2, Sl.1, K.2 tog., psso., M.2, K.2 tog., M.2, Yo., Sl.1, K.1, psso., K.2, * rep. 11 times more from * to *, K.1, K.2 tog., Yo., M.2, K.2 tog., M.2, Sl.1, K.2 tog., psso., M.2, K.3 tog., Yo., K.5, Yo.]

217th round—[Sl.2, K.1, p2sso., (M.2, K.2 tog.) twice, M.2, Yo., Sl.1, K.1, psso., K.1, * K.2 tog., Yo., (M.2, K.2 tog.) 6 times, M.2, Yo., Sl.1, K.1, psso., K.1, * rep. 11 times more from * to *, K.2 tog., Yo., (M.2, K.2 tog.) twice, M.2, K.3 tog., Yo., K.7, Yo.]

219th round—[Sl.2, K.1, p2sso., (M.2, K.2 tog.) twice, M.2, Sl.1, K.2 tog., psso., * (M.2, K.2 tog.) 7 times, M.2, Sl.1, K.2 tog., psso., * rep. 11 times more from * to *, (M.2, K.2 tog.) twice, M.2, K.3 tog., Yo., K.9, Yo.]

220th round—knit plain.

Now see FINISHING OF CHRISTENING SHAWL.

FINISHING OF CHRISTENING SHAWL

After knitting plain round 220, knit another 2 stitches and then finish the shawl with a chain of crochet as follows:

3 sts., 1 d.c., 9 ch. Work thus all round the shawl, finish with a slip stitch and break off. Secure thread invisibly.

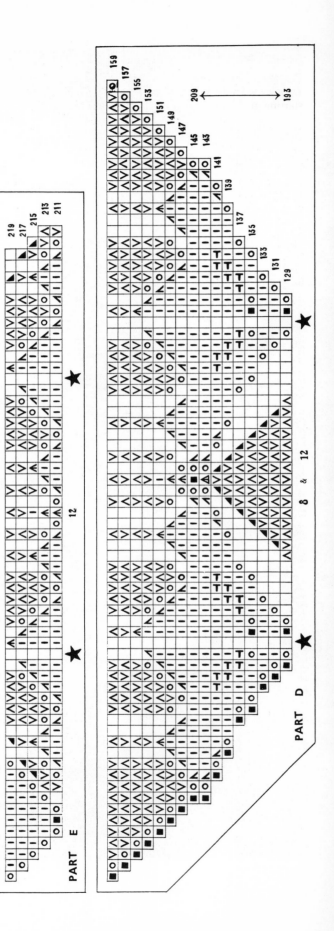

STRETCHING OF SHAWL

Prepare a paper pattern by drawing a square of 56 in. Divide each side of the square into 14 parts of 4 in. length, starting at the corners.

After washing and preparing the shawl start to pin it out by putting down the middle of the shawl on to the centre of the square.

Then place the corners into position shaping the same according to photo. The 2 loops of chain on both sides of the middle point of the leaf should be pinned down on both sides of the mark on the line. Now pin out the remaining 6 loops of chain at regular distances straight along the line.

Finish the shawl by treating it according to BASIC INSTRUCTIONS.

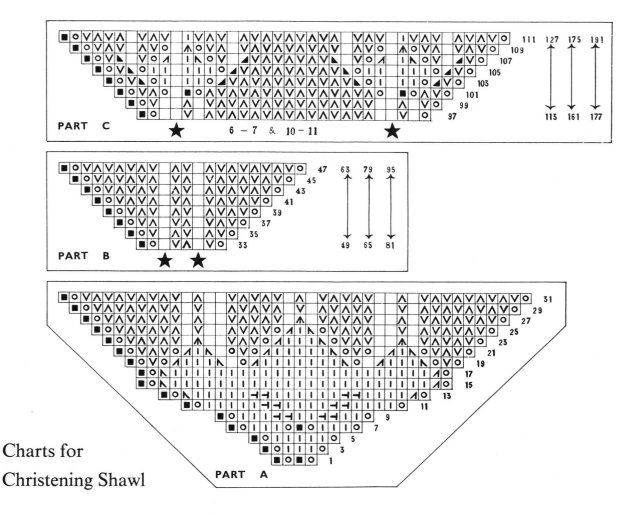

Charts for
Christening Shawl

Work PART A, PART B 4 times, PART C twice, PART D once, then again PART C twice, PART D up to round 209, and finish with PART E.

PART A

Every chart line to be knitted 4 times in one round.

PART B

Every chart line to be knitted 4 times in one round but work the section within the asterisks 16 times when working rounds 33 to 47.

24 times when working rounds 49 to 63.

32 times when working rounds 65 to 79.

40 times when working rounds 81 to 95.

PART C, D AND E

Every chart line to be knitted 4 times in one round, but work the section within the asterisks as many times as stated below.

When two or more numbers are given, the first refers to the first set of numbers beside the chart, the second to the second set, etc.

Every round of which the number is missing knit plain.

CHAPTER IV

OVAL - OBLONG - SQUARE DESIGNS

'Lilac Time' Design

OVAL DINNER CLOTH—TEA CLOTH—RUNNER

MATERIALS

DINNER CLOTH—12 balls of Crochet Cotton No. 50, or 10 oz. of Linen Thread No. 50.

TEA CLOTH—6 balls of Crochet Cotton No. 50, or 5 oz. of Linen Thread No. 50.

RUNNER—3 balls of Crochet Cotton No. 50, or 2 oz. of Linen Thread No. 50.

Four double pointed knitting needles No. 12, length 7 in.

One circular knitting needle No. 12, length 16 in., 1 of 24 in. length, and 1 of 36 in., or 42 in. length.

One steel crochet hook No. 5.

MEASUREMENTS

DINNER CLOTH—Length 78 in., width 64 in.

TEA CLOTH—Length 54 in., width 40 in.

RUNNER—Length 41 in. width 20 in.

The design can be adapted to other measurements as given in ADAPTATION OF PATTERN.

Dinner Cloth

CASTING-ON

Commence by casting on 200 stitches on to 3 needles having 52 stitches each on the first and second needles, and 96 stitches on the third needle, or cast all stitches on to a 16-in. circular needle, which will facilitate the work considerably. Now work one round of plain, knitting through the front of the stitches (not the back) since a loose, loopy selvedge is desired. Then start to work first pattern round of PART A.

Every round of which the number is missing knit plain.

L in front of pattern rounds: see ABBREVIATIONS.

PART A

Knit each section from [to] twice in one round

1st round—[(K.1B., Yo.) 4 times, ** (K.1B., Yo., Sl.1, K.1, psso., K.1, K.2 tog., Yo.) 4 times, ** rep. 3 times more from ** to **.]

3rd round—[(KM.1B., K.1, Yo., K.1B., Yo., KM.1B.) twice, ** KM.1B., K.1, (Yo., Sl.1, K.2 tog., psso.) 7 times, Yo., KM.1B., ** rep. 3 times more from ** to **.]

5th round—[(K.4, Yo., K.1B., Yo., K.3) twice, ** K.4, Yo., Sl.1, K.1, psso., (K.2, Yo., K.1B., Yo., K.1) twice, K.1, K.2 tog., Yo., K.3, ** rep. 3 times more from ** to **.]

7th round—[(K.1B., Yo., K.4, Yo.) 4 times, ** K.1B., Yo., K.4, (Yo., Sl.1, K.2 tog., psso.) 5 times, Yo., K.4, Yo., ** rep. 3 times more from ** to **.]

9th round—[(K.2, Yo., K.5, Yo., K.1B., Yo., K.5, Yo., K.1) twice, ** K.2, Yo., K.5, Yo., Sl.1, K.1, psso., K.2, Yo., K.1B., Yo., K.2, K.2 tog., Yo., K.5, Yo., K.1, ** rep. 3 times more from ** to **.]

11th round—[(K.3, Yo., K.6, Yo., K.1B., Yo., K.6, Yo., K.2) twice, ** K.3, Yo., K.6, (Yo., Sl.1, K.2 tog., psso.) 3 times, Yo., K.6, Yo., K.2, ** rep. 3 times more from ** to **.]

13th round—[(K.1B., Yo., K.8, Sl.1, K.1, psso., Yo., K.1B., Yo., K.2 tog., K.8, Yo.) twice, ** K.1B., Yo., K.8, Sl.1, K.1, psso., Yo., Sl.1, K.1, psso., K.1, K.2 tog., Yo., K.2 tog., K.8, Yo., ** rep. 3 times more from ** to **.]

15th round—[(K.2, Yo., K.8, Sl.1, K.1, psso., Yo., K.1B., Yo., K.2 tog., K.8, Yo., K.1) twice, ** K.2, Yo., K.8, Sl.1, K.1, psso., Yo., Sl.1, K.2 tog., psso., Yo., K.2 tog., K.8, Yo., K.1, ** rep. 3 times more from ** to **.]

17th round—[(K.3, Yo., K.7, K.2 tog., Yo., K.1, Yo., K.1B., Yo., K.1, Yo., Sl.1, K.1, psso., K.7, Yo., K.2) twice, ** K.3, Yo., K.7, K.2 tog., Yo., Sl.1, K.2 tog., psso., Yo., Sl.1, K.1, psso., K.7, Yo., K.2, ** rep. 3 times more from ** to **.]

19th round—[(K.10, K.2 tog., Yo., Sl.1, K.2 tog., psso., Yo., K.1B., Yo., Sl.1, K.2 tog., psso., Yo., Sl.1, K.1, psso., K.9) twice, ** K.10, K.2 tog., Yo., Sl.1, K.2 tog., psso., Yo., Sl.1, K.1, psso., K.9, ** rep. 3 times more from ** to **.]

L 21st round—[(Sl.1, K.2 tog., psso., K.7, K.2 tog., Yo., K.3, Yo., K.1B., Yo., K.3, Yo., Sl.1, K.1, psso., K.7) twice, ** Sl.1, K.2 tog., psso., K.7, K.2 tog., Yo., K.3, Yo., Sl.1, K.1, psso., K.7, ** rep. 3 times more from ** to **.]

23rd round—[(K.7, K.2 tog., Yo., K.1, Yo., Sl.1, K.2 tog., psso., Yo., K.1, Yo., K.1B., Yo., K.1, Yo., Sl.1, K.2 tog., psso., Yo., K.1, Yo., Sl.1, K.1, psso., K.6) twice, ** K.7, K.2 tog., Yo., K.1, Yo., Sl.1, K.2 tog., psso., Yo., K.1, Yo., Sl.1, K.1, psso., K.6, ** rep. 3 times more from ** to **.]

L 25th round—[* Sl.1, K.2 tog., psso., K.4, K.2 tog., (Yo., K.3, Yo., K.1B.) 3 times, Yo., K.3, Yo., Sl.1, K.1, psso., K.4, * rep. once more from * to *, ** Sl.1, K.2 tog., psso., K.4, K.2 tog., Yo., K.3, Yo., K.1B., Yo., K.3, Yo., Sl.1, K.1, psso., K.4, ** rep. 3 times more from ** to **.]

27th round—[* K.4, K.2 tog., Yo., K.1, (Yo., Sl.1, K.2 tog., psso.) 3 times, Yo., K.1, Yo., K.1B., Yo., K.1, (Yo., Sl.1, K.2 tog., psso.) 3 times, Yo., K.1, Yo., Sl.1, K.1, psso., K.3,

71

'Lilac Time' Design
Dinner Cloth

* rep. once more from * to *, ** K.4, K.2 tog., Yo., K.1, (Yo., Sl.1, K.2 tog., psso.) 3 times, Yo., K.1, Yo., Sl.1, K.1, psso., K.3, ** rep. 3 times more from ** to **.]

L 29th round—[* Sl.1, K.2 tog., psso., K.1, K.2 tog., (Yo., K.3, Yo., K.1B.) 5 times, Yo., K.3, Yo., Sl.1, K.1, psso., K.1, * rep. once more from * to *, ** Sl.1, K.2 tog., psso., K.1, K.2 tog., (Yo., K.3, Yo., K.1B.) twice, Yo., K.3, Yo., Sl.1, K.1, psso., K.1, ** rep. 3 times more from ** to **.]

31st round—[* K.1, K.2 tog., Yo., K.1, (Yo., Sl.1, K.2 tog., psso.) 5 times, Yo., K.1, Yo., K.1B., Yo., K.1, (Yo., Sl.1, K.2 tog., psso.) 5 times, Yo., K.1, Yo., Sl.1, K.1, psso., * rep. once more from * to *, ** K.1, K.2 tog., Yo., K.1, (Yo., Sl.1, K.2 tog., psso.) 5 times, Yo., K.1, Yo., Sl.1, K.1, psso., ** rep. 3 times more from ** to **.]

L 33rd round—[* Yo., Sl.1, K.2 tog., psso., (Yo., K.3, Yo., K.1B.) 7 times, Yo., K.3, * rep. once more from * to *, ** Yo., Sl.1, K.2 tog., psso., (Yo., K.3, Yo., K.1B.) 3 times, Yo., K.3, ** rep. 3 times more from ** to **.]

Now proceed with PART B.

PART B

Knit each section from [to] twice in one round

To contract the writing out, notice the following simplifications as from round 43:

Knit the pattern from * to * always 8 times, and the pattern from ** to ** always 16 times throughout PART B.

35th round—(Yo., Sl.1, K.2 tog., psso.) all round.

37th round—(K.3, Yo., K.1B., Yo.) all round.

39th round—(Sl.1, K.2 tog., psso., Yo.) all round.

41st round—(Yo., K.1B., Yo., K.3) all round.

43rd round—[* (Yo., Sl.1, K.2 tog., psso.) twice, Yo., K.1, Yo., K.1B., Yo., K.1, Yo., Sl.1, K.2 tog., psso., *—** (Yo., Sl.1, K.2 tog., psso.) twice. **]

45th round—(K.3, Yo., K.1B., Yo.) all round.

47th round—(Sl.1, K.2 tog., psso., Yo.) all round.

49th round—(Yo., K.1B. Yo., K.3) all round.

51st round—(Yo., Sl.1, K.2 tog., psso.) all round.

53rd round—(K.3, Yo., K.1B., Yo.) all round.

55th round—[* (Sl.1, K.2 tog., psso., Yo.) 3 times, K.1, Yo., K.1B., Yo., K.1, (Yo., Sl.1, K.2 tog., psso.) twice, Yo., *—** (Sl.1, K.2 tog., psso., Yo.) twice. **]

57th round—(Yo., K.1B., Yo., K.3) all round.

Now proceed with PART C.

PART C

Knit each section from [to] 24 times in one round

59th round—[(Yo., Sl.1, K.2 tog., psso.) 4 times, Yo., (KM.1B.) twice, K.1, (Yo., Sl.1, K.2 tog., psso.) 3 times.]

61st round—[K.3, Yo., K.1B., Yo., K.2, K.2 tog., Yo., K.7, Yo., Sl.1, K.1, psso., K.2, Yo., K.1B., Yo.]

63rd round—[(Sl.1, K.2 tog., psso., Yo.) 3 times, K.4, Yo., K.1B., Yo., K.4, Yo., (Sl.1, K.2 tog., psso., Yo.) twice.]

65th round—[Yo., K.1B., Yo., K.2, K.2 tog., Yo., K.5, Yo., K.3, Yo., K.5, Yo., Sl.1, K.1, psso., K.2.]

67th round—[(Yo., Sl.1, K.2 tog., psso.) twice, Yo., K.6, Yo., K.5, Yo., K.6, Yo., Sl.1, K.2 tog., psso.]

L 69th round—[Sl.1, K.1, psso., K.1, K.2 tog., Yo., K.2 tog., K.8, Yo., K.1B., Yo., K.8, Sl.1, K.1, psso., Yo.]

71st round—[Yo., Sl.1, K.2 tog., psso., Yo., K.2 tog., K.8, Yo., K.3, Yo., K.8, Sl.1, K.1, psso.]

73rd round—[Sl.1, K.2 tog., psso., Yo., Sl.1, K.1, psso., K.7, Yo., K.5, Yo., K.7, K.2 tog., Yo.]

75th round—[KM.1B., K.1, Yo., Sl.1, K.1, psso., K.19, K.2 tog., Yo., KM.1B.]

77th round—[K.4, Yo., Sl.1, K.1, psso., K.7, Sl.1, K.2 tog., psso., K.7, K.2 tog., Yo., K.3.]

79th round—[K.1B., Yo., K.4, Sl.1, K.1, psso., K.13, K.2 tog., Yo., K.4, Yo.]

81st round—[K.2, Yo., K.5, Yo., Sl.1, K.1, psso., K.4, Sl.1, K.2 tog., psso., K.4, K.2 tog., Yo., K.5, Yo., K.1.]

83rd round—[K.3, Yo., K.6, Yo., Sl.1, K.1, psso., K.7, K.2 tog., Yo., K.6, Yo., K.2.]

85th round—[K.1B., Yo., K.8, Sl.1, K.1, psso., Yo., Sl.1, K.1, psso., K.1, Sl.1, K.2 tog., psso., K.1, K.2 tog., Yo., K.2 tog., K.8, Yo.]

Now proceed with PART D.

PART D

Knit each section from [to] twice in one round

Notice: Work the pattern from * to * always 8 times, and the pattern from ** to ** always 4 times throughout PART D.

87th round—[* K.2, Yo., K.8, Sl.1, K.1, psso., Yo., Sl.1, K.1, psso., K.1, K.2 tog., Yo., K.2 tog., K.8, Yo., K.1, *—** K.2, Yo., K.8, Sl.1, K.1, psso., Yo., Sl.1, K.1, psso., K.1, K.2 tog., Yo., K.2 tog., K.8, Yo., K.1. **]

89th round—[* K.3, Yo., K.7, K.2 tog., Yo., K.1, Yo., Sl.1, K.2 tog., psso., Yo., K.1, Yo., Sl.1, K.1, psso., K.7, Yo., K.2, *—** K.3, Yo., K.7, Sl.2, K.1, p2sso., Yo., Sl.1, K.2 tog., psso., Yo., K.3 tog., K.7, Yo., K.2. **]

91st round—[* K.10, K.2 tog., Yo., Sl.1, K.2 tog., psso., Yo., K.1B., Yo., Sl.1, K.2 tog., psso., Yo., Sl.1, K.1, psso., K.9, * —** K.10, K.2 tog., Yo., Sl.1, K.2 tog., psso., Yo., Sl.1, K.1, psso., K.9. **]

L 93rd round—[* Sl.1, K.2 tog., psso., K.7, K.2 tog., Yo., K.3, Yo., K.1B., Yo., K.3, Yo., Sl.1, K.1, psso., K.7, *—** Sl.1, K.2 tog., psso., K.7, K.2 tog., Yo., K.3, Yo., Sl.1, K.1, psso., K.7. **]

95th round—[* K.7, K.2 tog., Yo., K.1, Yo., Sl.1, K.2 tog., psso., Yo., K.1, Yo., K.1B., Yo., K.1, Yo., Sl.1, K.2 tog., psso., Yo., K.1, Yo., Sl.1, K.1, psso., K.6, *—** K.7, K.2 tog., Yo., K.1, Yo., Sl.1, K.2 tog., psso., Yo., K.1, Yo., Sl.1, K.1, psso., K.6. **]

L 97th round—[* Sl.1, K.2 tog., psso., K.4, K.2 tog., (Yo., K.3, Yo., K.1B.) 3 times, Yo., K.3, Yo., Sl.1, K.1, psso., K.4, *—** Sl.1, K.2 tog., psso., K.4, K.2 tog., Yo., K.3, Yo., K.1B., Yo., K.3, Yo., Sl.1, K.1, psso., K.4. **]

99th round—[* K.4, K.2 tog., Yo., K.1, (Yo., Sl.1, K.2 tog., psso.) 7 times, Yo., K.1, Yo., Sl.1, K.1, psso., K.3, *—** K.4, K.2 tog., Yo., K.1, (Yo., Sl.1, K.2 tog., psso.) 3 times, Yo., K.1, Yo., Sl.1, K.1, psso., K.3. **]

L 101st round—[* Sl.1, K.2 tog., psso., K.1, K.2 tog., (Yo., K.3, Yo., K.1B.) 4 times, Yo., K.3, Yo., Sl.1, K.1, psso., K.1, *—** Sl.1, K.2 tog., psso., K.1, K.2 tog., (Yo., K.3, Yo., K.1B.) twice, Yo., K.3, Yo., Sl.1, K.1, psso., K.1. **]

103rd round—[* K.1, K.2 tog., Yo., K.1, (Yo., Sl.1, K.2 tog., psso.) 9 times, Yo., K.1, Yo., Sl.1, K.1, psso., *—** K.1, K.2 tog., Yo., K.1, (Yo., Sl.1, K.2 tog., psso.) 5 times, Yo., K.1, Yo., Sl.1, K.1, psso. **]

L 105th round—[* Yo., Sl.1, K.2 tog., psso., (Yo., K.3, Yo., K.1B.) 5 times, Yo., K.3, *—** Yo., Sl.1, K.2 tog., psso., (Yo., K.3, Yo., K.1B.) 3 times, Yo., K.3. **]

Now proceed with **PART E**.

PART E

Knit each section from [to] twice in one round

Notice the following simplification in round 119:
Knit the pattern from * to * 16 times and the pattern from ** to ** also 16 times.

107th round—(Yo., Sl.1, K.2 tog., psso.) all round.

109th round—(K.3, Yo., K.1B., Yo.) all round.

111th round—(Sl.1, K.2 tog., psso., Yo.) all round.

113th round—(Yo., K.1B., Yo., K.3) all round.

115th round—(Yo., Sl.1, K.2 tog., psso.) all round.

117th round—(K.3, Yo., K.1B., Yo.) all round.

119th round—[* (Sl.1, K.2 tog., psso., Yo.) 3 times, K.1, Yo., K.1B., Yo., K.1, Yo., (Sl.1, K.2 tog., psso., Yo.) twice, * —** (Sl.1, K.2 tog., psso., Yo.) twice. **]

121st round—(Yo., K.1B., Yo., K.3) all round.

Now proceed with **PART F**.

PART F

123rd round—(Yo., Sl.1, K.2 tog., psso.) all round.

125th round—(K.3, Yo., K.1B., Yo.) all round.

127th round—(Sl.1, K.2 tog., psso., Yo.) all round.

129th round—(Yo., K.1B., Yo., K.3) all round.

Now return to instructions of **PART C**. Work rounds 131 to 157 exactly the same way as rounds 59 to 85 but knit each section from [to] 40 times in one round.

Then follow once more the directions of **PART D**. Knit rounds 159 to 177 the same way as rounds 87 to 105 but **notice:** the section from * to * is knitted 16 times and not 8 times. The repetition of the section from ** to ** does not alter.

Now proceed with **PART G**.

PART G

Knit each section from [to] twice in one round

Notice: Knit the pattern from * to * 16 times, and from ** to ** also 16 times.

179th round—(Yo., Sl.1, K.2 tog., psso.) all round.

181st round—(K.3, Yo., K.1B., Yo.) all round.

183rd round—(Sl.1, K.2 tog., psso., Yo.) all round.

185th round—(Yo., K.1B., Yo., K.3) all round.

187th round—[* (Yo., Sl.1, K.2 tog., psso.) 4 times, Yo., K.1, Yo., Sl.1, K.1, psso., (Yo., Sl.1, K.2 tog., psso.) 3 times, Yo., K.2 tog., Yo., K.1, (Yo., Sl.1, K.2 tog., psso.) 3 times, *—** (Yo., Sl.1, K.2 tog., psso.) twice. **]

189th round—[* (K.3, Yo., K.1B., Yo.) twice, K.3, (Yo., Sl.1, K.1, psso.) twice, K.1, (K.2 tog., Yo.) twice, (K.3, Yo., K.1B., Yo.) twice, *—** K.3, Yo., K.1B., Yo. **]

191st round—[* (Sl.1, K.2 tog., psso., Yo.) 5 times, K.1, Yo., Sl.1, K.1, psso., Yo., Sl.1, K.2 tog., psso., Yo., K.2 tog., Yo., K.1, (Yo., Sl.1, K.2 tog., psso.) 4 times, Yo., *—** (Sl.1, K.2 tog., psso., Yo.) twice. **]

193rd round—[* (Yo., K.1B., Yo., K.3) 3 times, Yo., Sl.1, K.1, psso., K.1, K.2 tog., (Yo., K.3, Yo., K.1B.) twice, Yo., K.3, *—** Yo., K.1B., Yo., K.3. **]

195th round—[* (Yo., Sl.1, K.2 tog., psso.) 6 times, Yo., K.1, Yo., Sl.1, K.2 tog., psso., Yo., K.1, (Yo., Sl.1, K.2 tog., psso.) 5 times, *—** (Yo., Sl.1, K.2 tog., psso.) twice. **]

197th round—(K.3, Yo., K.1B., Yo.) all round.

Now proceed with **PART H**.

PART H

Knit each section from [to] twice in one round

Notice: Knit the pattern from * to * 16 times, and from ** to ** also 16 times.

199th round—(Sl.1, K.2 tog., psso., Yo.) all round.

201st round—(Yo., K.1B., Yo., K.3) all round.

203rd round—(Yo., Sl.1, K.2 tog., psso.) all round.

75

'Lilac Time' Design
Afternoon Tea Cloth

205th round—(K.3, Yo., K.1B., Yo.) all round.

207th round—[* (Sl.1, K.2 tog., psso., Yo.) 5 times, K.1, Yo., Sl.1, K.1, psso., (Yo., Sl.1, K.2 tog., psso.) 3 times, Yo., K.2 tog., Yo., K.1, Yo., (Sl.1, K.2 tog., psso., Yo.) 4 times, * —** (Sl.1, K.2 tog., psso., Yo.) twice. **]

209th round—[* (Yo., K.1B., Yo., K.3) 3 times, (Yo., Sl.1, K.1, psso.) twice, K.1, (K.2 tog., Yo.) twice, K.3, (Yo., K.1B., Yo., K.3) twice, *—** Yo., K.1B., Yo., K.3. **]

211th round—[* (Yo., Sl.1, K.2 tog., psso.) 6 times, Yo., K.1, Yo., Sl.1, K.1, psso., Yo., Sl.1, K.2 tog., psso., Yo., K.2 tog., Yo., K.1, (Yo., Sl.1, K.2 tog., psso.) 5 times, *—** (Yo., Sl.1, K.2 tog., psso.) twice. **]

213th round—[* (K.3, Yo., K.1B., Yo.) 3 times, K.3, Yo., Sl.1, K.1, psso., K.1, K.2 tog., Yo., (K.3, Yo., K.1B., Yo.) 3 times, *—** K.3, Yo., K.1B., Yo. **]

215th round—[* (Sl.1, K.2 tog., psso., Yo.) 7 times, K.1, Yo., Sl.1, K.2 tog., psso., Yo., K.1, Yo., (Sl.1, K.2 tog., psso., Yo.) 6 times, *—** (Sl.1, K.2 tog., psso., Yo.) twice. **]

217th round—(Yo., K.1B., Yo., K.3) all round.

Now proceed with PART I.

PART I

Knit each section from [to] 72 times in one round

219th round—(Yo., Sl.1, K.2 tog., psso.) all round.

221st round—(K.3, Yo., K.1B., Yo.) all round.

223rd round—(Sl.1, K.2 tog., psso., Yo.) all round.

225th round—(Yo., K.1B., Yo., K.3) all round.

227th round—[(Yo., Sl.1, K.2 tog., psso.) 4 times, Yo., (KM.1B.) twice, K.1, (Yo., Sl.1, K.2 tog., psso.) 3 times.]

229th round—[K.3, Yo., K.1B., Yo., K.2, K.2 tog., Yo., K.7, Yo., Sl.1, K.1, psso., K.2, Yo., K.1B., Yo.]

231st round—[(Sl.1, K.2 tog., psso., Yo.) 3 times, K.4, Yo., K.1B., Yo., K.4, Yo., (Sl.1, K.2 tog., psso., Yo.) twice.]

233rd round—[Yo., K.1B., Yo., K.2, K.2 tog., Yo., K.5, Yo., K.3, Yo., K.5, Yo., Sl.1, K.1, psso., K.2.]

235th round—[(Yo., Sl.1, K.2 tog., psso.) twice, Yo., K.6, Yo., K.5, Yo., K.6, Yo., Sl.1, K.2 tog., psso.]

L 237th round—[Sl.1, K.1, psso., K.1, K.2 tog., Yo., K.2 tog., K.8, Yo., K.1B., Yo., K.8, Sl.1, K.1, psso., Yo.]

239th round—[Yo., Sl.1, K.2 tog., psso., Yo., K.2 tog., K.8, Yo., K.3, Yo., K.8, Sl.1, K.1, psso.]

241st round—[Yo., Sl.1, K.2 tog., psso., Yo., Sl.1, K.1, psso., K.7, Yo., K.5, Yo., K.7, K.2 tog.]

243rd round—[Yo., (KM.1B.) twice, K.1, Yo., Sl.1, K.1, psso., K.19, K.2 tog.]

245th round—[Yo., K.7, Yo., Sl.1, K.1, psso., K.7, Sl.1, K.2 tog., psso., K.7, K.2 tog.]

247th round—[Yo., K.4, Yo., K.1B., Yo., K.4, Yo., Sl.1, K.1, psso., K.13, K.2 tog.]

249th round—[Yo., K.5, Yo., K.3, Yo., K.5, Yo., Sl.1, K.1, psso., K.4, Sl.1, K.2 tog., psso., K.4, K.2 tog.]

251st round—[Yo., K.6, Yo., K.5, Yo., K.6, Yo., Sl.1, K.1, psso., K.7, K.2 tog.]

253rd round—[Yo., K.2 tog., K.8, Yo., K.1B., Yo., K.8, Sl.1, K.1, psso., Yo., Sl.1, K.1, psso., K.1, Sl.1, K.2 tog., psso., K.1, K.2 tog.]

255th round—[Yo., K.2 tog., K.8, Yo., K.3, Yo., K.8, Sl.1, K.1, psso., Yo., Sl.1, K.1, psso., K.1, K.2 tog.]

257th round—[K.2 tog., K.8, Yo., K.5, Yo., K.8, Sl.1, K.1, psso., Yo., Sl.1, K.2 tog., psso., Yo.]

Now proceed with PART J.

PART J

Knit each section from [to] 72 times in one round

259th round—[Sl.1, K.1, psso., K.21, K.2 tog., Yo., Sl.1, K.2 tog., psso., Yo.]

261st round—[Sl.1, K.1, psso., K.8, Sl.1, K.2 tog., psso., K.8, K.2 tog., Yo., (KM.1B.) twice, K.1, Yo.]

263rd round—[Sl.1, K.1, psso., K.15, K.2 tog., Yo., K.7, Yo.]

265th round—[Sl.1, K.1, psso., K.5, Sl.1, K.2 tog., psso., K.5, K.2 tog., Yo., K.4, Yo., K.1B., Yo., K.4, Yo.]

267th round—[Sl.1, K.1, psso., K.9, K.2 tog., Yo., K.5, Yo., K.3, Yo., K.5, Yo.]

269th round—[Sl.1, K.1, psso., K.2, Sl.1, K.2 tog., psso., K.2, K.2 tog., Yo., K.6, Yo., K.5, Yo., K.6, Yo.]

271st round—[Sl.1, K.1, psso., K.3, K.2 tog., Yo., K.2 tog., K.8, Yo., K.1B., Yo., K.8, Sl.1, K.1, psso., Yo.]

273rd round—[Sl.1, K.1, psso., K.1, K.2 tog., Yo., K.2 tog., K.8, Yo., K.3, Yo., K.8, Sl.1, K.1, psso., Yo.]

275th round—[Yo., Sl.1, K.2 tog., psso., Yo., K.2 tog., K.8, Yo., K.5, Yo., K.8, Sl.1, K.1, psso.]

276th round—Knit plain.

FINISHING OF DINNER CLOTH

After knitting last plain round 276 finish the cloth by crocheting off as follows:

3 sts., 1 d.c., 6 ch., (4 sts., 1 d.c., 9 ch.) twice (3 sts., 1 d.c., 9 ch.) 3 times, 4 sts., 1 d.c., 9 ch., 4 sts., 1 d.c., 6 ch. Repeat 71 times. Finish with a slip stitch and break off. Secure thread invisibly.

Now the large hole left in the centre is stitched together by joining the opposite middle sections according to pattern.

Runner

The Runner is made up lengthwise of two more middle sections than the Dinner Cloth, a variation suggested in ADAPTATION OF PATTERN.

Cast on 296 stitches using for such a large number already a 16 in. circular needle.

Work now according to directions given for Dinner Cloth PARTS A, B, C, and D up to round 105 but **notice**: the pattern from ** to ** will repeat twice more in PART A and PART D, 8 times more in PART B. In PART C the section from [to] will be knitted 4 times more.

Round 106 knit plain, and then finish the edge with the usual chain of crochet as follows:

3 sts., 1 d.c., 9 ch., working thus all round the cloth. Finish with a slip stitch and break off. Secure thread invisibly.

The large hole left in the centre is stitched together by joining the opposite middle sections according to pattern.

Afternoon Tea Cloth

When working the Tea Cloth follow the instructions of CASTING-ON and PARTS A, B, C, D, E, F and C and D once more up to round 177, as given for Dinner Cloth. Round 178 knit plain and then finish the edge by crocheting off as follows:

3 sts., 1 d.c., 9 ch., working thus all round the cloth. Finish with a slip stitch and break off.

The large hole left in the centre is stitched together by joining the opposite middle sections according to pattern.

Chart Instructions

RUNNER

Work PARTS A, B, C, and D.

TEA CLOTH

Work PARTS A, B, C, D, E, F, and C and D.

DINNER CLOTH

Work PARTS A, B, C, D, E, F, once more C and D, and then PARTS G, H, I and J.

PARTS A, B, and D: Every chart line knitted twice in one round but knit the section from * to *, and from ** to ** as many times as stated.

PART C: Every chart line to be knitted 24 times in one round when working rounds 59 to 85 and 40 times when working rounds 131 to 157.

PARTS E, G and H: Every chart line to be knitted twice in one round but work the sections within the brackets as many times as stated below. The section from * to * is worked in all three PARTS 16 times.

PART F: Every chart line to be knitted 160 times in one round.

PARTS I and J: Every chart line to be knitted 72 times in one round.

Every round of which the number is missing knit plain.

Charts for Oval Design 'Lilac Time'

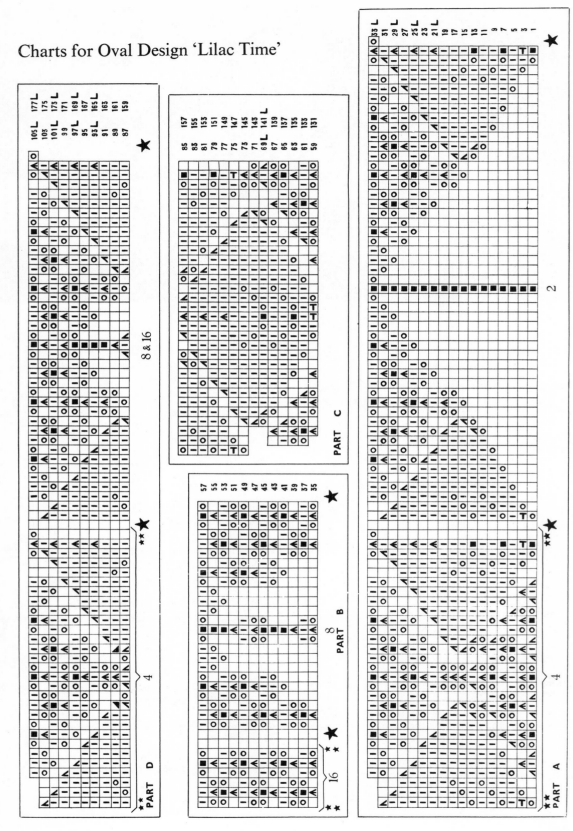

PART D

PART B

PART C

PART A

78

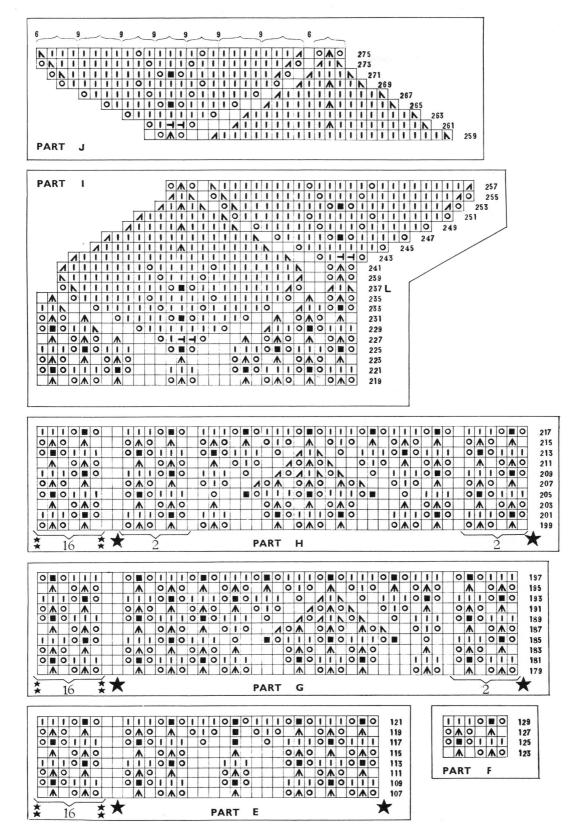

PART J

PART I

237 L

PART H

★ 16 ★★ ★ 2   PART H   2 ★

PART G

★ 16 ★★ ★   PART G   2 ★

PART F

PART E

★ 16 ★★ ★   PART E   ★

79

Stretching of 'Lilac Time' Design

DINNER CLOTH

Prepare a paper pattern by drawing a rectangle of 14 in. length and 64 in. width. Mark the middle of each width to be used as the centre for the semicircle of 32 in. radius which has to be added to each side of 64 in. Mark round the semicircle 32 points at a distance of $3\frac{1}{8}$ in. from each other.

Along the straight sides of 14 in. mark 4 points at a distance of $3\frac{1}{2}$ in. Now draw a second line all round at a distance of half an inch. This indicates the depth of the scallops.

After preparing the lace start to pin out the cloth trying to shape the scallops according to photo, pinning out the straight sides first. Put the two loops of 6 chain on to one pin only, placing it on to the mark of the inner line which gives the inner point of each scallop. The outer point of the scallop is obtained by pinning down the two centre loops of chain with one pin only in the middle of the scallop on to the outer line. Then pin down the remaining loops of chain, taking always two loops on to one pin.

TEA CLOTH

Prepare a paper pattern by drawing a rectangle of 14 in. length and 40 in. width. Mark the middle of each width to be used as the centre for the semicircle of 20 in. radius which has to be added to each side of 40 in. Mark round the semicircle 16 points at a distance of about 4 in. Along the straight sides of 14 in., mark 4 points at a distance of $3\frac{1}{2}$ in.

After preparing the lace start to pin out the cloth according to photo. The two loops of chain on both sides of the point of the leaf are pinned down with one pin only on to the marked point of the line, starting first along the straight sides. Then pin down the remaining loops of chain at regular distances all along the line, taking always two loops on to one pin only.

RUNNER

Prepare a paper pattern by drawing a rectangle of 21 in. length and 20 in. width. Mark the middle of each width to be used as the centre for the semicircle of 10 in. radius, which has to be added to each side of 20 in. Mark round the semicircle 8 points at a distance of about 4 in. from each other. Along the straight sides of 21 in. mark 6 points at distances of $3\frac{1}{2}$ in. Then take the prepared lace and pin out in the same manner as explained for Tea Cloth.

Adaptation of Pattern

The 'LILAC DESIGN' is made up lengthwise of a certain number of sections called middle sections and a semicircle on each end.

The pattern of the semicircle is given in the instructions as the part from * to *, and does not alter even when working a cloth of different length.

The design can be adapted for knitting a Dinner or Tea Cloth, etc., of a different length by altering the number of middle sections given in the directions as the part from ** to **.

48 stitches (24 for each side) are required to give one middle section which measures 3½ in. in length. By adding so many times 48 stitches to the already given number of cast-on stitches, the cloth can thus be lengthened by a multiple of 3½ in. The repetition from ** to ** will, of course, alter in all PARTS of the design according to the number of added middle sections.

If the adjustment of the pattern seems to be difficult to the knitter, then it is advisable to knit first the Tea Cloth or Runner according to the given instructions to get familiar with the pattern before working a cloth of a special length.

Alternative Adaptation

A good knitter could use the instructions given for the oval design to work also a round cloth. Cast on 8 stitches and work only the part from * to * according to the given instructions (omitting the section from ** to **). The sequence of working PARTS A, B, etc., are the same as for the oval Cloth. Thus one can produce a Tea Cloth of 40 in. diameter, or a Dinner Cloth of 64 in. diameter.

The above round cloth was worked as stated before, but only to round 106, giving a diameter of 22 in.

A small Cheval Set could also be worked according to the instructions of the oval runner up to and inclusive round 34. The two side mats can be worked as explained above, starting like a round cloth and also finishing at round 34.

The mats are crocheted off in the usual manner, taking 3 stitches together into a double crochet and making 9 chain in between.

'Trifolium' Design

OBLONG DINNER CLOTH—TROLLEY CLOTH—COFFEE TABLE CLOTH—DINNER MATS AND RUNNER—SQUARE TABLE CLOTH—SQUARE MATS

MATERIALS

OBLONG DINNER CLOTH—10 balls of Crochet Cotton No. 60, or 7 oz. of Linen Thread No. 60.

TROLLEY CLOTH—3 balls of Crochet Cotton No. 50 or 2 oz. of Linen Thread No. 50.

SQUARE TABLE CLOTH—5 balls of Crochet Cotton No. 50 or 4 oz. of Linen Thread No. 50.

Four double pointed knitting needles No. 13, length 7 in.

One circular knitting needle No. 13, length 16 in., 1 of 24 in. length, and 1 of 36 in., or 42 in.

One steel crochet hook No. 5.

COFFEE TABLE CLOTH—2 balls of Crochet Cotton No. 60 or 2 oz. of Linen Thread No. 60.

DINNER MAT—1 ball of Crochet Cotton No. 40 or 1 oz. of Linen Thread No. 40 is sufficient to work two mats.

RUNNER—2 balls of Crochet Cotton No. 40 or 2 oz. of Linen Thread No. 40.

SQUARE MAT—1 ball of Crochet Cotton No. 60 or 1 oz. Linen Thread No. 60 will be sufficient to work three to four mats.

Four double pointed knitting needles No. 14, length 7 in.

One circular knitting needle No. 14, length 16 in. and 1 circular needle No. 14 of 24 in. length.

MEASUREMENTS

DINNER CLOTH—60 in. by 48 in.

TROLLEY CLOTH—33 in. by 27 in.

COFFEE TABLE CLOTH—33 in. by 11 in.

DINNER MAT—16½ in. by 11 in.

RUNNER—22 in. by 11 in.

SQUARE TABLE CLOTH—39 in. square.

SQUARE MAT—11 in. square.

The design can easily be adapted to other measurements as given in ADAPTATION OF PATTERN.

Oblong Dinner Cloth

CASTING-ON

Commence by casting on 168 stitches on to 3 needles, having 44 stitches each on the first and second needles, and 80 stitches on the third needle, or cast all stitches on to a 16 in. circular needle (which would facilitate the work considerably). Now work one round of plain, knitting through the front of the stitches (not the back) since a loose, loopy selvedge is desired. Then start to work first pattern round of PART A.

Every round of which the number is missing knit plain.

PART A

Knit each section from [to] twice in one round

(Ignore double asterisks when working this cloth; they are only needed for the square cloth.)

1st round—[Yo., K.1B., * (Yo., K.9, Yo., K.1B.) 4 times, * rep. once more from * to *, Yo., K.1B., ** (Yo., K.1B.) twice. **]

3rd round—[Yo., (KM.1B.) twice, * (K.1, Yo., Sl.1, K.1, psso., K.5, K.2 tog., Yo., KM.1B., KM.1B.) 4 times, * rep. once more from * to *, K.1, Yo., K.1B., ** Yo., (KM.1B.) twice, K.1, Yo., K.1B. **]

5th round—[Yo., K.5, * (K.2, Yo., Sl.1, K.1, psso., K.3, K.2 tog., Yo., K.5) 4 times, * rep., once more from * to *, K.2, Yo., K.1B., ** Yo., K.7, Yo., K.1B. **]

7th round—[Yo., K.6, * (K.3, Yo., Sl.1, K.1, psso., K.1, K.2 tog., Yo., K.6) 4 times, * rep. once more from * to *, K.3, Yo., K.1B., ** Yo., K.9, Yo., K.1B. **]

9th round—[Yo., K.7, * (K.4, Yo., Sl.1, K.2 tog., psso., Yo., K.7) 4 times, * rep. once more from * to *, K.4, Yo., K.1B., ** Yo., K.11, Yo., K.1B. **]

11th round—[Yo., K.1, Yo., Sl.2, K.2 tog., p2sso., Yo., Sl.1, K.2 tog., psso., Yo., * (Sl.2, K.2 tog., p2sso., Yo., Sl.1, K.2 tog., psso., Yo.) 8 times, * rep. once more from * to *, Sl.2, K.2 tog., p2sso., Yo., K.1, Yo., K.1B., ** Yo., K.1, Yo., Sl.2, K.2 tog., p2sso., Yo., Sl.1, K.2 tog., psso., Yo., Sl.2, K.2 tog., p2sso., Yo., K.1, Yo., K.1B. **]

13th round—[Yo., K.3, Yo., K.1B., Yo., K.3, * (Yo., K.1B., Yo., K.3) 8 times, * rep. once more from * to *, Yo., K.1B., Yo., K.3, Yo., K.1B., ** (Yo., K.3, Yo., K.1B.) 3 times. **]

15th round—[Yo., K.1, (Yo., Sl.1, K.2 tog., psso.) 3 times, * (Yo., Sl.1, K.2 tog., psso.) 16 times, * rep. once more from * to *, (Yo., Sl.1, K.2 tog., psso.) twice, Yo., K.1, Yo., K.1B., ** Yo., K.1, (Yo., Sl.1, K.2 tog., psso.) 5 times, Yo., K.1, Yo., K.1B. **]

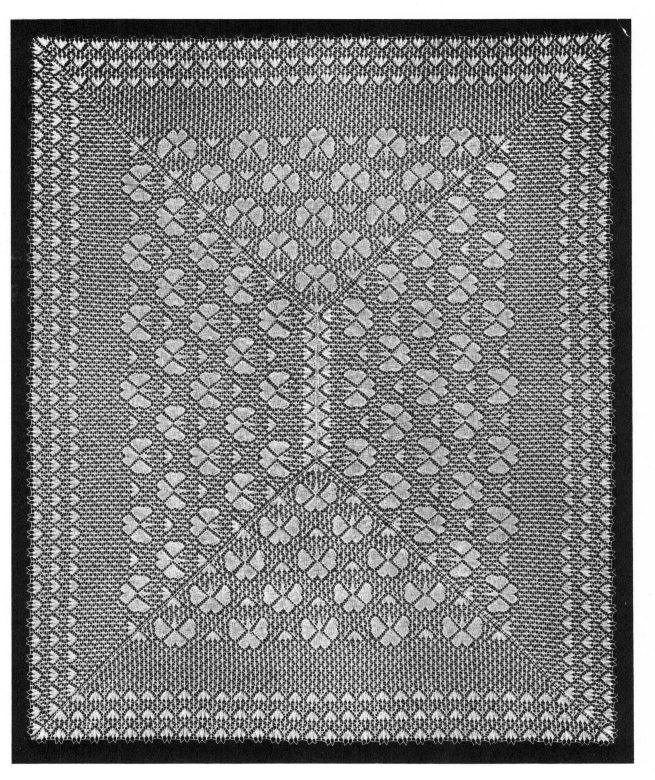

'Trifolium' Design
Dinner Cloth

17th round—[Yo., (K.3, Yo., K.1B., Yo.) twice, * (K.3, Yo., K.1B., Yo.) 8 times, * rep. once more from * to *, K.3, Yo., K.1B., Yo., K.3, Yo., K.1B., ** (Yo., K.3, Yo., K.1B.) 4 times. **]

19th round—[Yo., K.1, Yo., (Sl.1, K.2 tog., psso., Yo.) 4 times, * (Sl.1, K.2 tog., psso., Yo.) 16 times, * rep. once more from * to *, (Sl.1, K.2 tog., psso., Yo.) 3 times, K.1, Yo., K.1B., ** Yo., K.1, (Yo., Sl.1, K.2 tog.) 7 times, Yo., K.1, Yo., K.1B. **]

Now proceed with PART B.

PART B

Knit each section from [to] twice in one round
Work the part from * to * twice in succession
(Ignore double asterisks)
Take care of the working of Yo.2.

21st round—[Yo., K.3, Yo., M.3, Yo., K.3, Yo., K.1B., Yo., K.2, * K.1, Yo., K.1B., Yo., K.3, Yo., M.3, Yo., K.3, Yo., K.1B., (Yo., K.3, Yo., K.1B.) 3 times, Yo., K.3, Yo., M.3, Yo., K.3, Yo., K.1B., Yo., K.2, * K.1, Yo., K.1B., Yo., K.3, Yo., M.3, Yo., K.3, Yo., K.1B., ** Yo., K.3, Yo., M.3, (Yo., K.3, Yo., K.1B.) twice, Yo., K.3, Yo., M.3, Yo., K.3, Yo., K.1B. **]

23rd round—[Yo., K.1, Yo., Sl.1, K.2 tog., psso., Yo., K.5, (Yo., Sl.1, K.2 tog., psso.) twice, Yo., K.2, * K.1, (Yo., Sl.1, K.2 tog., psso.) twice, Yo., K.5, (Yo., Sl.1, K.2 tog., psso.) 9 times, Yo., K.5, (Yo., Sl.1, K.2 tog., psso.) twice, Yo., K.2, * K.1, (Yo., Sl.1, K.2 tog., psso.) twice, Yo., K.5, Yo., Sl.1, K.2 tog., psso., Yo., K.1, Yo., K.1B., ** Yo., K.1, Yo., Sl.1, K.2 tog., psso., Yo., K.5, (Yo., Sl.1, K.2 tog., psso.) twice, Yo., K.3, (Yo., Sl.1, K.2 tog., psso.) twice, Yo., K.5, Yo., Sl.1, K.2 tog., psso., Yo., K.1, Yo., K.1B. **]

25th round—[Yo., K.2, K.2 tog., Yo., K.2 tog., K.5, Yo., Sl.1, K.1, psso., K.2, Yo., K.2, * K.1, Yo., K.2, K.2 tog., Yo., K.5, Sl.1, K.1, psso., Yo., Sl.1, K.1, psso., K.1, (K.1, Yo., K.1B., Yo., K.2) 3 times, K.2 tog., Yo., K.2 tog., K.5, Yo., Sl.1, K.1, psso., K.2, Yo., K.2, * K.1, Yo., K.2, K.2 tog., Yo., K.5, Sl.1, K.1, psso., Yo., Sl.1, K.1, psso., K.2, Yo., K.1B., ** Yo., K.2, K.2 tog., Yo., K.2 tog., K.5, Yo., Sl.1, K.1, psso., (K.2, Yo., K.1) twice, K.1, K.2 tog., Yo., K.5, Sl.1, K.1, psso., Yo., Sl.1, K.1, psso., K.2, Yo., K.1B. **]

27th round—[Yo., K.1, Yo., Sl.1, K.2 tog., psso., Yo., K.2 tog., K.6, Yo., Sl.1, K.2 tog., psso., Yo., K.2 tog., K.1, * Sl.1, K.1, psso., Yo., Sl.1, K.2 tog., psso., Yo., K.6, Sl.1, K.1, psso., (Yo., Sl.1, K.2 tog., psso.) 7 times, Yo., K.2 tog., K.6, Yo., Sl.1, K.2 tog., psso., Yo., K.2 tog., K.1, * Sl.1, K.1, psso., Yo., Sl.1, K.2 tog., psso., Yo., K.6, Sl.1, K.1, psso., Yo., Sl.1, K.2 tog., psso., Yo., K.1, Yo., K.1B. ** Yo., K.1, Yo., Sl.1, K.2 tog., psso., Yo., K.2. tog., K.6, Yo., Sl.1, K.2 tog., psso., Yo., K.2 tog., K.1, Sl.1, K.1, psso., Yo., Sl.1, K.2 tog., psso., Yo., K.6, Sl.1, K.1, psso., Yo., Sl.1, K.2 tog., psso., Yo., K.1, Yo., K.1B. **]

29th round—[Yo., K.3, Yo., K.1B., Yo., K.2 tog., K.7, Yo., Sl.1, K.1, psso., K.2, * K.1, K.2 tog., Yo., K.7, Sl.1, K.1, psso., Yo., K.1B., (Yo., K.3, Yo., K.1B.) 3 times, Yo., K.2 tog., K.7, Yo., Sl.1, K.1, psso., K.2, * K.1, K.2 tog., Yo., K.7, Sl.1, K.1, psso., Yo., K.1B., Yo., K.3, Yo., K.1B., ** Yo., K.3, Yo., K.1B., Yo., K.2 tog., K.7, Yo., Sl.1, K.1, psso., K.3, K.2 tog., Yo., K.7, Sl.1, K.1, psso., Yo., K.1B., Yo., K.3, Yo., K.1B. **]

31st round—[Yo.2, K.1, (Yo., Sl.1, K.2 tog., psso.) twice, Yo., K.1B., K.8, Yo., Sl.1, K.1, psso., K.1, * K.2 tog., Yo., K.8, K.1B., (Yo., Sl.1, K.2 tog., psso.) 7 times, Yo., K.1B., K.8, Yo., Sl.1, K.1, psso., K.1, * K.2 tog., Yo., K.8, K.1B., (Yo., Sl.1, K.2 tog., psso.) twice, Yo., K.1, Yo.2, K.1B., ** Yo.2, K.1, Yo., (Sl.1, K.2 tog., psso., Yo.) twice, K.1B., K.8, Yo., Sl.1, K.1, psso., K.1, K.2 tog., Yo., K.8, K.1B., (Yo., Sl.1, K.2 tog., psso.) twice, Yo., K.1, Yo.2, K.1B. **]

Now proceed with PART C.

PART C

Knit each section from [to] 4 times in one round

But work the part from * to * 3 times when knitting the section for the first and third time (long sides), once when knitting the section for the second and fourth time (short sides).

33rd round—[Yo., K.1B., * (Yo., K.3, Yo., K.1B.) twice, K.9, Yo., Sl.1, K.2 tog., psso., Yo., K.9, K.1B., (Yo., K.3, Yo., K.1B.) twice, * Yo., K.1B.]

35th round—[Yo., (KM.1B.) twice, * K.1, (Yo., Sl.1, K.2 tog., psso.) 3 times, Yo., K.2 tog., K.7, K.2 tog., Yo., K.1, M.2, K.1, Yo., Sl.1, K.1, psso., K.7, Sl.1, K.1, psso., (Yo., Sl.1, K.2 tog., psso.) 3 times, Yo., (KM.1B.) twice, * K.1, Yo., K.1B.]

37th round—[Yo., K.5, * K.2, Yo., Sl.1, K.1, psso., K.2, Yo., K.1B., Yo., K.2 tog., K.6, K.2 tog., Yo., K.6, Yo., Sl.1, K.1, psso., K.6, Sl.1, K.1, psso., Yo., K.1B., Yo., K.2, K.2 tog., Yo., K.5, * K.2, Yo., K.1B.]

39th round—[Yo., K.6, * K.3, Yo., (Sl.1, K.2 tog., psso., Yo.) twice, Sl.1, K.1, psso., K.4, K.2 tog., Yo., K.8, Yo., Sl.1, K.1, psso., K.4, K.2 tog., (Yo., Sl.1, K.2 tog., psso.) twice, Yo., K.6, * K.3, Yo., K.1B.]

41st round—[Yo., K.7, * K.4, (Yo., Sl.1, K.1, psso., K.2) twice, K.2 tog., Yo., K.10, Yo., Sl.1, K.1, psso., (K.2, K.2 tog., Yo.) twice, K.7, * K.4, Yo., K.1B.]

43rd round—[Yo., K.1, Yo., Sl.2, K.2 tog., p2sso., Yo., Sl.1, K.2 tog., psso., Yo., * Sl.2, K.2 tog., p2sso., Yo., K.1, Yo., Sl.1, K.2 tog., psso., Yo., K.1, Yo., Sl.2, K.2 tog., p2sso., Yo., K.12, Yo., Sl.2, K.2 tog., p2sso., Yo., K.1, Yo., Sl.1, K.2 tog., psso., Yo., K.1, Yo., Sl.2, K.2 tog., p2sso., Yo., Sl.1, K.2 tog., psso., Yo., * Sl.2, K.2 tog., p2sso., Yo., K.1, Yo., K.1B.]

Charts for 'Trifolium' Design

All lace pieces of the Trifolium design are variations of the charts PARTS A, B, C, D, and E.

The great variety of combinations given already in the written instructions makes it impossible to give once more detailed directions to the charts. If you knit the first one or two rounds in each part from the written instructions, you will be able to follow the chart quite easily from there.

The section from [to] is always one chart line.

Every round of which the number is missing knit plain.

In PARTS A and B the part of chart line between the double * at beginning and end of line makes up the short side of the oblong cloth.

PART F of the chart is added just to illustrate how to crochet off round 225, etc.

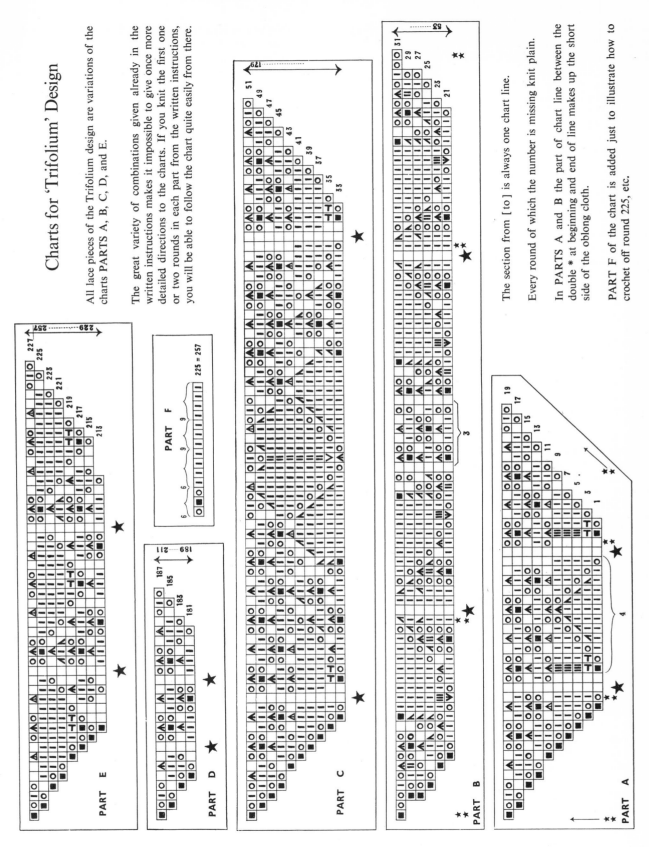

PART F   225 = 257

PART E

PART D

PART C

PART B

PART A

45th round—[Yo., K.3, Yo., K.1B., Yo., K.3, * (Yo., K.1B., Yo., K.3) twice, Yo., K.1B., Yo., K.14, (Yo., K.1B., Yo., K.3) 3 times, * Yo., K.1B., Yo., K.3, Yo., K.1B.]

47th round—[Yo., K.1, (Yo., Sl.1, K.2 tog., psso.) 3 times, * (Yo., Sl.1, K.2 tog., psso.) 5 times, Yo., Sl.1, K.1, psso., K.10, K.2 tog., (Yo., Sl.1, K.2 tog., psso.) 6 times, * (Yo., Sl.1, K.2 tog., psso.) twice, Yo., K.1, Yo., K.1B.]

49th round—[Yo., (K.3, Yo., K.1B., Yo.) twice, * (K.3, Yo., K.1B., Yo.) twice, K.3, (Yo., Sl.1, K.1, psso., K.2, K.2 tog.) twice, Yo., (K.3, Yo., K.1B., Yo.) 3 times, * K.3, Yo., K.1B., Yo., K.3, Yo., K.1B.]

51st round—[Yo., K.1, Yo., (Sl.1, K.2 tog., psso., Yo.) 4 times, * (Sl.1, K.2 tog., psso., Yo.) 5 times, (K.1, Yo., Sl.2, K.2 tog., p2sso., Yo.) twice, K.1, Yo., (Sl.1, K.2 tog., psso., Yo.) 6 times, * (Sl.1, K.2 tog., psso., Yo.) 3 times, K.1, Yo., K.1B.]

Now PARTS B and C are worked in their order 4 times more as follows:

Rounds 53 to 63 are the same as rounds 21 to 31 of PART B, but each section from [to] is worked 4 times in one round, *omitting* the part from ** to **. The part from * to * is worked 3 times when knitting the section for the first and third time (long sides) and once when knitting the section for the second and fourth time (short sides).

Rounds 65 to 83 are worked as rounds 33 to 51 of PART C, knitting each section from [to] also 4 times in one round. The part from * to * is knitted 4 times when working the section for the first and third times (long sides) and twice when knitting it for the second and fourth times (short sides).

Rounds 85 to 95 are worked as rounds 21 to 31 but work each section from [to] 4 times in one round, omitting the part from ** to **. The part from * to * is knitted 4 times when working the long sides and twice when working the short sides of the cloth.

Rounds 97 to 115 are worked as rounds 33 to 51 but knit the part from * to * 5 times when working the long sides and 3 times when working the short sides of the cloth.

Rounds 117 to 127 are worked as rounds 21 to 31. The section from [to] is worked 4 times in one round omitting again the part from ** to **. The part from * to * is knitted 5 times when working the long sides and 3 times when working the short sides of the cloth.

Rounds 129 to 147 are the same as rounds 33 to 51, but work the part from * to * 6 times when knitting the long sides and 4 times when knitting the short sides of the cloth.

Rounds 149 to 159 are worked as rounds 21 to 31. The section from [to] is knitted 4 times in one round omitting again the part from ** to **. The part from * to * is knitted 6

times when working the long sides and 4 times when working the short sides of the cloth.

Rounds 161 to 179 are the same as rounds 33 to 51, but knit the part from * to * 7 times when working the long sides and 5 times when working the short sides of the cloth.

Now proceed with PART D.

PART D

Knit each section from [to] 4 times in one round

but work the part from * to * 60 times when knitting the long sides and 44 times when knitting the short sides of the cloth.

181st round—[Yo., K.3, * Yo., K.1B., Yo., K.3, * Yo., K.1B.]

183rd round—[Yo., K.1, Yo., Sl.1, K.2 tog., psso., * (Yo., Sl.1, K.2 tog., psso.) twice, * Yo., K.1, Yo., K.1B.]

185th round—[Yo., K.3, Yo., K.1B., Yo., * K.3, Yo., K.1B., Yo., * K.3, Yo., K.1B.]

187th round—[Yo., K.1, Yo., (Sl.1, K.2 tog., psso., Yo.) twice, * (Sl.1, K.2 tog., psso., Yo.) twice, * Sl.1, K.2 tog., psso., Yo., K.1, Yo., K.1B.]

Now work PART D another 3 times with the following alterations:

Rounds 189 to 195 knit the part from * to * 62 times when working the long sides and 46 times when knitting the short sides.

Rounds 197 to 203 knit the part from * to * 64 times for the long sides and 48 times for the short sides.

Rounds 205 to 211 knit the part from * to * 66 times for the long sides and 50 times for the short sides.

Now proceed with PART E.

PART E

Knit each section from [to] 4 times in one round

but work the part from * to * 34 times when knitting the long sides and 26 times when knitting the short sides.

213th round—[Yo., K.3, * (Yo., K.1B., Yo., K.3) twice, * Yo., K.1B.]

215th round—[Yo.2, K.1, Yo., Sl.1, K.2 tog., psso., * (Yo., Sl.1, K.2 tog., psso.) 4 times, * Yo., K.1, Yo.2, K.1B.]

217th round—[Yo., K.1B., Yo., K.3, Yo., K.1B., Yo., * (K.3, Yo., K.1B., Yo.) twice, * K.3, (Yo., K.1B.) twice.]

219th round—[Yo., (KM.1B.) twice, K.1, Yo., (Sl.1, K.2 tog., psso., Yo.) twice, * Sl.1, K.2 tog., psso., Yo., (KM.1B.) twice, K.1, Yo., (Sl.1, K.2 tog., psso., Yo.) twice, * Sl.1, K.2 tog., psso., Yo., (KM.1B.) twice, K.1, Yo., K.1B.]

221st round—[Yo., K.7, Yo., Sl.1, K.1, psso., K.1, K.2 tog.,
* Yo., K.7, Yo., Sl.1, K.1, psso., K.1, K.2 tog., * Yo., K.7,
Yo., K.1B.]

223rd round—[Yo., K.9, Yo., Sl.1, K.2 tog., psso., * Yo.,
K.9, Yo., Sl.1, K.2 tog., psso., * Yo., K.9, Yo., K.1B.]

225th round—[Yo., K.11, Yo., K.1B., Yo., * K.11, Yo.,
K.1B., Yo., * K.11, Yo., K.1B.]

227th round—[Yo., K.1, Yo., (Sl.2, K.2 tog., p2sso., Yo.,
Sl.1, K.2 tog., psso., Yo.) twice, * (Sl.2, K.2 tog.,
p2sso., Yo., Sl.1, K.2 tog., psso., Yo.) twice, * Sl.2, K.2 tog., Yo.,
Sl.1, K.2 tog., psso., Yo., Sl.2, K.2 tog., p2sso., Yo., K.1,
Yo., K.1B.]

Now work **PART** E twice more with the following alterations:

Rounds 229 to 243; knit the part from * to * 36 times when
working the long sides and 28 times when knitting the short
sides of the Cloth.

Rounds 245 to 257 are the same as rounds 213 to 225 (notice:
omit the last round of **PART** E) but work the part from * to
* 38 times for the long sides and 30 times for the short sides.
Round 258 knit plain.

FINISHING OF DINNER CLOTH (see page 88).

Trolley Cloth

Commence by casting-on 88 stitches on to three needles,
having 24 stitches each on the first and second needles and
40 stitches on the third needle. Knit one round of plain and
then proceed working the pattern according to the instructions
given for Oblong Dinner Cloth.

Work **PARTS A, B, C** and one more repetition of B and C
up to round 83 inclusive. Then knit immediately **PART E**
3 times and a 4th time up to round 225 only. Now crochet

off the cloth according to the instructions of FINISHING
OF DINNER CLOTH.

Notice: When knitting **PART A** the section from * to * will
only be knitted once. In **PARTS B** and **C** the section from
* to * will also have one repeat less as for the Dinner Cloth
when working the long sides of the design. Knitting **PART
E** for the first time the section from * to * is worked 14 times
for the long sides and 10 times for the short sides of the cloth.
Working **PART E** for the second, third and fourth time,
the section from * to * repeats always twice more.

FINISHING OF OBLONG DINNER CLOTH

After knitting plain round 258 knit another stitch and finish the cloth by crocheting off as follows:

4 sts., 1 d.c., 9 ch., 3 sts., 1 d.c., 9 ch., 4 sts., 1 d.c., 6 ch., 3 sts., 1 d.c., 6 ch., thus working all round the cloth.

Finish with a slip stitch into first d.c. and break off and secure thread invisibly.

The large hole in the centre is then stitched together by joining the opposite middle sections according to the pattern.

Dinner Mat

Commence by casting-on 88 stitches on to three needles, having 24 stitches each on the first and second needles and 40 stitches on the third needle. Knit one round plain and then work according to the instructions for the Dinner Cloth knitting PARTS A, B and C up to rounds 51 only. Now work immediately PART E rounds 213 to 225 only and then crochet off according to FINISHING OF DINNER CLOTH.

Notice: When knitting the long sides of the Mat the repeat from * to * will be in PARTS A, B and C one less than for the Dinner Cloth.

In PART E the section from * to * will knit 10 times on the long sides and 6 times on the short sides of the Mat.

Square Mat

The casting-on and working is the same as for the Square Table Cloth but only up to round 51. Then knit immediately PART E rounds 213 to 225 working the section from [to] 4 times in one round and knitting the part from * to * 6 times in each section. Crochet off as given for the FINISHING OF DINNER CLOTH.

Coffee Table Cloth

Commence by casting on 328 stitches on to a 16 in. circular needle. Knit one round plain and then follow the instructions given for the Dinner Cloth.

Work PARTS A, B and C up to round 51 only, then knit immediately PART E rounds 213 to 225 only and crochet off according to the directions of FINISHING OF DINNER CLOTH.

Notice: When working the long sides of the cloth the section from * to * will repeat in PARTS A, B and C twice more than stated for the working of the Dinner Cloth. The repeats from * to * in PART E will adjust themselves accordingly.

The Coffee Cloth shown below is a shorter version (cast on 167 sts.) and is useful as a runner or as centre-piece for a luncheon setting.

Square Table Cloth

Commence by casting-on 8 stitches on to three needles having two stitches each on the first and second needle and four stitches on the third needle. Work one round into the back of the stitches and proceed working according to the directions of Oblong Dinner Cloth but knitting only the short sides 4 times in the round. For instance: In PART A work only the section from ** to ** but 4 times in each round. In PART B the section from ** to ** is also worked

4 times in the round. In PART C follow the directions given for the short sides only but again 4 times in the round. In the following repeats of PART B and C as well as in PART D and E always follow the instructions for the working of the short sides of the Dinner Cloth.

Also the crocheting off is the same as for the Dinner Cloth. The Square Cloth of 39 in. (photographed above) was worked the following way: PARTS A, B, C and repeats of B and C up to round 147 inclusive. PART D 4 times, and PART E 4 times but finished the 4th time with round 225.

Adaptation of Pattern

The pattern of the Oblong Cloth is made up lengthways of a certain number of sections on each side, called middle sections. By altering their number the pattern of the cloth can be adapted to different measurements.

80 cast-on stitches (40 for each side) are required to give one middle section which measures about 6 in. in length and is given in the instructions as the part from * to *. By adding so many times 80 stitches the cloth can thus be lengthened by a multiple of 6 in. The repetition from * to * will, of course, alter in all PARTS of the design according to the number of added middle sections.

The design can also be enlarged by adding additional rows of leaves. Each leaf is composed of PART B and PART C which have to be treated as one unit. Such a unit repeated adds always 3 in. all round to the size of the cloth.

Also the outer edge composed of PART E can be repeated any number of times and one repeat is always adding 1½ in. all round.

RUNNER (see photo above)

Another version of a Runner can be worked by casting on the required number of stitches and working PART A up to round 20 incl. Then knit immediately PART E rounds 213 to 227 and once more rounds 213 to 225 only. 226 knit plain and crochet off the usual way. (328 cast-on sts.)

Therefore, this design is adaptable to an endless number of combinations of oblong or square variations. Once one of the given patterns has been worked, it should not be difficult to make up any other variation as to taste and measurements.

STRETCHING OF TRIFOLIUM DESIGNS

Prepare paper pattern by drawing the shape of:

OBLONG DINNER CLOTH—rectangle 60 in. by 48 in.

TROLLEY CLOTH—rectangle 33 in. by 27 in.

SQUARE TABLE CLOTH—a square of 39 in.

Divide each side of either rectangle or square into parts of 2 in.

In the

COFFEE TABLE CLOTH—a rectangle 33 in. by 11 in.

DINNER MAT—a rectangle 16½ in. by 11 in.

RUNNER—a rectangle 22 in. by 11 in.

SQUARE MAT—a square of 11 in.

all sides are divided into parts of 1⅜ in.

Take the prepared lace and place the 4 corners into position by pinning out the corner loops of chain on the corners. The 2 loops of 6 chain are pinned out with one pin only on the points marked all round the oblong or square. The remaining loops of chain, of which there are 2 in between, are pinned down with one pin each slightly farther out from the line, thus forming a small scallop as seen on the photo.

Finish treating the lace as directed in BASIC INSTRUCTIONS.

CHAPTER V

ROUND DESIGNS

'Daffodil' Design

TEA CLOTH

MATERIALS

TEA CLOTH—4 balls of Crochet Cotton No. 60, or 3 oz. of Linen Thread No. 60.

Four double pointed knitting needles No. 12, length 7 in.

One circular knitting needle No. 12, length 24 in. or 30 in.

One steel crochet hook No. 5.

MEASUREMENTS

38 in. diameter.

CASTING-ON

Commence by casting-on (either method) 12 stitches on to 3 needles, having 4 stitches on each needle. Knit one round into the back of all stitches, and then work first pattern round of PART A.

Every round of which the number is missing knit plain.

L in front of pattern round see ABBREVIATIONS.

Also take care of Yo.2 as explained in BASIC INSTRUCTIONS.

PART A

1st round—Plain.

2nd round—(K.1, Yo.2, K.1) 6 times.

3rd round—(K.1, M.8 into Yo.2 of previous round, K.1) 6 times.

4 rounds plain.

8th round—(Yo.2, K.2 tog.) 30 times.

6 rounds plain.

15th round—[(KM.1B.) 14 times, K.1B.] 6 times all round.

Now proceed with PART B.

Notice that in the following PART B, PART C and PART D the stitches above the purl stitches of the pattern rounds must also be purled in the following plain round.

PART B

Knit each section from [to] 6 times in one round

17th round—[K.1B., (P.1, K.1) 13 times, P.1, K.1B.]

19th round—[K.1B., (P.1, K.1) 13 times, P.1, K.1B., Yo.2.]

21st round—[K.1B., (P.1, K.1) 13 times, P.1, K.1B., (Yo., K.1, Yo.) twice.]

23rd round—[K.1B., (P.1, K.1) 13 times, P.1, K.1B., Yo., K.1, Sl.1, K.1, psso., Yo.2, K.2 tog., K.1, Yo.]

25th round—[K.1B., (P.1, K.1) 13 times, P.1, K.1B., Yo., K.2, Sl.1, K.1, psso., Yo.2, K.2 tog., K.2, Yo.]

27th round—[K.1B., (P.1, K.1) 13 times, P.1, K.1B., Yo., K.3, Sl.1, K.1, psso., Yo.2, K.2 tog., K.3, Yo.]

29th round—[K.1B., (P.1, K.1) 13 times, P.1, K.1B., Yo., K.4, Sl.1, K.1, psso., Yo.2, K.2 tog., K.4, Yo.]

31st round—[K.1B., (P.1, K.1) 13 times, P.1, K.1B., Yo., K.5, Sl.1, K.1, psso., Yo.2, K.2 tog., K.5, Yo.]

Now proceed with PART C.

PART C

Knit each section from [to] 6 times in one round

33rd round—[K.1B., (P.1, K.1) 5 times, P.1, Sl.2, K.3 tog., p2sso., P.1, (K.1, P.1) 5 times, K.1B., Yo., K.6, Sl.1, K.1, psso., Yo.2, K.2 tog., K.6, Yo.]

35th round—[K.1B., (P.1, K.1) 4 times, P.1, Sl.2, K.3 tog., p2sso., P.1, (K.1, P.1) 4 times, K.1B., Yo., K.7, Sl.1, K.1, psso., Yo.2, K.2 tog., K.7, Yo.]

37th round—[K.1B., (P.1, K.1) 3 times, P.1, Sl.2, K.3 tog., p2sso., P.1, (K.1, P.1) 3 times, K.1B., Yo., K.1, Yo., K.1B., K.6, Sl.1, K.1, psso., Yo.2, K.2 tog., K.6, K.1B., Yo., K.1, Yo.]

39th round—[K.1B., (P.1, K.1) twice, P.1, Sl.2, K.3 tog., p2sso., P.1, (K.1, P.1) twice, K.1B., Yo., K.3, Yo., K.1B., K.6, Sl.1, K.1, psso., Yo.2, K.2 tog., K.6, K.1B., Yo., K.3, Yo.]

41st round—[K.1B., P.1, K.1, P.1, Sl.2, K.3 tog., p2sso., P.1, K.1, P.1, K.1B., Yo., K.1, Yo., Sl.1, K.2 tog., psso., Yo., K.1, Yo., K.1B., K.6, Sl.1, K.1, psso., Yo.2, K.2 tog., K.6, K.1B., Yo., K.1, Yo., Sl.1, K.2 tog., psso., Yo., K.1, Yo.]

43rd round—[K.1B., P.1, Sl.2, K.3 tog., p2sso., P.1, K.1B., (Yo., K.3, Yo., K.1B.) twice, K.6, Sl.1, K.1, psso., Yo.2, K.2 tog., K.6, (K.1B., Yo., K.3, Yo.) twice.]

45th round—[Sl.2, K.3 tog., p2sso., Yo., K.1, (Yo., Sl.1, K.2 tog., psso.) 3 times, Yo., K.1, Yo., K.1B., K.6, Sl.1, K.1, psso., Yo.2, K.2 tog., K.6, K.1B., Yo., K.1, (Yo., Sl.1, K.2 tog., psso.) 3 times, Yo., K.1, Yo.]

47th round—[(Yo., K.1B., Yo., K.3) 3 times, Yo., K.1B., K.6, Sl.1, K.1, psso., Yo.2, K.2 tog., K.6, K.1B., Yo., K.3, (Yo., K.1B., Yo., K.3) twice.]

49th round—[(Yo., Sl.1, K.2 tog., psso.) 6 times, Yo., K.1, Yo., K.1B., K.6, Sl.1, K.1, psso., Yo.2, K.2 tog., K.6, K.1B., Yo., K.1, (Yo., Sl.1, K.2 tog., psso.) 5 times.]

Now proceed with PART D.

'Daffodil' Design

PART D

Knit each section from [to] 6 times in one round

51st round—[(K.3, Yo., K.1B., Yo.) 3 times, K.3, Yo., K.1B., K.6, Sl.1, K.1, psso., Yo.2, K.2 tog., K.6, K.1B., Yo., (K.3, Yo., K.1B., Yo.) 3 times.]

53rd round—[(Sl.1, K.2 tog., psso., Yo.) 7 times, K.2 tog., K.6, K.1B., Yo., K.2 tog., Yo., K.1B., K.6, Sl.1, K.1, psso., Yo., (Sl.1, K.2 tog., psso., Yo.) 6 times.]

55th round—[(Yo., K.1B., Yo., K.3) 3 times, Yo., K.1B., Yo., K.2 tog., K.6, K.1B., Yo., (KM.1B.) twice, K.1, Yo., K.1B., K.6, Sl.1, K.1, psso., (Yo., K.1B., Yo., K.3) 3 times.]

57th round—[(Yo., Sl.1, K.2 tog., psso.) 7 times, Yo., K.1B., K.6, K.1B., Yo., K.2 tog., (KM.1B.) twice, K.1, Sl.1, K.1, psso., Yo., K1.B., K.6, K.1B., (Yo., Sl.1, K.2 tog., psso.) 6 times.]

59th round—[(K.3, Yo., K.1B., Yo.) 3 times, K.3, Yo., K.1B., K.6, K.1B., Yo., K.2 tog., (KM.1B.) 4 times, K.1, Sl.1, K.1, psso., Yo., K.1B., K.6, K.1B., Yo., (K.3, Yo., K.1B., Yo.) 3 times.]

61st round—[(Sl.1, K.2 tog., psso., Yo.) 7 times, K.2 tog., K.6, K.1B., Yo., K.2 tog., (K.1, P.1) 4 times, K.1, Sl.1, K.1, psso., Yo., K.1B., K.6, Sl.1, K.1, psso., Yo., (Sl.1, K.2 tog., psso., Yo.) 6 times.]

63rd round—[(Yo., K.1B., Yo., K.3) 3 times, Yo., K.1B., Yo., K.2 tog., K.6, K.1B., Yo., K.2 tog., (K.1, P.1) 4 times, K.1, Sl.1, K.1, psso., Yo., K.1B., K.6, Sl.1, K.1, psso., (Yo., K.1B., Yo., K.3) 3 times.]

65th round—[(Yo., Sl.1, K.2 tog., psso.) 7 times, Yo., K.1B., K.6, K.1B., Yo., K.2 tog., (K.1, P.1) 4 times, K.1, Sl.1, K.1, psso., Yo., K.1B., K.6, K.1B., (Yo., Sl.1, K.2 tog., psso.) 6 times.]

67th round—[(K.3, Yo., K.1B., Yo.) 3 times, K.3, Yo., K.1B., K.6, K.1B., Yo.2, K.2 tog., (K.1, P.1) 4 times, K.1, Sl.1, K.1, psso., Yo.2, K.1B., K.6, (K.3, Yo., K.1B., Yo.) 3 times.]

69th round—[(Sl.1, K.2 tog., psso., Yo.) 7 times, K.2 tog., K.6, K.1B., Yo., M.2, K.2 tog., (K.1, P.1) 4 times, K.1, Sl.1, K.1, psso., Yo., M.2, Yo., K.1B., K.6, Sl.1, K.1, psso., Yo., (Sl.1, K.2 tog., psso., Yo.) 6 times.]

71st round—[(Yo., K.1B., Yo., K.3) 3 times, Yo., K.1B., Yo., K.2 tog., K.6, K.1B., Yo., M.2, K.2 tog., Yo., K.2 tog., (K.1, P.1) 4 times, K.1, Sl.1, K.1, psso., Yo., K.2 tog., M.2, Yo., K.1B., K.6, Sl.1, K.1, psso., (Yo., K.1B., Yo., K.3) 3 times.]

Now proceed with **PART E**.

Notice that in the following PART E the stitches above the purl stitches of pattern rounds 73, 75 and 77 must also be purled in their following plain rounds.

PART E

Knit each section from [to] 6 times in one round

73rd round—[(Yo., Sl.1, K.2 tog., psso.) 6 times, (Yo., K.2 tog.) twice, K.6, K.1B., Yo., M.2, K.2 tog., M.2, Yo., K.2 tog., (K.1, P.1) 4 times, K.1, Sl.1, K.1, psso., Yo., M.2, K.2 tog., M.2, Yo., K.1B., K.6, Sl.1, K.1, psso., Yo., Sl.1, K.1, psso., (Yo., Sl.1, K.2 tog., psso.) 5 times.]

75th round—[(K.3, Yo., K.1B., Yo.) 3 times, K.2 tog., Yo., K.2 tog., K.6, K.1B., Yo., (M.2, K.2 tog.) twice, Yo., K.2 tog., (K.1, P.1) 4 times, K.1, Sl.1, K.1, psso., Yo., (K.2 tog., M.2) twice, Yo., K.1B., K.6, (Sl.1, K.1, psso., Yo.) twice, K.1B., Yo., (K.3, Yo., K.1B., Yo.) twice.]

77th round—[(Sl.1, K.2 tog., psso., Yo.) 5 times, (K.2 tog., Yo.) twice, K.2 tog., K.6, K.1B., Yo., (M.2, K.2 tog.) twice, M.2, (Yo., K.1B.) twice, K.1, P.1, Sl.2, K.3 tog., p2sso., P.1, K.1, (K.1B., Yo.) twice, (M.2, K.2 tog.) twice, M.2, Yo., K.1B., K.6, (Sl.1, K.1, psso., Yo.) 3 times, (Sl.1, K.2 tog., psso., Yo.) 4 times.]

79th round—[(Yo., K.1B., Yo., K.3) twice, Yo., K.1B., (Yo., K.2 tog.) 3 times, K.6, K.1B., Yo., (M.2, K.2 tog.) 3 times, Yo., KM.1B, K.1, (Yo., K.1B.) twice, Sl.2, K.3 tog., p2sso., (K.1B., Yo.) twice, KM.1B., K.1, Yo., (K.2 tog., M.2) 3 times, Yo., K.1B., K.6, Sl.1, K.1, psso., (Yo., Sl.1, K.1, psso.) twice, (Yo., K.1B., Yo., K.3) twice.]

81st round—[(Yo., Sl.1, K.2 tog., psso.) 4 times, (Yo., K.2 tog.) 4 times, K.6, K.1B., Yo., (M.2, K.2 tog.) twice, M.2, K.3 tog., Yo., K.2 tog., KM.1B., K.1, Yo., K.2 tog., K.1, Yo., Sl.1, K.2 tog., psso., Yo., K.1, Sl.1, K.1, psso., Yo., KM.1B., K.1, Sl.1, K.1, psso., Yo., Sl.2, K.1, p2sso., (M.2, K.2 tog.) twice, M.2, Yo., K.1B., K.6, (Sl.1, K.1, psso., Yo.) 4 times, (Sl.1, K.2 tog., psso., Yo.) twice, Sl.1, K.2 tog., psso.]

83rd round—[(K.3, Yo., K.1B., Yo.) twice, (K.2 tog., Yo.) 3 times, K.2 tog., K.6, K.1B., Yo., (M.2, K.2 tog.) twice, M.2, K.3 tog., Yo., K.2 tog., K.1, KM.1B., K.1, Yo., K.2 tog., K.5, Sl.1, K.1, psso., Yo., KM.1B., K.2, Sl.1, K.1, psso., Yo., Sl.2, K.1, p2sso., (M.2, K.2 tog.) twice, M.2, Yo., K.1B., K.6, (Sl.1, K.1, psso., Yo.) 4 times, K.1B., Yo., K.3, Yo., K.1B., Yo.]

85th round—[(Sl.1, K.2 tog., psso., Yo.) 3 times, (K.2 tog., Yo.) 4 times, K.2 tog., K.6, K.1B., Yo., (M.2, K.2 tog.) twice, M.2, K.3 tog., Yo., K.2 tog., K.2, KM.1B., K.1, Yo., K.2 tog., K.1, (KM.1B.) twice, K.2, Sl.1, K.1, psso., Yo., KM.1B., K.3, Sl.1, K.1, psso., Yo., Sl.2, K.1, p2sso., (M.2, K.2 tog.) twice, M.2, Yo., K.1B., K.6, (Sl.1, K.1, psso., Yo.) 5 times, (Sl.1, K.2 tog., psso., Yo.) twice.]

87th round—[Yo., K.1B., Yo., K.3, Yo., K.1B., (Yo., K.2 tog.) 5 times, K.6, K.1B., Yo., (M.2, K.2 tog.) twice, M.2, K.3 tog., Yo., K.2 tog., K.3, KM.1B., K.1, Yo., K.2 tog., K.2, (KM.1B.) twice, K.3, Sl.1, K.1, psso., Yo., KM.1B., K.4, Sl.1, K.1, psso., Yo., Sl.2, K.1, p2sso., (M.2, K.2 tog.) twice, M.2, Yo., K.1B., K.6, (Sl.1, K.1, psso., Yo.) 5 times, K.1B., Yo., K.3.]

89th round—[(Yo., Sl.1, K.2 tog., psso.) twice, (Yo., K.2 tog.) 6 times, K.6, K.1B., Yo., (M.2, K.2 tog.) 3 times, M.2, Yo., K.2 tog., K.4, KM.1B., K.1, Yo., K.2 tog., K.3, (KM.1B.) twice, K.4, Sl.1, K.1, psso., Yo., KM.1B., K.5, Sl.1, K.1, psso., Yo., (M.2, K.2 tog.) 3 times, M.2, Yo., K.1B., K.6, (Sl.1, K.1, psso., Yo.) 6 times, Sl.1, K.2 tog., psso.]

91st round—[K.3, Yo., K.1B., (Yo., K.2 tog.) 6 times, K.6, K.1B., Yo., (M.2, K.2 tog.) 4 times, Yo., K.2 tog., K.5, KM.1B., K.1, Yo., K.2 tog., K.4, (KM.1B.) twice, K.5, Sl.1, K.1, psso., Yo., KM.1B., K.6, Sl.1, K.1, psso., Yo., (K.2 tog., M.2) 4 times, Yo., K.1B., K.6, (Sl.1, K.1, psso., Yo.) 6 times, K.1B., Yo.]

93rd round—[Yo., Sl.1, K.2 tog., psso., (Yo., K.2 tog.) 7 times, K.6, K.1B., Yo., (M.2, K.2 tog.) 3 times, M.2, K.3 tog., Yo., K.2 tog., K.6, KM.1B., K.1, Yo., K.2 tog., K.5, (KM.1B.) twice, K.6, Sl.1, K.1, psso., Yo., KM.1B., K.7, Sl.1, K.1, psso., Yo., Sl.2, K.1, p2sso., (M.2, K.2 tog.) 3 times, M.2, Yo., K.1B., K.6, (Sl.1, K.1, psso., Yo.) 6 times, Sl.1, K.1, psso.]

L *95th round*—[Sl.1, K.1, psso., K.1, K.2 tog., (Yo., K.2 tog.) 6 times, K.6, K.1B., Yo., (M.2, K.2 tog.) 3 times, M.2, K.3 tog., Yo., K.2 tog., K.9, Yo., M.2, Yo., K.1B., K.15, K.1B., Yo., M.2, Yo., K.9, Sl.1, K.1, psso., Yo., Sl.2, K.1, p2sso., (M.2, K.2 tog.) 3 times, M.2, Yo., K.1B., K.6, (Sl.1, K.1, psso., Yo.) 6 times.]

97th round—[Yo., Sl.1, K.2 tog., psso., (Yo., K.2 tog.) 6 times, K.3, K.2 tog., K.1, K.1B., Yo., (M.2, K.2 tog.) 4 times, M.2, Yo., K.2 tog., K.7, K.2 tog., Yo., M.2, K.2 tog., M.2, Yo., K.1B., K.15, K.1B., Yo., M.2, K.2 tog., M.2, Yo., Sl.1, K.1, psso., K.7, Sl.1, K.1, psso., Yo., (M.2, K.2 tog.) 4 times, M.2, Yo., K.1B., K.1, Sl.1, K.1, psso., K.3, (Sl.1, K.1, psso. Yo.) 5 times, Sl.1, K.1, psso.]

L *99th round*—[Sl.1, K.1, psso., K.1, K.2 tog., (Yo., K.2 tog.) 5 times, K.5, K.1B., Yo., (M.2, K.2, tog.) 5 times, Yo., K.2 tog., K.6, K.2 tog., Yo., (M.2, K.2 tog.) twice, M.2, Yo., Sl.1, K.1, psso., K.13, K.2 tog., Yo., (M.2, K.2 tog.) twice, M.2, Yo., Sl.1, K.1, psso., K.6, Sl.1, K.1, psso., Yo., (K.2 tog., M.2) 5 times, Yo., K.1B., K.5, (Sl.1, K.1, psso., Yo.) 5 times.]

101st round—[Yo., Sl.1, K.2 tog., psso., (Yo., K.2 tog.) 5 times, K.2, K.2 tog., K.1, K.1B., Yo., (M.2, K.2 tog.) 4 times, M.2, K.3 tog., Yo., K.2 tog., K.5, K.2 tog., Yo., (M.2, K.2 tog.) 3 times, M.2, Yo.2, Sl.2, K.1, p2sso., K.9, K.3 tog., Yo.2, (M.2, K.2 tog.) 3 times, M.2, Yo., Sl.1, K.1, psso., K.5, Sl.1, K.1, psso., Yo., Sl.2, K.1, p2sso., (M.2, K.2 tog.) 4 times, M.2, Yo., K.1B., K.1, Sl.1, K.1, psso., K.2, (Sl.1, K.1, psso., Yo.) 4 times, Sl.1, K.1, psso.]

L *103rd round*—[Sl.1, K.1, psso., K.1, K.2 tog., (Yo., K.2 tog.) 4 times, K.4, K.1B., Yo., (M.2, K.2 tog.) 4 times, M.2, K.3 tog., Yo., K.2 tog., K.4, K.2 tog., Yo., (M.2, K.2 tog.) 4 times, M.2, Yo., K.1B., Yo., Sl.2, K.1, p2sso., K.5, K.3 tog., Yo., K.1B., Yo., (M.2, K.2 tog.) 4 times, M.2, Yo., Sl.1, K.1, psso., K.4, Sl.1, K.1, psso., Yo., Sl.2, K.1, p2sso., (M.2, K.2 tog.) 4 times, M.2, Yo., K.1B., K.4, (Sl.1, K.1, psso., Yo.) 4 times.]

105th round—[Yo., Sl.1, K.2 tog., psso., (Yo., K.2 tog.) 4 times, K.1, K.2 tog., K.1, K.1B., Yo., (M.2, K.2 tog.) 4 times, M.2, K.3 tog., Yo., K.2 tog., K.3, K.2 tog., Yo., (M.2, K.2 tog.) 5 times, M.2, Yo., KM.1B., K.1, Yo., Sl.1, K.1, psso., K.3, K.2 tog., Yo., KM.1B., K.1B., Yo., (M.2, K.2 tog.) 5 times, M.2, Yo., Sl.1, K.1, psso., K.3, Sl.1, K.1, psso., Yo., Sl.2, K.1, p2sso., (M.2, K.2 tog.) 4 times, M.2, Yo., K.1B., K.1, Sl.1, K.1, psso., K.1, (Sl.1, K.1, psso., Yo.) 3 times, Sl.1, K.1, psso.]

L *107th round*—[Sl.1, K.1, psso., K.1, K.2 tog., (Yo., K.2 tog.) 3 times, K.3, K.1B., Yo., (M.2, K.2 tog.) 4 times, M.2, K.3 tog., Yo., K.2 tog., K.1, K.3 tog., Yo., (M.2, K.2 tog.) 6 times, M.2, Yo., K.1B., P.1, KM.1B., K.1, Yo., Sl.1, K.1, psso., K.1, K.2 tog., Yo., KM.1B., K.1B., P.1, K.1B., Yo., (M.2, K.2 tog.) 6 times, M.2, Yo., Sl.2, K.1, p2sso., K.1, Sl.1, K.1, psso., Yo., Sl.2, K.1, p2sso., (M.2, K.2 tog.) 4 times, M.2, Yo., K.1B., K.3, (Sl.1, K.1, psso., Yo.) 3 times.]

109th round—[Yo., Sl.1, K.2 tog., psso., (Yo., K.2 tog.) 3 times, K.2 tog., K.1, K.1B., Yo., (M.2, K.2 tog.) 4 times, M.2, K.3 tog., Yo., (K.2 tog.) twice, Yo., (M.2, K.2 tog.) 7 times, M.2, Yo., (K.1B., P.1) twice, KM.1B., K.1, Yo., Sl.1, K.2 tog., psso., Yo., KM.1B., (K.1B., P.1) twice, K.1B., Yo., (M.2, K.2 tog.) 7 times, M.2, Yo., (Sl.1, K.1, psso.) twice, Yo., Sl.2, K.1, p2sso., (M.2, K.2 tog.) 4 times, M.2, Yo., K.1B., K.1, (Sl.1, K.1, psso.) twice, (Yo., Sl.1, K.1, psso.) twice.]

L *111th round*—[Sl.1, K.1, psso., K.1, K.2 tog., (Yo. K.2 tog.) twice, K.2, K.1B., Yo., (M.2, K.2 tog.) 4 times, M.2, K.3 tog., (M.2, K.2 tog.) 9 times, M.2, Yo., (K.1B., P.1) 3 times, (KM.1B.) 4 times, (K.1B., P.1) 3 times, K.1B., Yo., (M.2, K.2 tog.) 8 times, M.2, Sl.1, K.1, psso., M.2, Sl.2, K.1, p2sso., (M.2, K.2 tog.) 4 times, M.2, Yo., K.1B., K.2, (Sl.1, K.1, psso., Yo.) twice.]

Now proceed with PART F.

PART F

Knit each section from [to] 6 times in one round

113th round—[Yo., Sl.1, K.2 tog., psso., (Yo., K.2 tog.) twice, K.2 tog., K.1B., Yo., (M.2, K.2 tog.) 15 times, Yo., K.2 tog., (P.1, K.1B.) 9 times, P.1, Sl.1, K.1, psso., Yo., (K.2 tog., M.2) 15 times, Yo., K.1B., (Sl.1, K.1, psso.) twice, Yo., Sl.1, K.1, psso.]

L *115th round*—[Sl.1, K.1, psso., K.1, K.2 tog., Yo., (K.2 tog.) twice, Yo., M.2, (K.2 tog., M.2) 15 times, Yo., K.2 tog., (P.1, K.1B.) 9 times, P.1, Sl.1, K.1, psso., Yo., (M.2, K.2 tog.) 15 times, M.2, Yo., (Sl.1, K.1, psso.) twice, Yo.]

117th round—[Yo., Sl.1, K.2 tog., psso., Yo., K.3 tog., Yo., (M.2, K.2 tog.) 16 times, Yo., K.2 tog., (P.1, K.1B.) 9 times, P.1, Sl.1, K.1, psso., Yo., (K.2 tog., M.2) 16 times, Yo., Sl.2, K.1, p2sso.]

L *119th round*—[Sl.1, K.1, psso., K.1, K.2 tog., Yo., M.2, (K.2 tog., M.2) 16 times, Yo., K.2 tog., (P.1, K.1B.) 9 times, P.1, Sl.1, K.1, psso., Yo., (M.2, K.2 tog.) 16 times, M.2, Yo.]

121st round—[Sl.1, K.2 tog., psso., (M.2, K.2 tog.) 17 times, Yo., K.2 tog., (P.1, K.1B.) 9 times, P.1, Sl.1, K.1, psso., Yo., (K.2 tog., M.2) 17 times.]

123rd round—[M.2, (K.2 tog., M.2) 16 times, K.3 tog., (Yo., K.2 tog.) 5 times, Yo., Sl.1, K.2 tog., psso., Yo., (Sl.1, K.1, psso., Yo.) 5 times, Sl.2, K.1, p2sso., (M.2, K.2 tog.) 16 times.]

125th round—[(K.2 tog., M.2) 16 times, K.3 tog., (M.2, K.1) 11 times, M.2, Sl.2, K.1, p2sso., (M.2, K.2 tog.) 15 times, M.2.]

127th round—[(M.2, K.2 tog.) 44 times.]

129th round—[(K.2 tog., M.2) 44 times.]

131st round—same as 127th round.

133rd round—same as 129th round.

Now proceed with PART G.

PART G

Knit each section from [to] 24 times in one round

135th round—[(M.2, K.2 tog.) 5 times, M.2, Yo., K.2 tog., Yo., (M.2, K.2 tog.) 5 times.]

137th round—[(K.2 tog., M.2) 5 times, K.2 tog., Yo., (KM.1B.) twice, K.1, Yo., (K.2 tog., M.2) 5 times.]

139th round—[(M.2, K.2 tog.) 5 times, M.2, Yo., K.2, (KM.1B.) twice, K.3, Yo., (M.2, K.2 tog.) 5 times.]

141st round—[(K.2 tog., M.2) 5 times, K.2 tog., Yo., K.2 tog., K.2, (KM.1B.) twice, K.3, Sl.1, K.1, psso., Yo., (K.2 tog., M.2) 5 times.]

143rd round—[(M.2, K.2 tog.) 5 times, M.2, Yo., K.2 tog., K.3, (KM.1B.) twice, K.4, Sl.1, K.1, psso., Yo., (M.2, K.2 tog.) 5 times.]

145th round—[(K.2 tog., M.2) 5 times, K.2 tog., Yo., K.2 tog., K.4, (KM.1B.) twice, K.5, Sl.1, K.1, psso., Yo., (K.2 tog., M.2) 5 times.]

147th round—[(M.2, K.2 tog.) 4 times, M.2, K.3 tog., Yo., K.2 tog., K.5, (KM.1B.) twice, K.6, Sl.1, K.1, psso., Yo., Sl.2, K.1, p2sso., (M.2, K.2 tog.) 4 times.]

149th round—[(K.2 tog., M.2) 4 times, K.3 tog., Yo., K.2 tog., K.6, (K.1B., Yo.) twice, K.1B., K.6, Sl.1, K.1, psso., Yo., Sl.2, K.1, p2sso., (M.2, K.2 tog.) 3 times, M.2.]

151st round—[(M.2, K.2 tog.) 3 times, M.2, K.3 tog., Yo., K.2 tog., K.6, K.1B., Yo., K.3, Yo., K.1B., K.6, Sl.1, K.1, psso., Yo., Sl.2, K.1, p2sso., (M.2, K.2 tog.) 3 times.]

153rd round—[(K.2 tog., M.2) 3 times, K.3 tog., Yo., K.2 tog., K.6, K.1B., Yo., K.1, Yo., Sl.1, K.2 tog., psso., Yo., K.1, Yo., K.1B., K.6, Sl.1, K.1, psso., Yo., Sl.2, K.1, p2sso., (M.2, K.2 tog.) twice, M.2.]

155th round—[(M.2, K.2 tog.) twice, M.2, K.3 tog., Yo., K.2 tog., K.3, K.2 tog., K.1, K.1B., (Yo., K.3, Yo., K.1B.) twice, K.1, Sl.1, K.1, psso., K.3, Sl.1, K.1, psso., Yo., Sl.2, K.1, p2sso., (M.2, K.2 tog.) twice.]

157th round—[(K.2 tog., M.2) twice, K.3 tog., Yo., K.2 tog., K.2, K.2 tog., K.1, K.1B., Yo., K.1, (Yo., Sl.1, K.2 tog., psso.) 3 times, Yo., K.1, Yo., K.1B., K.1, Sl.1, K.1, psso., K.2, Sl.1, K.1, psso., Yo., Sl.2, K.1, p2sso., M.2, K.2 tog., M.2.]

159th round—[M.2, K.2 tog., M.2, K.3 tog., Yo., K.2 tog., K.1, K.2 tog., K.1, K.1B., (Yo., K.3, Yo., K.1B.) 3 times, K.1, Sl.1, K.1, psso., K.1, Sl.1, K.1, psso., Yo., Sl.2, K.1, p2sso., M.2, K.2 tog.]

161st round—[K.2 tog., M.2, K.3 tog., Yo., (K.2 tog.) twice, K.1, K.1B., Yo., K.1, (Yo., Sl.1, K.2 tog., psso.) 5 times, Yo., K.1, Yo., K.1B., K.1, (Sl.1, K.1, psso.) twice, Yo., Sl.2, K.1, p2sso., M.2.]

163rd round—[M.2, K.3 tog., Yo., (K.2 tog.) twice, K.1B., (Yo., K.3, Yo., K.1B.) 4 times, (Sl.1, K.1, psso.) twice, Yo., Sl.2, K.1, p2sso.]

L *165th round*—[Sl.2, K.2 tog., p2sso., Yo., (K.2 tog.) twice, Yo., K.1, (Yo., Sl.1, K.2 tog., psso.) 7 times, Yo., K.1, Yo., (Sl.1, K.1, psso.) twice, Yo.]

167th round—[K.1, K.3 tog., (Yo., K.3, Yo., K.1B.) 4 times, Yo., K.3, Yo., Sl.2, K.1, p2sso.]

168th round—knit plain.

Now see FINISHING OF CLOTH.

FINISHING OF TEA CLOTH

After knitting plain round 168 knit another two stitches, and then finish the cloth with a chain of crochet as follows:

4 sts., 1 d.c., 9 ch., (3 sts., 1 d.c., 9 ch.) 7 times, 4 sts., 1 d.c., 6 ch., 3 sts., 1 d.c., 6 ch. Repeat 23 times. Finish with a slip stitch and break off.

STRETCHING OF TEA CLOTH

Prepare a paper pattern by drawing a circle of 37 in. diameter. Mark round the circle 24 points at a distance of 4¾ in. from each other. Now draw a second outer circle of 38 in. diameter. This indicates the depth of the scallops.

After preparing the lace start to pin out the cloth, trying to shape the scallops according to photo. First pin down the middle of the cloth on to the centre of the circle. Then put the 2 loops of 6 chain on to one pin only, placing it on to the mark of the inner circle, which gives the inner point of each scallop. The outer point of the scallop is obtained by pinning down the two central loops of chain in the middle of the scallop, separately, on to the outer circle. Then pin down the remaining loops of chain according to photo or to one's own liking.

Finish treating the lace as directed in the BASIC INSTRUCTIONS.

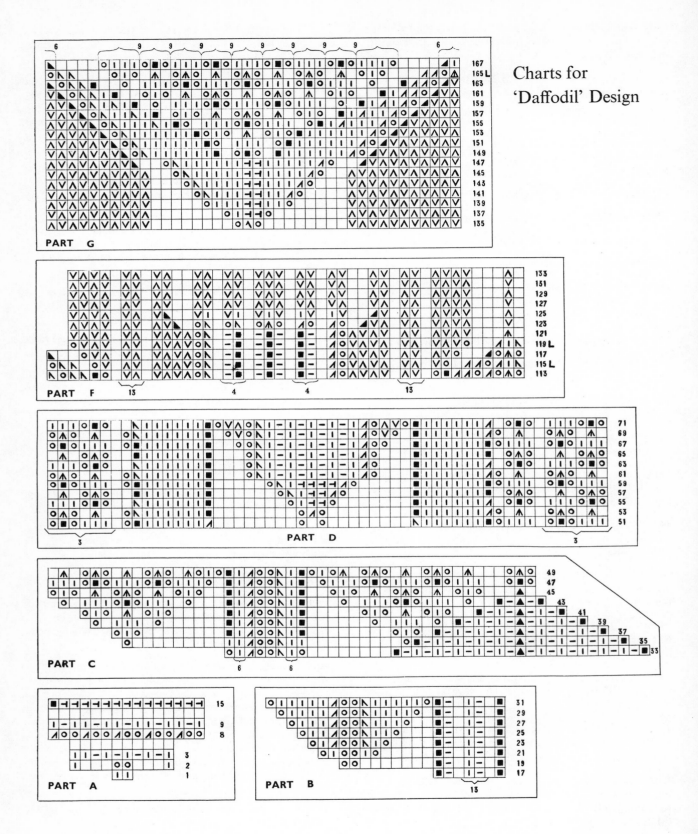

Charts for
'Daffodil' Design

PART G

PART F

PART D

PART C

PART A

PART B

98

PART E₂

PART E₁

Tea Cloth. Work PARTS A, B, C, D, E1 and E2 (as one chart), F, and G.

Parts A, B, C, D, and F. Every chart line to be knitted 6 times in one round, but work the sections within the brackets as many times as indicated by the number below.

Parts E1 and E2. Both belong together and when reading the chart lines a line of E1 has to be followed immediately by the line of the same number of E2. For instance: line 73 of PART E1 is continued forthwith by the line 73 of PART E2, etc.

Every such chart line comprised of E1 and E2 is to be repeated 6 times in one round.

Part G. Every chart line to be knitted 24 times in one round.

Every round of which the number is missing knit plain, but special attention should be paid as occasionally more than one round of plain is worked between pattern rounds. **Notice:** in PARTS B, C, D, and E up to round 77 the stitches above the purl stitches of the pattern rounds must also be purled in their following plain rounds.

Charts for 'Daffodil' Design

99

Thistle Design 'Balmoral'
COFFEE CLOTH AND DINNER CLOTH

MATERIALS

COFFEE CLOTH—3 balls of Crochet Cotton No. 50 or 60, or 2 oz. of Linen Thread No. 60.

DINNER CLOTH—9 balls of Crochet Cotton No. 50 or 60, or 6 oz. of Linen Thread No. 60.

Four double pointed knitting needles No. 12, length 7 in.

One circular knitting needle No. 12, length 24 in. and one circular knitting needle No. 12, length 36 in. or 42 in. (The long circular needle is required for the Dinner Cloth only).

One Cotton Crochet Hook No. 5.

MEASUREMENTS

COFFEE CLOTH—32 in. diameter.

DINNER CLOTH—62 in. diameter.

Coffee Cloth and Dinner Cloth

The Casting-on and the Instructions of PARTS A, B, C, D, and E are the same for the working of Coffee and Dinner cloths. Then follow directions for Finishing of Coffee Cloth when knitting the Cloth of 32 in. diameter.

When working the Dinner Cloth of 62 in. diameter proceed with PARTS F, G, H, work PART E, once more, and then see Finishing of Dinner Cloth.

CASTING-ON

Start from the centre of the cloth by casting-on 12 stitches on to three needles, having 4 stitches on each needle. Work 1 round into the back of all stitches, and knit another round plain. Now start to knit first pattern round of PART A.

Every round of which the number is missing knit plain.

X and L in front of pattern round: see ABBREVIATIONS.

PART A

Knit each section from [to] 6 times in one round

1st round—[K.1B., Yo., K.1, Yo.]

3rd round—[K.1B., Yo., K.3, Yo.]

5th round—[K.1B., Yo., K.5, Yo.]

7th round—[K.1B., Yo., K.2, (KM.1B.) twice, K.3, Yo.]

9th round—[K.1B., Yo., K.4, (KM.1B.) twice, K.5, Yo.]

11th round—[K.1B., Yo., K.6, (KM.1B.) twice, K.7, Yo.]

13th round—[K.1B., Yo., K.8, (KM.1B.) twice, K.9, Yo.]

15th round—[K.1B., Yo., K.5, K.3 tog., Yo., K.2, (KM.1B.) twice, K.3, Yo., Sl.2, K.1, p2sso., K.5, Yo.]

17th round—[K.1B., Yo., K.4, K.3 tog., Yo., M.2, Yo., K.3, (KM.1B.) twice, K.4, Yo., M.2, Yo., Sl.2, K.1, p2sso., K.4, Yo.]

19th round—[K.1B., Yo., K.3, K.3 tog., Yo., M.2, K.2 tog., Yo., K.2 tog., K.3, (KM.1B.) twice, K.4, Sl.1, K.1, psso., Yo., K.2 tog., M.2, Yo., Sl.2, K.1, p2sso., K.3, Yo.]

21st round—[K.1B., Yo., K.2, K.3 tog., Yo., M.2, K.2 tog., M.2, Yo., K.2 tog., K.4, (KM.1B.) twice, K.5, Sl.1, K.1, psso., Yo., M.2, K.2 tog., M.2, Yo., Sl.2, K.1, p2sso., K.2, Yo.]

23rd round—[K.1B., Yo., K.1, K.3 tog., Yo., (M.2, K.2 tog.) twice, Yo., K.2 tog., K.5, (KM.1B.) twice, K.6, Sl.1, K.1, psso., Yo., (K.2 tog., M.2) twice, Yo., Sl.2, K.1, p2sso., K.1, Yo.]

25th round—[K.1B., K.3 tog., Yo., (M.2, K.2 tog.) twice, M.2, Yo., K.2 tog., K.15, Sl.1, K.1, psso., Yo., (M.2, K.2 tog.) twice, M.2, Yo., Sl.2, K.1, p2sso.]

L *27th round*—[Sl.1, K.2 tog., psso., Yo., (M.2, K.2 tog.) 3 times, Yo., K.2 tog., K.3, K.2 tog., Yo., K.5, Yo., Sl.1, K.1, psso., K.3, Sl.1, K.1, psso., Yo., (K.2 tog., M.2) 3 times, Yo.]

29th round—[K.1, (M.2, K.2 tog.) 3 times, M.2, Yo., K.2 tog., K.2, K.2 tog., Yo., M.2, Yo., K.5, Yo., M.2, Yo., Sl.1, K.1, psso., K.2, Sl.1, K.1, psso., Yo., (M.2, K.2 tog.) 3 times, M.2.]

31st round—[(M.2, K.2 tog.) 4 times, Yo., K.2 tog., K.1, K.2 tog., Yo., M.2, K.2 tog., Yo., K.2 tog., K.3, Sl.1, K.1, psso., Yo., K.2 tog., M.2, Yo., Sl.1, K.1, psso., K.1, Sl.1, K.1, psso., Yo., (K.2 tog., M.2) 3 times, K.2 tog.]

33rd round—[(K.2 tog., M.2) 3 times, K.3 tog., Yo., (K.2 tog.) twice, Yo., M.2, K.2 tog., M.2, Yo., K.2 tog., K.3, Sl.1, K.1, psso., Yo., M.2, K.2 tog., M.2, Yo., (Sl.1, K.1, psso.) twice, Yo., K.3 tog., (M.2, K.2 tog.) twice, M.2.]

Thistle Design 'Balmoral'
Dinner Cloth

35th round—[(M.2, K.2 tog.) twice, M.2, (K.3 tog., Yo.) twice, (M.2, K2 tog.) twice, Yo., K.2 tog., K.3, Sl.1, K.1, psso., Yo., (K.2 tog., M.2) twice, Yo., Sl.2, K.1, p2sso., Yo., K.3 tog., (M.2, K.2 tog.) twice.]

37th round—[(K.2 tog., M.2) twice, K.3 tog., M.2, K.1, (M.2, K.2 tog.) twice, M.2, Yo., K.2 tog., K.3, Sl.1, K.1, psso., Yo., (M.2, K.2 tog.) twice, M.2, K.1, M.2, K.3 tog., M.2, K.2 tog., M.2.]

PART B

Knit each section from [to] 6 times in one round

39th round—[(M.2, K.2 tog.) 6 times, Yo., K.2 tog., K.3, Sl.1, K.1, psso., Yo., (K.2 tog., M.2) 5 times, K.2 tog.]

41st round—[(K.2 tog., M.2) 6 times, Yo., K.2 tog., K.3, Sl.1, K.1, psso., Yo., (M.2, K.2 tog.) 5 times, M.2.]

43rd round—[(M.2, K.2 tog.) 6 times, Yo., K.3 tog., K.1, Sl.2, K.1, p2sso., Yo., (K.2 tog., M.2) 5 times, K.2 tog.]

45th round—[(K.2 tog., M.2) 5 times, K.3 tog., Yo., K.1, C.3L., K.1, Yo., K.3 tog., (M.2, K.2 tog.) 4 times, M.2.]

47th round—[(M.2, K.2 tog.) 4 times, M.2, K.3 tog., Yo., K.1, KM.1B., K.1, M.3, KM.1B., K.2, Yo., K.3 tog., (M.2, K.2 tog.) 4 times.]

49th round—[(K.2 tog., M.2) 4 times, K.3 tog., Yo., K.2 tog., K.1, KM.1B., K.4, KM.1B., K.2, Sl.1, K.1, psso., Yo., K.3 tog., (M.2, K.2 tog.) 3 times, M.2.]

51st round—[(M.2, K.2 tog.) 3 times, M.2, K.3 tog., Yo., K.2 tog., (KM.1B.) twice, K.2, Yo., Sl.1, K.2, psso.2, Yo., K.1, (KM.1B.) twice, K.1, Sl.1, K.1, psso., Yo., K.3 tog., (M.2, K.2 tog.) 3 times.]

53rd round—[(K.2 tog., M.2) 4 times, Yo., K.2 tog., K.1, (KM.1B.) twice, K.2, (Yo., Sl.1, K.2, psso.2) twice, Yo., K.1, (KM.1B.) twice, K.2, Sl.1, K.1, psso., Yo., (M.2, K.2 tog.) 3 times, M.2.]

55th round—[(M.2, K.2 tog.) 4 times, Yo., K.2 tog., K.2, (KM.1B.) twice, K.2, (Yo., Sl.1, K.2, psso.2) 3 times, Yo., K.1, (KM.1B.) twice, K.3, Sl.1, K.1, psso., Yo., (K.2 tog., M.2) 3 times, K.2 tog.]

57th round—[(K.2 tog., M.2) 4 times, Yo., K.2 tog., K.3, (KM.1B.) twice, K.2, (Yo., Sl.1, K.2, psso.2) 4 times, Yo., K.1, (KM.1B.) twice, K.4, Sl.1, K.1, psso., Yo., (M.2, K.2 tog.) 3 times, M.2.]

59th round—[(M.2, K.2 tog.) 4 times, Yo., K.2 tog., K.5, KM.1B., K.2, Sl.1, K.2 tog., psso., (Yo., Sl.1, K.2, psso.2) 3 times, Yo., Sl.1, K.2 tog., psso., K.1, KM.1B., K.6, Sl.1, K.1, psso., Yo., (K.2 tog., M.2) 3 times, K.2 tog.]

61st round—[(K.2 tog., M.2) 4 times, Yo., K.2 tog., K.9, (Yo., Sl.1, K.2, psso.2) 4 times, Yo., K.9, Sl.1, K.1, psso., Yo., (M.2, K.2 tog.) 3 times, M.2.]

63rd round—[(M.2, K.2 tog.) 4 times, M.2, Yo., K.9, Sl.1, K.2 tog., psso., (Yo., Sl.1, K.2, psso.2) 3 times, Yo., Sl.1, K.2 tog., psso., K.9, Yo., (M.2, K.2 tog.) 4 times.]

65th round—[(K.2 tog., M.2) 5 times, Yo., K.9, Sl.1, K.2 tog., psso., (Yo., Sl.1, K.2, psso.2) twice, Yo., Sl.1, K.2 tog., psso., K.9, Yo., (M.2, K.2 tog.) 4 times, M.2.]

67th round—[Yo., K.1B., Yo., (K.2 tog., M.2) 5 times, Yo., K.9, Sl.1, K.2 tog., psso., Yo., Sl.1, K.2, psso.2, Yo., Sl.1, K.2 tog., psso., K.9, Yo., (M.2, K.2 tog.) 5 times.]

69th round—[Yo., Sl.1, K.2 tog., psso., Yo., (M.2, K.2 tog.) 5 times, M.2, Yo., Sl.1, K.1, psso., K.7, Sl.1, K.2 tog., psso., Yo., Sl.1, K.2 tog., psso., K.7, K.2 tog., Yo., (M.2, K.2 tog.) 5 times, M.2.]

71st round—[Yo., (KM.1B.) twice, K.1, Yo., (K.2 tog., M.2) 6 times, Yo., Sl.1, K.1, psso., K.6, Sl.1, K.2 tog., psso., K.6, K.2 tog., Yo., (M.2, K.2 tog.) 6 times.]

73rd round—[Yo., K.2 tog., (KM.1B.) twice, K.1, Sl.1, K.1, psso., Yo., (M.2, K.2 tog.) 6 times, M.2, (Yo., C.3L) twice, Yo., Sl.1, K.2 tog., psso., (Yo., C.3R) twice, Yo., (M.2, K.2 tog.) 6 times, M.2.]

75th round—[Yo., K.2 tog., K.1, (KM.1B.) twice, K.2, Sl.1, K.1, psso., Yo., (K.2 tog., M.2) 6 times, K.2 tog., (Yo., K.2 tog., K.2) twice, Yo., K.1, M.2, K.1, (Yo., K.2, Sl.1, K.1, psso.) twice, Yo., (K.2 tog., M.2) 6 times, K.2 tog.]

77th round—[Yo., K.2 tog., K.2, (KM.1B.) twice, K.3, Sl.1, K.1, psso., Yo., (M.2, K.2 tog.) 5 times, M.2, K.3 tog., (Yo., K.2, K.2 tog.) twice, Yo., K.6, (Yo., Sl.1, K.1, psso., K.2) twice, Yo., K.3 tog., (M.2, K.2 tog.) 5 times, M.2.]

79th round—[Yo., K.2 tog., K.3, (KM.1B.) twice, K.4, Sl.1, K.1, psso., Yo., (K.2 tog., M.2) 5 times, K.3 tog., (Yo., K.2, K.2 tog.) 3 times, (Sl.1, K.1, psso., K.2, Yo.) 3 times, K.3 tog., (M.2, K.2 tog.) 5 times.]

81st round—[Yo., K.2 tog., K.4, (KM.1B.) twice, K.5, Sl.1, K.1, psso., Yo., (M.2, K.2 tog.) 4 times, M.2, K.3 tog., (Yo., K.2, K.2 tog.) 3 times, (Sl.1, K.1, psso., K.2, Yo.) 3 times, K.3 tog., (M.2, K.2 tog.) 4 times, M.2.]

83rd round—[Yo., K.2 tog., K.13, Sl.1, K.1, psso., Yo., (K.2 tog., M.2) 4 times, K.3 tog., (Yo., K.2, K.2 tog.) 3 times, Yo., (Sl.1, K.1, psso., K.2, Yo.) 3 times, K.3 tog., (M.2, K.2 tog.) 4 times.]

85th round—[Yo., K.2 tog., K.4, K.2 tog., Yo., K.1B., Yo., Sl.1, K.1, psso., K.4, Sl.1, K.1, psso., Yo., (M.2, K.2 tog.) 4 times, (M.2, Yo.) twice, Sl.1, K.2 tog., psso., (Yo., K.2, K.2 tog.) twice, Yo., K.1, Yo., (Sl.1, K.1, psso., K.2, Yo.) twice, Sl.1, K.2 tog., psso., (Yo., M.2) twice, (K.2 tog., M.2) 4 times.]

87th round—[Yo., K.2 tog., K.3, K.2 tog., Yo., K.3, Yo., Sl.1, K.1, psso., K.3, Sl.1, K.1, psso., Yo., (K.2 tog., M.2) 6 times, K.1, M.2, Yo., Sl.1, K.2 tog., psso., Yo., K.2, K.2 tog., Yo., K.3, Yo., Sl.1, K.1, psso., K.2, Yo., Sl.1, K.2 tog., psso., Yo., M.2, K.1, (M.2, K.2 tog.) 6 times.]

89th round—[Yo., K.2 tog., K.2, K.2 tog., Yo., K.5, Yo., Sl.1, K.1, psso., K.2, Sl.1, K.1, psso., Yo., (M.2, K.2 tog.) 7 times, M.2, K.1, M.2, (Yo., Sl.1, K.2 tog., psso., Yo., M.2) 3 times, K.1, (M.2, K.2 tog.) 7 times, M.2.]

91st round—[Yo., K.2 tog., K.1, K.2 tog., Yo., M.2, Yo., Sl.1, K.1, psso., K.1, K.2 tog., Yo., M.2, Yo., Sl.1, K.1, psso., K.1, Sl.1, K.1, psso., Yo., (K.2 tog., M.2) 9 times, (K.1, M.2, K.2 tog., M.2) twice, K.1, (M.2, K.2 tog.) 9 times.]

PART C

Knit each section from [to] 6 times in one round

93rd round—[Yo., (K.2 tog.) twice, Yo., M.2, K.2 tog., M.2, Yo., Sl.1, K.2 tog., psso., Yo., M.2, K.2 tog., M.2, Yo., (Sl.1, K.1, psso.) twice, Yo., K.3 tog., M.2, (K.2 tog., M.2) 20 times, K.3 tog.]

95th round—[Yo., K.3 tog., Yo., (M.2, K.2 tog.) twice, M.2, K.1, M.2, (K.2 tog., M.2) twice, Yo., Sl.2, K.1, p2sso., Yo., K.3 tog., (M.2, K.2 tog.) 19 times, M.2, K.3 tog.]

97th round—[M.2, K.1, (M.2, K.2 tog.) 6 times, M.2, K.1, M.2, K.3 tog., M.2, (K.2 tog., M.2) 18 times, K.3 tog.]

PART D

Knit each section from [to] 168 times in one round

99th round—[K.2 tog., M.2.]

101st round—[M.2, K.2 tog.]

103rd round—[K.2 tog., M.2.]

105th round—[M.2, K.2 tog.]

PART E

Knit each section from [to] 24 times in one round

XX *107th round*—[Yo., M.2, Yo., (K.2 tog., M.2) 6 times, K.2 tog.]

109th round—[Yo., K.4, Yo., (M.2, K.2 tog.) 6 times, M.2.]

111th round—[Yo., K.6, Yo., (K.2 tog., M.2) 6 times, K.2 tog.]

113th round—[Yo., K.2, KM.1B., K.1, KM.1B., K.3, Yo., K.3 tog., (M.2, K.2 tog.) 4 times, M.2, K.3 tog.]

115th round—[(Yo., K.6) twice, Yo., K.3 tog., (M.2, K.2 tog.) 3 times, M.2, K.3 tog.]

117th round—[Yo., K.7, Yo., K.1B., Yo., K.7, Yo., K.3 tog. (M.2, K.2 tog.) twice, M.2, K.3 tog.]

119th round—[Yo., K.8, Yo., Sl.1, K.2 tog., psso., Yo., K.8, Yo., K.3 tog., M.2, K.2 tog., M.2, K.3 tog.]

121st round—[Yo., K.9, Yo., K.3, Yo., K.9, Yo., K.3 tog., M.2, K.3 tog.]

123rd round—[Yo., K.10, Yo., K.1, Yo., Sl.1, K.2 tog., psso., Yo., K.1, Yo., K.10, Yo., Sl.2, K.2 tog., p2sso.]

125th round—[K.11, Yo., K.3, Yo., K.1B., Yo., K.3, Yo., K.12.]

127th round—[K6, Yo., Sl.1, K.1, psso., K2, Sl.1, K.1, psso., (Yo., Sl.1, K.2 tog., psso.) 3 times, Yo., K.2 tog., K2, K.2 tog., Yo., K.7.]

129th round—[K.4, K.2 tog., Yo., K.1B., Yo., Sl.1, K.1, psso., K.1, Sl.1, K.1, psso., Yo., K.1B., Yo., K.3, Yo., K.1B., Yo., K.2 tog., K.1, K.2 tog., Yo., K.1B., Yo., Sl.1, K.1, psso., K.5.]

131st round—[K.3, K.2 tog., Yo., Sl.1, K.2 tog., psso., Yo., Sl.2, K.1, p2sso., (Yo., Sl.1, K.2 tog., psso.) 3 times, Yo., K.3 tog., Yo., Sl.1, K.2 tog., psso., Yo., Sl.1, K.1, psso., K.4.]

133rd round—[K.2, K.2 tog., (Yo., K.3, Yo., K.1B.) 3 times, Yo., K.3, Yo., Sl.1, K.1, psso., K.3.]

135th round—[K.1, K.2 tog., Yo., K.1, (Yo., Sl.1, K.2 tog., psso.) 7 times, Yo., K.1, Yo., Sl.1, K.1, psso., K.2.]

137th round—[K.2 tog., (Yo., K.3, Yo., K.1B.) 4 times, Yo., K.3, Yo., Sl.1, K.1, psso., K.1.]

For Coffee Cloth of 32 in. diameter see now FINISHING OF COFFEE CLOTH on page 105.

If working Dinner Cloth proceed with PART F.

PART F

Knit each section from [to] 24 times in one round

LL *139th round*—[Sl.1, K.2 tog., psso., Yo., K.1, Yo., (Sl.1, K.2 tog., psso., Yo.) 9 times, K.1, Yo.]

141st round—[(Yo., K.1B., Yo., K.3) 6 times.]

143rd round—[(Yo., Sl.1, K.2 tog., psso.) 12 times.]

145th round—[(K.3, Yo., K.1B., Yo.) 6 times.]

147th round—[(Sl.1, K.2 tog., psso., Yo.) 12 times.]

149th round—[(Yo., K.1B., Yo., K.3) 6 times.]

151st round—[(Yo., Sl.1, K.2 tog., psso.) twice, Yo., K.2 tog., Yo., K.1, Yo., (Sl.1, K.2 tog., psso., Yo.) 7 times, K.1, Yo., Sl.1, K.1, psso., Yo., Sl.1, K.2 tog., psso.]

L *153rd round*—[Sl.1, K.1, psso., K.1, (K.2 tog., Yo.) twice, K.3, (Yo., K.1B., Yo., K.3) 4 times, Yo., Sl.1, K.1, psso., Yo.]

155th round—[Yo., Sl.1, K.2 tog., psso., Yo., K.2 tog., Yo., K.1, (Yo., Sl.1, K.2 tog., psso.) 9 times, Yo., K.1, Yo., Sl.1, K.1, psso.]

L *157th round*—[Sl.1, K.1, psso., K.1, K.2 tog., (Yo., K.3, Yo., K.1B.) 5 times, Yo., K.3, Yo.]

159th round—[Sl.1, K.2 tog., psso., Yo., K.1, (Yo., Sl.1, K.2 tog., psso.) 11 times, Yo., K.1, Yo.]

161st round—[(Yo., K.1B., Yo., K.3) 7 times.]

163rd round—[(Yo., Sl.1, K.2 tog., psso.) 14 times.]

165th round—[(K.3, Yo., K.1B., Yo.) 7 times.]

167th round—[(Sl.1, K.2 tog., psso., Yo.) 14 times.]

169th round—[(Yo., K.1B., Yo., K.3) 7 times.]

171st round—[(Yo., Sl.1, K.2 tog., psso.) twice, Yo., K.2 tog., Yo., K.1, Yo., (Sl.1, K.2 tog., psso., Yo.) 9 times, K.1, Yo., Sl.1, K.1, psso., Yo., Sl.1, K.2 tog., psso.]

L *173rd round*—[Sl.1, K.1, psso., K.1, (K.2 tog., Yo.) twice, K.3, (Yo., K.1B., Yo., K.3) 5 times, Yo., Sl.1, K.1, psso., Yo.]

175th round—[Yo., Sl.1, K.2 tog., psso., Yo., K.2 tog., Yo., K.1, (Yo., Sl.1, K.2 tog., psso.) 11 times, Yo., K.1, Yo., Sl.1, K.1, psso.]

L *177th round*—[Sl.1, K.1, psso., K.1, K.2 tog., (Yo., K.3, Yo., K.1B.) 6 times, Yo., K.3, Yo.]

179th round—[Sl.1, K.2 tog., psso., Yo., K.1, (Yo., Sl.1, K.2 tog., psso.) 13 times, Yo., K.1, Yo.]

181st round—[(Yo., K.1B., Yo., K.3) 8 times.]

183rd round—[(Yo., Sl.1, K.2 tog., psso.) 16 times.]

185th round—[(K.3, Yo., K.1B., Yo.) 8 times.]

187th round—[(Sl.1, K.2 tog., psso., Yo.) 16 times.]

189th round—[(Yo., K.1B., Yo., K.3) 8 times.]

PART G

Knit each section from [to] 48 times in one round

191st round—[(Yo., Sl.1, K.2 tog., psso.) 4 times, Yo., (KM.1B.) twice, K.1, (Yo., Sl.1, K.2 tog., psso.) 3 times.]

193rd round—[(K.3, Yo., K.1B., Yo.) twice, K.2 tog., (KM.1B.) twice, K.1, Sl.1, K.1, psso., Yo., K.1B., Yo., K.3, Yo., K.1B., Yo.]

195th round—[(Sl.1, K.2 tog., psso., Yo.) 3 times, K.2 tog., Yo., K.2 tog., K.1, (KM.1B.) twice, K.2, (Sl.1, K.1, psso., Yo.) twice, (Sl.1, K.2 tog., psso., Yo.) twice.]

197th round—[Yo., K.1B., Yo., K.3, Yo., K.1B., (Yo., K.2 tog.) twice, K.2, (KM.1B.) twice, K.3, (Sl.1, K.1, psso., Yo.) twice, K.1B., Yo., K.3.]

199th round—[(Yo., Sl.1, K.2 tog., psso.) twice, (Yo., K.2 tog.) 3 times, K.3, (KM.1B.) twice, K.4, (Sl.1, K.1, psso., Yo.) 3 times, Sl.1, K.2 tog., psso.]

L *201st round*—[Sl.1, K.1, psso., K.1, K.2 tog., (Yo., K.2 tog.) 3 times, K.4, (KM.1B.) twice, K.5, (Sl.1, K.1, psso., Yo.) 3 times.]

203rd round—[Yo., Sl.1, K.2 tog., psso., (Yo., K.2 tog.) 3 times, K.13, (Sl.1, K.1, psso., Yo.) twice, Sl.1, K.1, psso.]

L *205th round*—[Sl.1, K.1, psso., K.1, K.2 tog., (Yo., K.2 tog.) twice, K.4, K.2 tog., Yo., K.1B., Yo., Sl.1, K.1, psso., K.4, (Sl.1, K.1, psso., Yo.) twice.]

207th round—[Yo., Sl.1, K.2 tog., psso., (Yo., K.2 tog.) twice, K.3, K.2 tog., Yo., K.3, Yo., Sl.1, K.1, psso., K.3, Sl.1, K.1, psso., Yo., Sl.1, K.1, psso.]

L *209th round*—[Sl.1, K.1, psso., K.1, K.2 tog., Yo., K.2 tog., K.2, K.2 tog., Yo., K.5, Yo., Sl.1, K.1, psso., K.2, Sl.1, K.1, psso., Yo.]

211th round—[Sl.1, K.2 tog., psso., Yo., K.2 tog., K.1, K.2 tog., Yo., M.2, Yo., Sl.1, K.1, psso., K.1, K.2 tog., Yo., M.2, Yo., Sl.1, K.1, psso., K.1, Sl.1, K.1, psso., Yo.]

213th round—[K.1, Yo., (K.2 tog.) twice, Yo., M.2, K.2 tog., M.2, Yo., Sl.1, K.2 tog., psso., Yo., M.2, K.2 tog., M.2, Yo., (Sl.1, K.1, psso.) twice, Yo.]

215th round—[K.1, K.3 tog., Yo., (M.2, K.2 tog.) twice, M.2, K.1, (M.2, K.2 tog.) twice, M.2, Yo., Sl.2, K.1, p2sso.]

L *217th round*—[Sl.1, K.2 tog., psso., (M.2, K.2 tog.) 6 times, M.2.]

104

PART H

Knit each section from [to] 336 times in one round

219th round—[M.2, K.2 tog.]

221st round—[K.2 tog., M.2.]

223rd round—[M.2, K.2 tog.]

225th round—[K.2 tog., M.2.]

After working plain round 226 knit once more PART E, but knit section from [to] 48 times in one round instead of 24 times. This brings the rounds from 227 to 257. Round 258 knit plain and then see FINISHING OF DINNER CLOTH.

NOTICE

When working round 227, which is the same as round 107 DO NOT move the two stitches before starting the round.

FINISHING OF COFFEE CLOTH

After knitting last plain round 138 knit another stitch and then start to finish the edge of the cloth with a chain of crochet as follows:

4 sts., 1 d.c., 9 ch., (3 sts., 1 d.c., 9 ch.) 7 times, 4 sts., 1 d.c., 9 ch., 3 sts., 1 d.c., 9 ch. Repeat 23 times.

Finish with a slip stitch into first d.c., and break off.

Secure thread invisibly with few stitches into chain.

FINISHING OF DINNER CLOTH

After knitting last plain round 258 knit another stitch, and then start to finish the edge of the cloth with a chain of crochet as follows:

4 sts., 1 d.c., 9 ch., (3 sts., 1 d.c., 9 ch.) 7 times, 4 sts., 1 d.c., 9 ch., 3 sts., 1 d.c., 9 ch. Repeat 47 times.

Finish with a slip stitch into first d.c. and break off.

Secure thread invisibly with few stitches into chain.

STRETCHING

COFFEE CLOTH

Draw a circle of 32 in. diameter. Mark round the circle 24 points at a distance of about 4 in. from each other.

DINNER CLOTH

Draw a circle of 62 in. diameter. Mark round the circle 48 points at a distance of about 4 in. from each other.

Take the washed, rinsed and starched lace and pin down the middle of the cloth on to the centre of the circle. Take the two loops of chain beside the point of the leaf and pin them, with one pin only, on to the points marked on the circle. (24 for the Coffee Cloth, and 48 for the Dinner Cloth.

The remaining loops of chain are pinned down evenly between these points always taking two loops of chain on one pin.

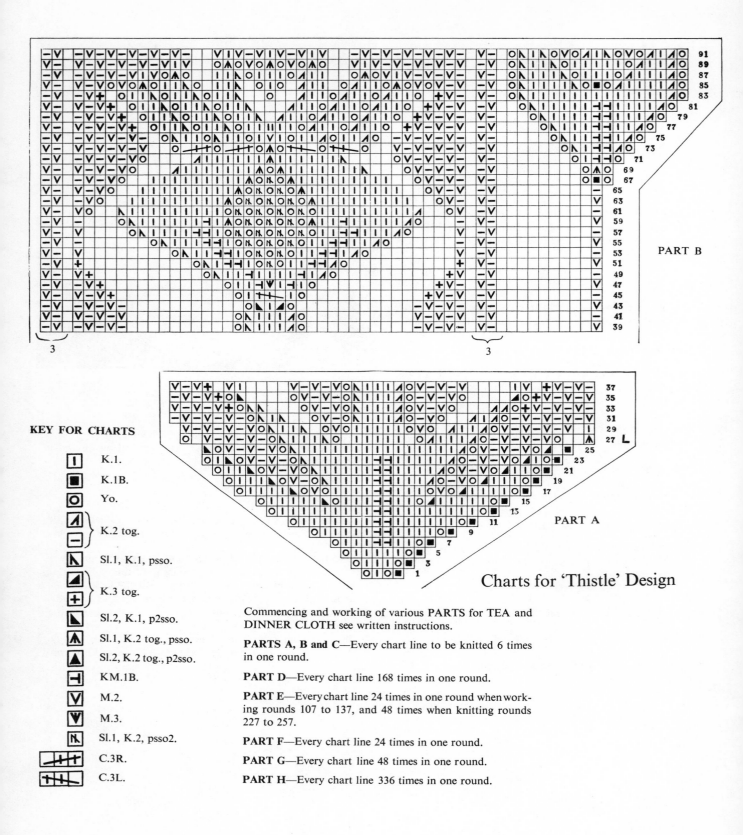

PART B

PART A

KEY FOR CHARTS

- K.1.
- K.1B.
- Yo.
- } K.2 tog.
- Sl.1, K.1, psso.
- } K.3 tog.
- Sl.2, K.1, p2sso.
- Sl.1, K.2 tog., psso.
- Sl.2, K.2 tog., p2sso.
- KM.1B.
- M.2.
- M.3.
- Sl.1, K.2, psso2.
- C.3R.
- C.3L.

Charts for 'Thistle' Design

Commencing and working of various PARTS for TEA and DINNER CLOTH see written instructions.

PARTS A, B and C—Every chart line to be knitted 6 times in one round.

PART D—Every chart line 168 times in one round.

PART E—Every chart line 24 times in one round when working rounds 107 to 137, and 48 times when knitting rounds 227 to 257.

PART F—Every chart line 24 times in one round.

PART G—Every chart line 48 times in one round.

PART H—Every chart line 336 times in one round.

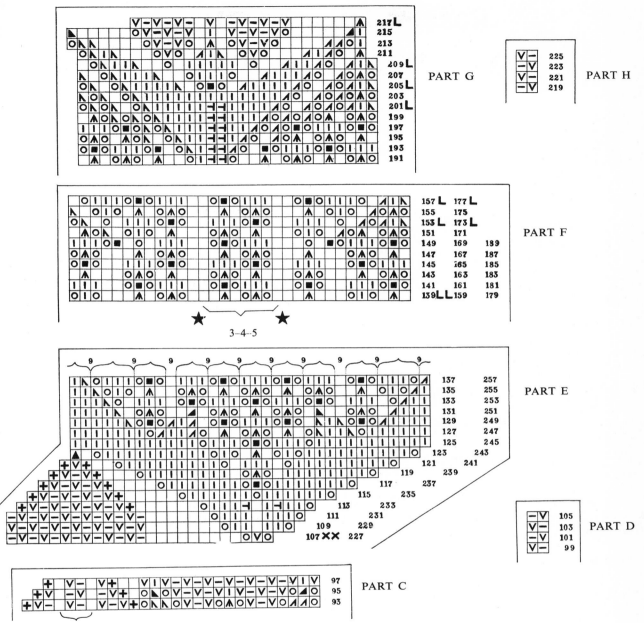

PART G

PART H

PART F

3-4-5

PART E

PART D

PART C

18

Every section of a chart line within a bracket is worked as
many times as stated below. Where 3 numbers are given,
the first refers to the first row of numbers beside the chart,
the second to the second row, etc.

Every round of which the number is missing knit plain.

X and L in front of a chart line: see ABBREVIATIONS.

'Rose of England' Design

AFTERNOON TEA CLOTH AND DINNER CLOTH

MATERIALS

TEA CLOTH—4 balls of Crochet Cotton No. 60, or 3 oz. of Linen Thread No. 60.

DINNER CLOTH—12 balls of Crochet Cotton No. 60, or 10 oz. of Linen Thread No. 60.

Four double pointed knitting needles No. 12, length 7 in.

One circular knitting needle No. 12, length 24 in. and one circular knitting needle No. 12, length 36 in., or better 42 in.

One cotton Crochet Hook No. 5.

MEASUREMENTS

TEA CLOTH—36 in. diameter.

DINNER CLOTH—72 in. diameter.

NOTICE

The Casting-on and the instructions of PARTS A, B, C, D, E, F and G are the same for the working of Tea and Dinner Cloth.

Then follow directions for FINISHING OF TEA CLOTH when working Cloth of 36 in. diameter.

When working Dinner Cloth of 72 in. diameter proceed with knitting PARTS H, J, K, L and M and then see FINISHING OF DINNER CLOTH.

Every round of which the number is missing knit plain.

Great care must be taken in the working of Yo.2, as fully explained in the BASIC INSTRUCTIONS.

X and L in front of pattern round: see ABBREVIATIONS.

CASTING-ON

Commence from the centre of the cloth by casting on 10 stitches on to one needle. Then rearrange the stitches on to other needles by transferring 4 stitches on to one needle, 4 stitches on to a second needle, leaving 2 stitches on the original needle. By help of this arrangement of stitches four sections of one round of PART A will be knitted on the first needle, four sections on the second needle, and two sections on the third needle. After casting-on and rearrangement of stitches knit one round into the back of all stitches. Then start to knit PART A.

PART A

Knit each section from [to] 10 times in one round

1st round—[K.1.]

2nd round—[Yo.2, K.1B.]

3rd round—[M.3 into Yo.2 of previous round, K.1.]

4th, 5th and 6th round—Knit plain.

7th round—[Yo.2, K.4.]

X *9th round*—[Yo.2, Sl.1, K.1, psso., K.2, K.2 tog.]

X *11th round*—[K.2 tog., Yo.2, K.2, Yo.2, Sl.1, K.1. psso.]

13th round—[(Yo.2, Sl.1, K.1, psso., K.2 tog.) twice.]

X *15th round*—[(K.2 tog., Yo.2, Sl.1, K.1, psso.) twice.]

17th round—[(Yo.2, Sl.1, K.1, psso., K.2 tog.) twice.]

18th round—[(M.5 into Yo.2 of previous round, K.2) twice.]

19th, 20th, 21st and 22nd round—Knit plain.

PART B

Knit each section from [to] 5 times in one round

X *23rd round*—[Yo.2, Sl.1, K.2 tog., psso., Yo.2, K.2 tog., (K.1, M.3) 3 times, Yo., K.3, Sl.1, K.2 tog., psso., K.3, Yo., (M.3, K.1) 3 times, Sl.1, K.1, psso.]

X *25th round*—[Yo.2, Sl.1, K.2 tog., psso., Yo.2, K.2 tog., (M.3, P.3 tog.) 3 times, M.3, Yo., K.2, Sl.1, K.2 tog., psso., K.2, Yo., (M.3, P.3 tog.) 3 times, M.3, Sl.1, K.1, psso.]

X *27th round*—[Yo.2, Sl.1, K.2 tog., psso., Yo.2, K.2 tog., (P.3 tog., M.3) 4 times, Yo., K.1, Sl.1, K.2 tog., psso., K.1, Yo., (M.3, P.3 tog.) 4 times, Sl.1, K.1, psso.]

X *29th round*—[Yo.2, Sl.1, K.2 tog., psso., Yo.2, K.2 tog., (M.3, P.3 tog.) 4 times, M.3, Sl.1, K.2 tog., psso., (M.3, P.3 tog.) 4 times, M.3, Sl.1, K.1, psso.]

X *31st round*—[Yo.2, Sl.1, K.2 tog., psso., Yo.2, K.2 tog., (P.3 tog., M.3) 9 times, P.3 tog., Sl.1, K.1, psso.]

X *33rd round*—[Yo.2, Sl.1, K.2 tog., psso., Yo.2, K.2 tog., (M.3, P.3 tog.) 9 times, M.3, Sl.1, K.1, psso.]

X *35th round*—same as 31st round.

X *37th round*—same as 33rd round.

X *39th round*—same as 31st round.

*'Rose of England' Design
Dinner Cloth*

109

PART C

Knit each section from [to] 5 times in one round

X *41st round*—[Yo.2, Sl.1, K.2 tog., psso., Yo.2, K.2 tog., (M.3, P.3 tog.) 4 times, M.4, K.3, M.4, (P.3 tog., M.3) 4 times, Sl.1, K.1, psso.]

X *43rd round*—[Yo.2, K.1B., M.3, K.1B., Yo.2, K.2 tog., (P.3 tog., M.3) 3 times, P.3 tog., M.4, K.11, M.4, P.3 tog., (M.3, P.3 tog.) 3 times, Sl.1, K.1, psso.]

X *45th round*—[Yo.2, K.2 tog., (K.1–M.1B.) twice, K.1, Sl.1, K.1, psso., Yo.2, K.2 tog., M.4, (P.3 tog., M.3) twice, P.3 tog., M.4, K.19, M.4, (P.3 tog., M.3) twice, P.3 tog., M.4, Sl.1, K.1, psso.]

X *47th round*—[Yo.2, K.2 tog., K.1, (K.1–M.1B.) twice, K.2, Sl.1, K.1, psso., Yo.2, K.2 tog., K.4, M.4, P.3 tog., M.3, P.3 tog., M.4, K.27, M.4, P.3 tog., M.3, P.3 tog., M.4, K.4, Sl.1, K.1, psso.]

X *49th round*—[Yo., K.2 tog., K.2, (K.1–M.1B.) twice, K.3, Sl.1, K.1, psso., Yo., K.2 tog., K.8, M.4, P.3 tog., M.4, K.35, M.4, P.3 tog., M.4, K.8, Sl.1, K.1, psso.]

51st round—[Yo., K.2 tog., K.3, (K.1–M.1B.) twice, K.4, Sl.1, K.1, psso., Yo., Sl.1, K.1, psso., K.67, K.2 tog.]

53rd round—[Yo., K.2 tog., K.5, Yo., M.9, Yo., K.5, Sl.1, K.1, psso., Yo., Sl.1, K.1, psso., K.65, K.2 tog.]

PART D

Notice that every round of this part is a pattern round and K.1, P.1, K.1, is always worked into Yo.3 of previous round.

Knit each section from [to] 5 times in one round

55th round—[Yo., K.2 tog., K.3, K.2 tog., Yo., K.11, Yo., Sl.1, K.1, psso., K.3, Sl.1, K.1, psso., Yo., Sl.1, K.1, psso., K.29, K.2 tog., Yo.3, K.1B., Yo.3, Sl.1, K.1, psso., K.29, K.2 tog.]

56th round—[K.53, K.3 tog., K.1, P.1, K.3, P.1, K.1, Sl.2, K.1, p2sso., K.28.]

57th round—[Yo., K.2 tog., K.2, K.2 tog., Yo., K.13, Yo., Sl.1, K.1, psso., K.2, Sl.1, K.1, psso., Yo., Sl.2, K.1, p2sso., K.23, K.3 tog., Yo.3, K.3, Yo., K.1B., Yo., K.3, Yo.3, Sl.2, K.1, p2sso., K.23, K.3 tog.]

58th round—[K.47, K.3 tog., K.1, P.1, K.11, P.1, K.1, Sl.2, K.1, p2sso., K.22.]

59th round—[Yo., K.2 tog., K.1, K.2 tog., Yo., K.15, Yo., Sl.1, K.1, psso., K.1, Sl.1, K.1, psso., Yo., Sl.2, K.1, p2sso., K.17, K.3 tog., Yo.3, (Sl.1, K.2 tog., psso., Yo.) 4 times, Sl.1, K.2 tog., psso., Yo.3, Sl.2, K.1, p2sso., K.17, K.3 tog.]

60th round—[K.41, K.3 tog., K.1, P.1, K.11, P.1, K.1, Sl.2, K.1, p2sso., K.16.]

61st round—[Yo., K.2 tog., K.2, Yo., K.17, Yo., K.2, Sl.1, K.1, psso., Yo., Sl.2, K.1, p2sso., K.11, K.3 tog., Yo.3, K.2 tog., (Yo., K.3, Yo., K.1B.) twice, Yo., K.3, Yo., Sl.1, K.1, psso., Yo.3, Sl.2, K.1, p2sso., K.11, K.3 tog.]

62nd round—[K.37, K.3 tog., K.1, P.1, K.21, P.1, K.1, Sl.2, K.1, p2sso., K.10.]

63rd round—[Yo., K.1, Yo., K.3 tog., Yo., K.1, Yo., K.17, (Yo., K.1, Yo., Sl.2, K.1, p2sso.) twice, K.5, K.3 tog., Yo.3, K.2 tog., (Yo., Sl.1, K.2 tog., psso.) 7 times, Yo., Sl.1, K.1, psso., Yo.3, Sl.2, K.1, p2sso., K.5, K.3 tog.]

64th round—[K.31, Sl.2, K.1, p2sso., K.1, K.3 tog., K.1, P.1, K.19, P.1, K.1, Sl.2, K.1, p2sso., K.1, K.3 tog.]

65th round—[Yo.3, K.3, Yo., K.1B., Yo., K.3, Yo., Sl.1, K.1, psso., K.13, K.2 tog., Yo., K.3, Yo., K.1B., Yo., K.3, Yo.3, Sl.1, K.2 tog., psso., Yo.3, (K.3, Yo., K.1B., Yo.) 5 times, K.3, Yo.3, Sl.1, K.2 tog., psso.]

66th round—[K.1, P.1, K.37, P.1, K.3, P.1, K.35, P.1, K.2.]

67th round—[(Yo., Sl.1, K.2 tog., psso.) 4 times, Yo., K.1, Yo., Sl.1, K.1, psso., K.11, K.2 tog., Yo., K.1, (Yo., Sl.1, K.2 tog., psso.) 4 times, Yo., K.1B., (Yo., Sl.1, K.2 tog., psso.) 13 times, Yo., K.1B.]

PART E

Knit each section from [to] 5 times in one round

69th round—[(K.3, Yo., K.1B., Yo.) twice, K.3, Yo., Sl.1, K.1, psso., K.9, K.2 tog., Yo., (K.3, Yo., K.1B., Yo.) 10 times.]

71st round—[(Sl.1, K.2 tog., psso., Yo.) 5 times, K.1, Yo., Sl.1, K.1, psso., K.7, K.2 tog., Yo., K.1, Yo., (Sl.1, K.2 tog., psso., Yo.) 20 times.]

73rd round—[(Yo., K.1B., Yo., K.3) 3 times, Yo., Sl.1, K.1, psso., K.5, K.2 tog., Yo., K.3, (Yo., K.1B., Yo., K.3) 10 times.]

75th round—[(Yo., Sl.1, K.2 tog., psso.) 6 times, Yo., K.1, Yo., Sl.1, K.1, psso., K.3, K.2 tog., Yo., K.1, (Yo., Sl.1, K.2 tog., psso.) 21 times.]

77th round—[(K.3, Yo., K.1B., Yo.) 3 times, K.3, Yo., Sl.1, K.1, psso., K.1, K.2 tog., Yo., (K.3, Yo., K.1B., Yo.) 11 times.]

79th round—[(Sl.1, K.2 tog., psso., Yo.) 7 times, K.1, Yo., Sl.1, K.2 tog., psso., Yo., K.1, Yo., (Sl.1, K.2 tog., psso., Yo.) 22 times.]

PART F

Knit each section from [to] 80 times in one round

81st round—[Yo., K.1B., Yo., K.3.]

83rd round—[(Yo., Sl.1, K.2 tog., psso.) twice.]

85th round—[K.3, Yo., K.1B., Yo.]

87th round—[(Sl.1, K.2 tog., psso., Yo.) twice.]

89th round—[Yo., K.1B., Yo., K.3.]

91st round—[(Yo., Sl.1, K.2 tog., psso.) twice.]

93rd round—[K.3, Yo., K.1B., Yo.]

PART G

Knit each section from [to] 40 times in one round

95th round—[(Sl.1, K.2 tog., psso., Yo.) 4 times.]

96th round—[(K.1, M.4 into Yo.2 of previous round) 4 times.]

97th, 98th, 99th, 100th, 101st and 102nd round—Knit plain.

LL *103rd round*—[(Sl.2, K.3 tog., p2sso., Yo.2) 4 times.]

104th round—[(K.1, M.4 into Yo.2 of previous round) 4 times.]

105th, 106th, 107th, 108th, 109th and 110th round—Knit plain.

111th round—[Yo., K.9, K.2 tog., K.9.]

113th round—[Yo., K.1B., Yo., K.8, Sl.1, K.2 tog., psso., K.8.]

115th round—[Sl.1, K.2 tog., psso., Yo., K.7, Sl.1, K.2 tog., psso., K.7, Yo.]

117th round—[K.1B., Yo., K.1, Yo., K.6, Sl.1, K.2 tog., psso., K.6, Yo., K.1, Yo.]

119th round—[K.1B., Yo., Sl.1, K.2 tog., psso., Yo., K.5, Sl.1, K.2 tog., psso., K.5, Yo., Sl.1, K.2 tog., psso., Yo.]

121st round—[K.1B., Yo., K.3, Yo., K.4, Sl.1, K.2 tog., psso., K.4, Yo., K.3, Yo.]

123rd round—[(K.1B., Yo.) twice, Sl.1, K.2 tog., psso., Yo., K.1, Yo., K.3, Sl.1, K.2 tog., psso., K.3, Yo., K.1, Yo., Sl.1, K.2 tog., psso., Yo., K.1B. Yo.]

125th round—[(Yo., K.1B.) 4 times, Yo., Sl.1, K.1, psso., K.2, Yo., K.2, Sl.1, K.2 tog., psso., K.2, Yo., K.2, K.2 tog., (Yo., K.1B.) 3 times.]

127th round—[Yo., Sl.1, K.2 tog., psso., Yo., K.2, Yo., K.1B., Yo., K.1, Sl.1, K.1, psso., Yo., Sl.1, K.2 tog., psso., (Yo., K.1) twice, Sl.1, K.2 tog., psso., (K.1, Yo.) twice, Sl.1, K.2 tog., psso., Yo., K.2 tog., K.1, Yo., K.1B., Yo., K.2.]

129th round—[Yo., Sl.1, K.2 tog., psso., Yo., K.3, Yo., K.1B., Yo., K.2, Sl.1, K.1, psso., Yo., Sl.1, K.1, psso., K.2, Yo., Sl.1, K.2 tog., psso., Yo., K.2, K.2 tog., Yo., K.2 tog., K.2, Yo., K.1B., Yo., K.3.]

131st round—[Yo., Sl.1, K.2 tog., psso., Yo., K.4, Yo., K.1B., Yo., K.3, Sl.1, K.1, psso., (Yo., Sl.1, K.2 tog., psso.) 3 times, Yo., K.2 tog., K.3, Yo., K.1B., Yo., K.4.]

133rd round—[Yo., Sl.1, K.2 tog., psso., Yo., K.10, Sl.1, K.1, psso., Yo., Sl.1, K.1, psso., K.1, K.2 tog., Yo., K.2 tog., K.10.]

135th round—[Sl.1, K.2 tog., psso., Yo., Sl.1, K.1, psso., K.7, Sl.2, K.1, p2sso., Yo., Sl.1, K.2 tog., psso., Yo., Sl.2, K.1, p2sso., K.7, K.2 tog., Yo.]

137th round—[K.1B., Yo., K.1, Yo., Sl.1, K.1, psso., K.5, K.2 tog., Yo., Sl.1, K.2 tog., psso., Yo., Sl.1, K.1, psso., K.5, K.2 tog., Yo., K.1, Yo.]

139th round—[K.1B., Yo., K.3, Yo., Sl.1, K.1, psso., K.3, Sl.2, K.1, p2sso., Yo., K.1B., Yo., Sl.2, K.1, p2sso., K.3, K.2 tog., Yo., K.3, Yo.]

141st round—[(K.1B., Yo.) twice, Sl.1, K.2 tog., psso., Yo., K.1, Yo., Sl.1, K.1, psso., K.1, K.2 tog., Yo., Sl.1, K.2 tog., psso., Yo., Sl.1, K.1, psso., K.1, K.2 tog., Yo., K.1, Yo., Sl.1, K.2 tog., psso., Yo., K.1B., Yo.]

143rd round—[(Yo., K.1B.) 4 times, Yo., Sl.1, K.1, psso., K.2, Yo., Sl.1, K.2 tog., psso., Yo., K.3, Yo., Sl.1, K.2 tog., psso., Yo., K.2, K.2 tog., (Yo., K.1B.) 3 times.]

145th round—[Yo., Sl.1, K.2 tog., psso., Yo., K.2, Yo., K.1B., Yo., K.1, Sl.1, K.1, psso., (Yo., Sl.1, K.2 tog., psso.) 5 times, Yo., K.2 tog., K.1, Yo., K.1B., Yo., K.2.]

147th round—[Yo., Sl.1, K.2 tog., psso., Yo., K.3, Yo., K.1B., Yo., K.2, Sl.1, K.1, psso., Yo., Sl.1, K.1, psso., K.2, Yo., K.1B., Yo., K.2, K.2 tog., Yo., K.2 tog., K.2, Yo., K.1B., Yo., K.3.]

149th round—[Yo., Sl.1, K.2 tog., psso., Yo., K.4, Yo., K.1B., Yo., K.3, Sl.1, K.1, psso., (Yo., Sl.1, K.2 tog., psso.) 3 times, Yo., K.2 tog., K.3, Yo., K.1B., Yo., K.4.]

151st round—[Yo., Sl.1, K.2 tog., psso., Yo., K.5, Yo., K.1B., Yo., K.4, Sl.1, K.1, psso., Yo., Sl.1, K.1, psso., K.1, K.2 tog., Yo., K.2 tog., K.4, Yo., K.1B., Yo., K.5.]

For TEA CLOTH of 36 in. diameter see now FINISHING OF TEA CLOTH on page 117.

If working DINNER CLOTH proceed with PART H.

PART H

Knit each section from [to] 40 times in one round

153rd round—[Sl.1, K.2 tog., psso., Yo., K.12, Sl.1, K.1, psso., Yo., Sl.1, K.2 tog., psso., Yo., K.2 tog., K.12, Yo.]

155th round—[K.1B., Yo., K.1, Yo., Sl.1, K.1, psso., K.9, K.2 tog., Yo., Sl.1, K.2 tog., psso., Yo., Sl.1, K.1, psso., K.9, K.2 tog., Yo., K.1, Yo.]

157th round—[K.1B., Yo., K.3, Yo., Sl.1, K.1, psso., K.7, Sl.2, K.1, p2sso., Yo., K.1B., Yo., Sl.2, K.1, p2sso., K.7, K.2 tog., Yo., K.3, Yo.]

159th round—[(K.1B., Yo.) twice, Sl.1, K.2 tog., psso., Yo., K.1, Yo., Sl.1, K.1, psso., K.5, K.2 tog., Yo., Sl.1, K.2 tog., psso., Yo., Sl.1, K.1, psso., K.5, K.2 tog., Yo., K.1, Yo., Sl.1, K.2 tog., psso., Yo., K.1B., Yo.]

161st round—[(Yo., K.1B.) 4 times, Yo., Sl.1, K.1, psso., K.2, Yo., Sl.1, K.1, psso., K.3, Sl.2, K.1, p2sso., Yo., K.1B., Yo., Sl.2, K.1, p2sso., K.3, K.2 tog., Yo., K.2, K.2 tog., (Yo., K.1B.) 3 times.]

163rd round—[Yo., Sl.1, K.2 tog., psso., Yo., K.2, Yo., K.1B., Yo., K.1, Sl.1, K.1, psso., Yo., Sl.1, K.2 tog., psso., Yo., K.1, Yo., Sl.1, K.1, psso., K.1, K.2 tog., Yo., Sl.1, K.2 tog., psso., Yo., Sl.1, K.1, psso., K.1, K.2 tog., Yo., K.1, Yo., Sl.1, K.2 tog., psso., Yo., K.2 tog., K.1, Yo., K.1B., Yo., K.2.]

165th round—[Yo., Sl.1, K.2 tog., psso., Yo., K.3, Yo., K.1B., Yo., K.2, Sl.1, K.1, psso., Yo., Sl.1, K.1, psso., K.2, Yo., Sl.1, K.2 tog., psso., Yo., K.3, Yo., Sl.1, K.2 tog., psso., Yo., K.2, K.2 tog., Yo., K.2 tog., K.2, Yo., K.1B., Yo., K.3.]

167th round—[Yo., Sl.1, K.2 tog., psso., Yo., K.4, Yo., K.1B., Yo., K.3, Sl.1, K.1, psso., (Yo., Sl.1, K.2 tog., psso.) 5 times, Yo., K.2 tog., K.3, Yo., K.1B., Yo., K.4.]

169th round—[Yo., Sl.1, K.2 tog., psso., Yo., K.5, Yo., K.1B., Yo., K.4, Sl.1, K.1, psso., Yo., Sl.1, K.1, psso., K.2, Yo., K.1B., Yo., K.2, K.2 tog., Yo., K.2 tog., K.4, Yo., K.1B., Yo., K.5.]

171st round—[Yo., Sl.1, K.2 tog., psso., Yo., K.6, Yo., K.1B., Yo., K.5, Sl.1, K.1, psso., (Yo., Sl.1, K.2 tog., psso.) 3 times, Yo., K.2 tog., K.5, Yo., K.1B., Yo., K.6.]

173rd round—[Sl.1, K.2 tog., psso., Yo., Sl.1, K.1, psso., K.11, Sl.2, K.1, p2sso., Yo., Sl.1, K.1, psso., K.1, K.2 tog., Yo., Sl.2, K.1, p2sso., K.11, K.2 tog., Yo.]

175th round—[K.1B., Yo., K.1, Yo., Sl.1, K.1, psso., K.9, Sl.2, K.1, p2sso., Yo., Sl.1, K.2 tog., psso., Yo., Sl.2, K.1, p2sso., K.9, K.2 tog., Yo., K.1, Yo.]

177th round—the same as 157th round.

179th round—the same as 159th round.

181st round—the same as 161st round.

183rd round—the same as 163rd round.

185th round—the same as 165th round.

187th round—the same as 167th round.

189th round—the same as 169th round.

191st round—[Sl.1, K.2 tog., psso., Yo., K.6, Yo., K.1B., Yo., K.5, Sl.1, K.1, psso., (Yo., Sl.1, K.2 tog., psso.) 3 times, Yo., K.2 tog., K.5, Yo., K.1B., Yo., K.6, Yo.]

193rd round—[K.1B., Yo., K.1, Yo., K.14, Sl.1, K.1, psso., Yo., Sl.1, K.1, psso., K.1, K.2 tog., Yo., K.2 tog., K.14, Yo., K.1, Yo.]

195th round—[K.1B., Yo., K.3, Yo., Sl.1, K.1, psso., K.11, Sl.2, K.1, p2sso., Yo., Sl.1, K.2 tog., psso., Yo., Sl.2, K.1, p2sso., K.11, K.2 tog., Yo., K.3, Yo.]

197th round—[(K.1B., Yo.) twice, Sl.1, K.2 tog., psso., Yo., K.1, Yo., Sl.1, K.1, psso., K.9, K.2 tog., Yo., Sl.1, K.2 tog., psso., Yo., Sl.1, K.1, psso., K.9, K.2 tog., Yo., K.1, Yo., Sl.1, K.2 tog., psso., Yo., K.1B., Yo.]

199th round—[(Yo., K.1B.) 4 times Yo., Sl.1, K.1, psso., K.2, Yo., Sl.1, K.1, psso., K.7, Sl.2, K.1, p2sso., Yo., K.1B., Yo., Sl.2, K.1, p2sso., K.7, K.2 tog., Yo., K.2, K.2 tog., (Yo., K.1B.) 3 times.]

201st round—[Yo., Sl.1, K.2 tog., psso., Yo., K.2, Yo., K.1B., Yo., K.1, Sl.1, K.1, psso., Yo., Sl.1, K.2 tog., psso., Yo., K.1, Yo., Sl.1, K.1, psso., K.5, K.2 tog., Yo., Sl.1, K.2 tog., psso., Yo., Sl.1, K.1, psso., K.5, K.2 tog., Yo., K.1, Yo., Sl.1, K.2 tog., psso., Yo., K.2 tog., K.1, Yo., K.1B., Yo., K.2.]

203rd round—[Yo., Sl.1, K.2 tog., psso., Yo., K.3, Yo., K.1B., Yo., K.2, Sl.1, K.1, psso., Yo., Sl.1, K.1, psso., K.2, Yo., Sl.1, K.1, psso., K.3, Sl.2, K.1, p2sso., Yo., K.1B., Yo., Sl.2, K.1, p2sso., K.3, K.2 tog., Yo., K.2, K.2 tog., Yo., K.2 tog., K.2, Yo., K.1B., Yo., K.3.]

205th round—[Yo., Sl.1, K.2 tog., psso., Yo., K.4, Yo., K.1B., Yo., K.3, Sl.1, K.1, psso., Yo., Sl.1, K.2 tog., psso., Yo., K.1, Yo., Sl.1, K.1, psso., K.1, K.2 tog., Yo., Sl.1, K.1, psso., K.1, K.2 tog., Yo., K.1, Yo., Sl.1, K.2 tog., psso., Yo., K.2 tog., K.3, Yo., K.1B., Yo., K.4.]

207th round—[Yo., Sl.1, K.2 tog., psso., Yo., K.5, Yo., K.1B., Yo., K.4, Sl.1, K.1, psso., Yo., Sl.1, K.1, psso., K.2, Yo., Sl.1, K.2 tog., psso., Yo., K.3, Yo., Sl.1, K.2 tog., psso., Yo., K.2, K.2 tog., Yo., K.2 tog., K.4, Yo., K.1B., Yo., K.5.]

209th round—[Yo., Sl.1, K.2 tog., psso., Yo., K.6, Yo., K.1B., Yo., K.5, Sl.1, K.1, psso., (Yo., Sl.1, K.2 tog., psso.) 5 times, Yo., K.2 tog., K.5, Yo., K.1B., Yo., K.6.]

112

211th round—[Sl.1, K.2 tog., psso., Yo., K.7, Yo., K.1B., Yo., K.6, Sl.1, K.1, psso., Yo., Sl.1, K.1, psso., K.2, Yo., K.1B., Yo., K.2, K.2 tog., Yo., K.2 tog., K.6, Yo., K.1B., Yo., K.7, Yo.]

PART J

Knit each section from [to] 40 times in one round

213th round—[K.1B., Yo., K.1, Yo., Sl.1, K.1, psso., K.13, Sl.2, K.1, p2sso., (Yo., Sl.1, K.2 tog., psso.) 3 times, Yo., Sl.2, K.1, p2sso., K.13, K.2 tog., Yo., K.1, Yo.]

215th round—[K.1B., Yo., K.3, Yo., Sl.1, K.1, psso., K.11, Sl.2, K.1, p2sso., Yo., K.1B., Yo., K.3, Yo., K.1B., Yo., Sl.2, K.1, p2sso., K.11, K.2 tog., Yo., K.3, Yo.]

217th round—[K.1B., Yo., K.1, Yo., Sl.1, K.2 tog., psso., Yo., K.1, Yo., Sl.1, K.1, psso., K.9, K.2 tog., (Yo., Sl.1, K.2 tog., psso.) 3 times, Yo., Sl.1, K.1, psso., K.9, K.2 tog., Yo., K.1, Yo., Sl.1, K.2 tog., psso., Yo., K.1, Yo.]

219th round—[K.1B., Yo., K.3, Yo., Sl.1, K.1, psso., K.2, Yo., Sl.1, K.1, psso., K.7, K.2 tog., Yo., K.3, Yo., K.1B., Yo., K.3, Yo., Sl.1, K.1, psso., K.7, K.2 tog., Yo., K.2, K.2 tog., Yo., K.3, Yo.]

221st round—[K.1B., Yo., K.5, Yo., Sl.1, K.2 tog., psso., Yo., K.1, Yo., Sl.1, K.1, psso., K.5, Sl.2, K.1, p2sso., (Yo., Sl.1, K.2 tog., psso.) 3 times, Yo., Sl.2, K.1, p2sso., K.5, K.2 tog., Yo., K.1, Yo., Sl.1, K.2 tog., psso., Yo., K.5, Yo.]

223rd round—[K.1B., Yo., K.5, Sl.1, K.1, psso., (Yo., Sl.1, K.1, psso., K.2) twice, K.1, Sl.2, K.1, p2sso., Yo., K.1B., Yo., K.3, Yo., K.1B., Yo., Sl.2, K.1, p2sso., K.1, (K.2, K.2 tog., Yo.) twice, K.2 tog., K.5, Yo.]

225th round—[K.1B., Yo., K.6, Sl.1, K.1, psso., Yo., Sl.1, K.2 tog., psso., Yo., K.1, Yo., Sl.1, K.1, psso., K.1, K.2 tog., (Yo., Sl.1, K.2 tog., psso.) 3 times, Yo., Sl.1, K.1, psso., K.1, K.2 tog., Yo., K.1, Yo., Sl.1, K.2 tog., psso., Yo., K.2 tog., K.6, Yo.]

227th round—[K.1B., Yo., K.7, Sl.1, K.1, psso., Yo., Sl.1, K.1, psso., K.2, Yo., Sl.1, K.2 tog., psso., Yo., K.3, Yo., K.1B., Yo., K.3, Yo., Sl.1, K.2 tog., psso., Yo., K.2, K.2 tog., Yo., K.2 tog., K.7, Yo.]

229th round—[K.1B., Yo., K.8, Sl.1, K.1, psso., (Yo., Sl.1, K.2 tog., psso.) 7 times, Yo., K.2 tog., K.8, Yo.]

231st round—[K.10, Sl.1, K.1, psso., (Yo., K.1B., Yo., K.3) 3 times, Yo., K.1B., Yo., K.2 tog., K.9.]

PART K

Knit each section from [to] 40 times in one round

233rd round—[K.9, K.2 tog., (Yo., Sl.1, K.2 tog., psso.) 7 times, Yo., Sl.1, K.1, psso., K.8.]

235th round—[K.8, K.2 tog., (Yo., K.3, Yo., K.1B.) 3 times, Yo., K.3, Yo., Sl.1, K.1, psso., K.7.]

237th round—[K.7, K.2 tog., Yo., K.1, (Yo., Sl.1, K.2 tog., psso.) 7 times, Yo., K.1, Yo., Sl.1, K.1, psso., K.6.]

239th round—[K.6, K.2 tog., (Yo., K.3, Yo., K.1B.) 4 times, Yo., K.3, Yo., Sl.1, K.1, psso., K.5.]

241st round—[K.5, K.2 tog., Yo., K.1, (Yo., Sl.1, K.2 tog., psso.) 9 times, Yo., K.1, Yo., Sl.1, K.1, psso., K.4.]

243rd round—[K.4, K.2 tog., (Yo., K.3, Yo., K.1B.) 5 times, Yo., K.3, Yo., Sl.1, K.1, psso., K.3.]

245th round—[K.3, K.2 tog., Yo., K.1, (Yo., Sl.1, K.2 tog., psso.) 11 times, Yo., K.1, Yo., Sl.1, K.1, psso., K.2.]

247th round—[K.2, K.2 tog., (Yo., K.3, Yo., K.1B.) 6 times, Yo., K.3, Yo., Sl.1, K.1, psso., K.1.]

LL *249th round*—[Yo., Sl.2, K.3 tog., p2sso., Yo., Sl.2, K.2 tog., p2sso., (Yo., Sl.1, K.2 tog., psso.) 11 times, Yo., Sl.2, K.2 tog., p2sso.]

PART L

Knit each section from [to] 280 times in one round

251st round—[K.3, Yo., K.1B., Yo.]

253rd round—[(Sl.1, K.2 tog., psso., Yo.) twice.]

255th round—[Yo., K.1B., Yo., K.3.]

257th round—[(Yo., Sl.1, K.2 tog., psso.) twice.]

259th round—[K.3, Yo., K.1B., Yo.]

261st round—[(Sl.1, K.2 tog., psso., Yo.) twice.]

263rd round—[Yo., K.1B., Yo., K.3.]

PART M

Knit each section from [to] 280 times in one round

265th round—[(Sl.1, K.2 tog., psso., Yo.2) twice.]

266th round—[(K.1, M.3 into Yo.2 of previous round) twice.]

267th, 268th, 269th, 270th, 271st and 272nd round—Knit plain.

LL *273rd round*—[(Sl.2, K.2 tog., p2sso., Yo.2) twice.]

274th round—[(K.1, M.3 into Yo.2 of previous round) twice.]

275th, 276th, 277th, 278th, 279th and 280th round—Knit plain.

Chart for 'Rose of England' Design

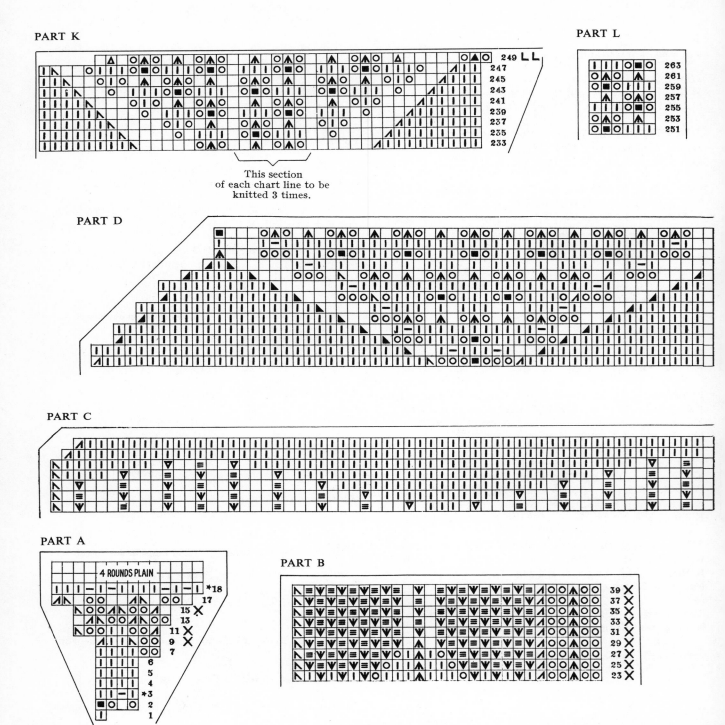

PART K

249 L L
247
245
243
241
239
237
235
233

This section
of each chart line to be
knitted 3 times.

PART L

263
261
259
257
255
253
251

PART D

PART C

PART A

4 ROUNDS PLAIN

*18
17
15 X
13
11 X
9 X
7
6
5
4
*3
2
1

PART B

39 X
37 X
35 X
33 X
31 X
29 X
27 X
25 X
23 X

114

Commencing and working of various PARTS for TEA and DINNER CLOTH see written instructions.

PART A

Every chart line to be knitted 10 times in one round.

PARTS B, C, D and E

Every chart line 5 times in one round.

PART F

Every chart line 80 times in one round.

PARTS G, H, J and K

Every chart line 40 times in one round.

PARTS L and M

Every chart line 280 times in one round.

Every section of a chart line within a bracket is worked as many times as stated below.

NOTICE

PART D. Every round is a pattern round.

Every round of which the number is missing knit plain.

X, L and LL: see ABBREVIATIONS.

* This sign in front of round 3, 266 and 274 draws attention that three stitches (K.1, P.1, K.1) are worked into Yo.2 of previous round. Notice further that in 18th round 5 stitches are knitted into Yo.2 of previous round.

Knitting round 96 and 104 knit 4 stitches into Yo.2 of previous round.

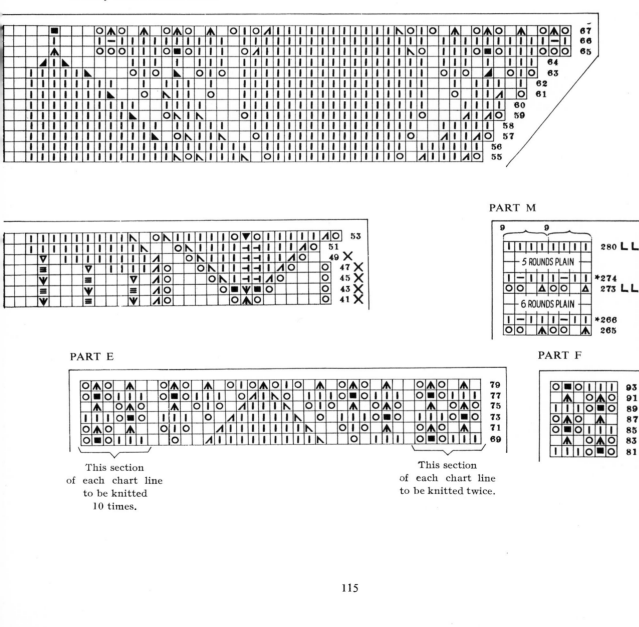

PART M

PART E

This section
of each chart line
to be knitted
10 times.

This section
of each chart line
to be knitted twice.

PART F

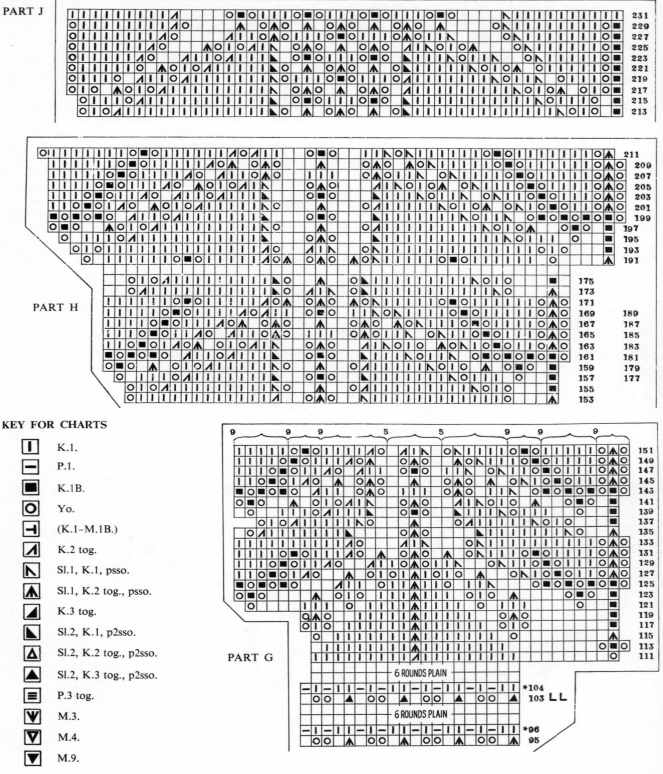

PART J

PART H

PART G

KEY FOR CHARTS

K.1.
P.1.
K.1B.
Yo.
(K.1–M.1B.)
K.2 tog.
Sl.1, K.1, psso.
Sl.1, K.2 tog., psso.
K.3 tog.
Sl.2, K.1, p2sso.
Sl.2, K.2 tog., p2sso.
Sl.2, K.3 tog., p2sso.
P.3 tog.
M.3.
M.4.
M.9.

116

FINISHING OF DINNER CLOTH

After knitting last plain round knit another 2 stitches and then finish the edge of your cloth with a chain of crochet. 4 sts. are crocheted together into one group with 1 d.c. and 9 chain are made between each group 560 times all round. Finish with a slip stitch into first d.c. and break off. Secure thread with few stitches into chain.

FINISHING OF TEA CLOTH

After knitting last plain round 152 start to finish the edge of the cloth with a chain of crochet as follows:

3 sts., 1 d.c., 9 ch., 5 sts., 1 d.c., 9 ch., 3 sts., 1 d.c., 9 ch., 6 sts., 1 d.c., 5 ch., 3 sts., 1 d.c., 5 ch., 6 sts., 1 d.c., 9 ch., 3 sts., 1 d.c., 9 ch., 5 sts., 1 d.c., 9 ch. Repeat 39 times. Finish with a slip stitch into first d.c. and break off.

Secure thread with few stitches into chain.

STRETCHING

Soak and wash the finished work in warm lather of soap flakes. Rinse thoroughly and use starch for final rinse. Do not wring out the lace cloth, squeeze gently and leave it wet for stretching.

TEA CLOTH

Draw a circle of 36 in. diameter. Mark round the circle 40 points at a distance of about 2¾ in. from each other. Now proceed with stretching trying to shape the scallops according to photo. First pin down the 2 centre loops of chain in the middle of the scallop on both sides of the mark of the paper. The 2 loops of 5 chain are the inside points of the scallop and are pinned out with one pin only.

DINNER CLOTH

Draw a circle of 72 in. diameter. Mark round the circle 40 points at a distance of about 5½ in. from each other. On each of these points pin down with one pin the two loops of chain above the middle leaf of each branch as there are 40 all round. The remaining loops of chain are pinned down evenly between these points, always two loops with one pin only.

Finish by treating the lace as directed in **BASIC INSTRUCTIONS**.

Dover Books on Art

PRINCIPLES OF ART HISTORY, H. Wölfflin. This remarkably instructive work demonstrates the tremendous change in artistic conception from the 14th to the 18th centuries, by analyzing 164 works by Botticelli, Dürer, Hobbema, Holbein, Hals, Titian, Rembrandt, Vermeer, etc., and pointing out exactly what is meant by "baroque," "classic," "primitive," "picturesque," and other basic terms of art history and criticism. "A remarkable lesson in the art of seeing," SAT. REV. OF LITERATURE. Translated from the 7th German edition. 150 illus. 254pp. 6⅛ x 9¼.   20276-3 Paperbound $2.50

FOUNDATIONS OF MODERN ART, A. Ozenfant. Stimulating discussion of human creativity from paleolithic cave painting to modern painting, architecture, decorative arts. Fully illustrated with works of Gris, Lipchitz, Léger, Picasso, primitive, modern artifacts, architecture, industrial art, much more. 226 illustrations. 368pp. 6⅛ x 9¼.   20215-1 Paperbound $3.00

METALWORK AND ENAMELLING, H. Maryon. Probably the best book ever written on the subject. Tells everything necessary for the home manufacture of jewelry, rings, ear pendants, bowls, etc. Covers materials, tools, soldering, filigree, setting stones, raising patterns, repoussé work, damascening, niello, cloisonné, polishing, assaying, casting, and dozens of other techniques. The best substitute for apprenticeship to a master metalworker. 363 photos and figures. 374pp. 5½ x 8½.

22702-2 Paperbound $3.50

SHAKER FURNITURE, E. D. and *F. Andrews.* The most illuminating study of Shaker furniture ever written. Covers chronology, craftsmanship, houses, shops, etc. Includes over 200 photographs of chairs, tables, clocks, beds, benches, etc. "Mr. & Mrs. Andrews know all there is to know about Shaker furniture," Mark Van Doren, NATION. 48 full-page plates. 192pp. 7⅞ x 10¾.   20679-3 Paperbound $2.75

LETTERING AND ALPHABETS, J. A. Cavanagh. An unabridged reissue of "Lettering," containing the full discussion, analysis, illustration of 89 basic hand lettering styles based on Caslon, Bodoni, Gothic, many other types. Hundreds of technical hints on construction, strokes, pens, brushes, etc. 89 alphabets, 72 lettered specimens, which may be reproduced permission-free. 121pp. 9¾ x 8.   20053-1 Paperbound $1.50

THE HUMAN FIGURE IN MOTION, Eadweard Muybridge. The largest collection in print of Muybridge's famous high-speed action photos. 4789 photographs in more than 500 action-strip-sequences (at shutter speeds up to 1/6000th of a second) illustrate men, women, children—mostly undraped—performing such actions as walking, running, getting up, lying down, carrying objects, throwing, etc. "An unparalleled dictionary of action for all artists," AMERICAN ARTIST. 390 full-page plates, with 4789 photographs. Heavy glossy stock, reinforced binding with headbands. 7⅞ x 10¾.   20204-6 Clothbound $12.50

ANIMALS IN MOTION, Eadweard Muybridge. The largest collection of animal action photos in print. 34 different animals (horses, mules, oxen, goats, camels, pigs, cats, lions, gnus, deer, monkeys, eagles—and 22 others) in 132 characteristic actions. All 3919 photographs are taken in series at speeds up to 1/1600th of a second, offering artists, biologists, cartoonists a remarkable opportunity to see exactly how an ostrich's head bobs when running, how a lion puts his foot down, how an elephant's knee bends, how a bird flaps his wings, thousands of other hard-to-catch details. "A really marvellous series of plates," NATURE. 380 full-page plates. Heavy glossy stock, reinforced binding with headbands. 7⅞ x 10¾.   20203-8 Clothbound $10.00

THE BOOK OF SIGNS, R. Koch. 493 symbols—crosses, monograms, astrological, biological symbols, runes, etc.—from ancient manuscripts, cathedrals, coins, catacombs, pottery. May be reproduced permission-free. 493 illustrations by Fritz Kredel. 104pp. 6⅛ x 9¼.   20162-7 Paperbound $1.25

A HANDBOOK OF EARLY ADVERTISING ART, C. P. Hornung. The largest collection of copyright-free early advertising art ever compiled. Vol. I: 2,000 illustrations of animals, old automobiles, buildings, allegorical figures, fire engines, Indians, ships, trains, more than 33 other categories! Vol. II: Over 4,000 typographical specimens; 600 Roman, Gothic, Barnum, Old English faces; 630 ornamental type faces; hundreds of scrolls, initials, flourishes, etc. "A remarkable collection," PRINTERS' INK.
Vol. I: Pictorial Volume. Over 2000 illustrations. 256pp. 9 x 12.
               20122-8 Clothbound $10.00
Vol. II: Typographical Volume. Over 4000 specimens. 319pp. 9 x 12.   20123-6 Clothbound $10.00
               Two volume set, Clothbound, only $20.00

THE UNIVERSAL PENMAN, George Bickham. Exact reproduction of beautiful 18th-century book of handwriting. 22 complete alphabets in finest English roundhand, other scripts, over 2000 elaborate flourishes, 122 calligraphic illustrations, etc. Material is copyright-free. "An essential part of any art library, and a book of permanent value," AMERICAN ARTIST. 212 plates. 224pp. 9 x 13¾.   20020-5 Clothbound $12.50

AN ATLAS OF ANATOMY FOR ARTISTS, F. Schider. This standard work contains 189 full-page plates, more than 647 illustrations of all aspects of the human skeleton, musculature, cutaway portions of the body, each part of the anatomy, hand forms, eyelids, breasts, location of muscles under the flesh, etc. 59 plates illustrate how Michelangelo, da Vinci, Goya, 15 others, drew human anatomy. New 3rd edition enlarged by 52 new illustrations by Cloquet, Barcsay. "The standard reference tool," AMERICAN LIBRARY ASSOCIATION. "Excellent," AMERICAN ARTIST. 189 plates, 647 illustrations. xxvi + 192pp. 7⅞ x 10⅝.   20241-0 Clothbound $6.50

MASTERPIECES OF FURNITURE, Verna Cook Salomonsky. Photographs and measured drawings of some of the finest examples of Colonial American, 17th century English, Windsor, Sheraton, Hepplewhite, Chippendale, Louis XIV, Queen Anne, and various other furniture styles. The textual matter includes information on traditions, characteristics, background, etc. of various pieces. 101 plates. Bibliography. 224pp. 7⅞ x 10¾.
21381-1 Paperbound $3.00

PRIMITIVE ART, Franz Boas. In this exhaustive volume, a great American anthropologist analyzes all the fundamental traits of primitive art, covering the formal element in art, representative art, symbolism, style, literature, music, and the dance. Illustrations of Indian embroidery, paleolithic paintings, woven blankets, wing and tail designs, totem poles, cutlery, earthenware, baskets and many other primitive objects and motifs. Over 900 illustrations. 376pp. 5⅜ x 8.   20025-6 Paperbound $2.50

AN INTRODUCTION TO A HISTORY OF WOODCUT, A. M. Hind. Nearly all of this authoritative 2-volume set is devoted to the 15th century—the period during which the woodcut came of age as an important art form. It is the most complete compendium of information on this period, the artists who contributed to it, and their technical and artistic accomplishments. Profusely illustrated with cuts by 15th century masters, and later works for comparative purposes. 484 illustrations. 5 indexes. Total of xi + 838pp. 5⅜ x 8½. Two-vols. 20952-0, 20953-0 Paperbound $7.50

A HISTORY OF ENGRAVING AND ETCHING, A. M. Hind. Beginning with the anonymous masters of 15th century engraving, this highly regarded and thorough survey carries you through Italy, Holland, and Germany to the great engravers and beginnings of etching in the 16th century, through the portrait engravers, master etchers, practicioners of mezzotint, crayon manner and stipple, aquatint, color prints, to modern etching in the period just prior to World War I. Beautifully illustrated —sharp clear prints on heavy opaque paper. Author's preface. 3 appendixes. 111 illustrations. xviii + 487 pp. 5⅜ x 8½.
20954-7 Paperbound $3.50

ART STUDENTS' ANATOMY, E. J. Farris. Teaching anatomy by using chiefly living objects for illustration, this study has enjoyed long popularity and success in art courses and home-study programs. All the basic elements of the human anatomy are illustrated in minute detail, diagrammed and pictured as they pass through common movements and actions. 158 drawings, photographs, and roentgenograms. Glossary of anatomical terms. x + 159pp. 5⅝ x 8⅜.   20744-7 Paperbound $1.50

COLONIAL LIGHTING, A. H. Hayward. The only book to cover the fascinating story of lamps and other lighting devices in America. Beginning with rush light holders used by the early settlers, it ranges through the elaborate chandeliers of the Federal period, illustrating 647 lamps. Of great value to antique collectors, designers, and historians of arts and crafts. Revised and enlarged by James R. Marsh. xxxi + 198pp. 5⅝ x 8¼.
20975-X Paperbound $2.50

GRAPHIC WORLDS OF PETER BRUEGEL THE ELDER, H. A. Klein. 64 of the finest etchings and engravings made from the drawings of the Flemish master Peter Bruegel. Every aspect of the artist's diversified style and subject matter is represented, with notes providing biographical and other background information. Excellent reproductions on opaque stock with nothing on reverse side. 63 engravings, 1 woodcut. Bibliography. xviii + 289pp. 11⅜ x 8¼. 21132-0 Paperbound $4.00

THE COMPLETE WOODCUTS OF ALBRECHT DURER, edited by Dr. Willi Kurth. Albrecht Dürer was a master in various media, but it was in woodcut design that his creative genius reached its highest expression. Here are all of his extant woodcuts, a collection of over 300 great works, many of which are not available elsewhere. An indispensable work for the art historian and critic and all art lovers. 346 plates. Index. 285pp. 8½ x 12¼. 21097-9 Paperbound $4.00

GRAPHIC REPRODUCTION IN PRINTING, H. Curwen. A behind-the-scenes account of the various processes of graphic reproduction—relief, intaglio, stenciling, lithography, line methods, continuous tone methods, photogravure, collotype— and the advantages and limitations of each. Invaluable for all artists, advertising art directors, commercial designers, advertisers, publishers, and all art lovers who buy prints as a hobby. 137 illustrations, including 13 full-page plates, 10 in color. xvi + 171pp. 5¼ x 8½. 20512-6 Clothbound $7.50

WILD FOWL DECOYS, Joel Barber. Antique dealers, collectors, craftsmen, hunters, readers of Americana, etc. will find this the only thorough and reliable guide on the market today to this unique folk art. It contains the history, cultural significance, regional design variations; unusual decoy lore; working plans for constructing decoys; and loads of illustrations. 140 full-page plates, 4 in color. 14 additional plates of drawings and plans by the author. xxvii + 156pp. 7⅞ x 10¾. 20011-6 Paperbound $4.00

1800 WOODCUTS BY THOMAS BEWICK AND HIS SCHOOL. This is the largest collection of first-rate pictorial woodcuts in print—an indispensable part of the working library of every commercial artist, art director, production designer, packaging artist, craftsman, manufacturer, librarian, art collector, and artist. And best of all, when you buy your copy of Bewick, you buy the rights to reproduce individual illustrations—no permission needed, no acknowledgments, no clearance fees! Classified index. Bibliography and sources. xiv + 246pp. 9 x 12.
20766-8 Paperbound $4.00

THE SCRIPT LETTER, Tommy Thompson. Prepared by a noted authority, this is a thorough, straightforward course of instruction with advice on virtually every facet of the art of script lettering. Also a brief history of lettering with examples from early copy books and illustrations from present day advertising and packaging. Copiously illustrated. Bibliography. 128pp. 6½ x 9⅛. 21311-0 Paperbound $1.25

ART ANATOMY, Dr. William Rimmer. One of the few books on art anatomy that are themselves works of art, this is a faithful reproduction (rearranged for handy use) of the extremely rare masterpiece of the famous 19th century anatomist, sculptor, and art teacher. Beautiful, clear line drawings show every part of the body—bony structure, muscles, features, etc. Unusual are the sections on falling bodies, foreshortenings, muscles in tension, grotesque personalities, and Rimmer's remarkable interpretation of emotions and personalities as expressed by facial features. It will supplement every other book on art anatomy you are likely to have. Reproduced clearer than the lithographic original (which sells for $500 on up on the rare book market.) Over 1,200 illustrations. xiii + 153pp. 7¾ x 10¾.
20908-3 Paperbound $2.50

THE CRAFTSMAN'S HANDBOOK, Cennino Cennini. The finest English translation of IL LIBRO DELL' ARTE, the 15th century introduction to art technique that is both a mirror of Quatrocento life and a source of many useful but nearly forgotten facets of the painter's art. 4 illustrations. xxvii + 142pp. D. V. Thompson, translator. 5⅜ x 8.   20054-X Paperbound $2.00

THE BROWN DECADES, Lewis Mumford. A picture of the "buried renaissance" of the post-Civil War period, and the founding of modern architecture (Sullivan, Richardson, Root, Roebling), landscape development (Marsh, Olmstead, Eliot), and the graphic arts (Homer, Eakins, Ryder). 2nd revised, enlarged edition. Bibliography. 12 illustrations. xiv + 266 pp. 5⅜ x 8.
20200-3 Paperbound $2.00

THE STYLES OF ORNAMENT, A. Speltz. The largest collection of line ornament in print, with 3750 numbered illustrations arranged chronologically from Egypt, Assyria, Greeks, Romans, Etruscans, through Medieval, Renaissance, 18th century, and Victorian. No permissions, no fees needed to use or reproduce illustrations. 400 plates with 3750 illustrations. Bibliography. Index. 640pp. 6 x 9.   20577-6 Paperbound $3.00

THE ART OF ETCHING, E. S. Lumsden. Every step of the etching process from essential materials to completed proof is carefully and clearly explained, with 24 annotated plates exemplifying every technique and approach discussed. The book also features a rich survey of the art, with 105 annotated plates by masters. Invaluable for beginner to advanced etcher. 374pp. 5⅜ x 8.   20049-3 Paperbound $3.00

OF THE JUST SHAPING OF LETTERS, Albrecht Dürer. This remarkable volume reveals Albrecht Dürer's rules for the geometric construction of Roman capitals and the formation of Gothic lower case and capital letters, complete with construction diagrams and directions. Of considerable practical interest to the contemporary illustrator, artist, and designer. Translated from the Latin text of the edition of 1535 by R. T. Nichol. Numerous letterform designs, construction diagrams, illustrations. iv + 43pp. 7⅞ x 10¾.   21306-4 Paperbound $2.00

Dover Books on Art

LANDSCAPE GARDENING IN JAPAN, Josiah Conder. A detailed picture of Japanese gardening techniques and ideas, the artistic principles incorporated in the Japanese garden, and the religious and ethical concepts at the heart of those principles. Preface. 92 illustrations, plus all 40 full-page plates from the Supplement. Index. xv + 299pp. 8⅜ x 11¼.

21216-5 Paperbound $3.50

DESIGN AND FIGURE CARVING, E. J. Tangerman. "Anyone who can peel a potato can carve," states the author, and in this unusual book he shows you how, covering every stage in detail from very simple exercises working up to museum-quality pieces. Terrific aid for hobbyists, arts and crafts counselors, teachers, those who wish to make reproductions for the commercial market. Appendix: How to Enlarge a Design. Brief bibliography. Index. 1298 figures. x + 289pp. 5⅜ x 8½.

21209-2 Paperbound $2.00

THE STANDARD BOOK OF QUILT MAKING AND COLLECTING, M. Ickis. Even if you are a beginner, you will soon find yourself quilting like an expert, by following these clearly drawn patterns, photographs, and step-by-step instructions. Learn how to plan the quilt, to select the pattern to harmonize with the design and color of the room, to choose materials. Over 40 full-size patterns. Index. 483 illustrations. One color plate. xi + 276pp. 6¾ x 9½.   20582-7 Paperbound $2.50

LOST EXAMPLES OF COLONIAL ARCHITECTURE, J. M. Howells. This book offers a unique guided tour through America's architectural past, all of which is either no longer in existence or so changed that its original beauty has been destroyed. More than 275 clear photos of old churches, dwelling houses, public buildings, business structures, etc. 245 plates, containing 281 photos and 9 drawings, floorplans, etc. New Index. xvii + 248pp. 7⅞ x 10¾.   21143-6 Paperbound $3.00

A HISTORY OF COSTUME, Carl Köhler. The most reliable and authentic account of the development of dress from ancient times through the 19th century. Based on actual pieces of clothing that have survived, using paintings, statues and other reproductions only where originals no longer exist. Hundreds of illustrations, including detailed patterns for many articles. Highly useful for theatre and movie directors, fashion designers, illustrators, teachers. Edited and augmented by Emma von Sichart. Translated by Alexander K. Dallas. 594 illustrations. 464pp. 5⅛ x 7⅛.

21030-8 Paperbound $3.00

Dover publishes books on commercial art, art history, crafts, design, art classics; also books on music, literature, science, mathematics, puzzles and entertainments, chess, engineering, biology, philosophy, psychology, languages, history, and other fields. For free circulars write to Dept. DA, Dover Publications, Inc., 180 Varick St., New York, N.Y. 10014.